The Art of Southern Cooking

MILDRED EVANS WARREN

Illustrated by Mel Klapholz

Gramercy Books
New York

Dedicated to those many friends whose
encouragement and contributions
have made my "Southern Cooking" possible

This 2003 edition published by Gramercy Books, an imprint of Random House Value Publishing, a division of Random House, Inc., New York, by arrangement with Doubleday & Company, Inc.

Gramercy is a registered trademark and the colophon is a trademark of Random House, Inc.

Random House
New York • Toronto • London • Sydney • Auckland
www.randomhouse.com

Printed in the United States of America

Library of Congress Cataloging-in-Publication Data

Warren, Mildred Evans.
The art of southern cooking.
Selected from the author's column The cook's nook, published in
the Houston home journal, Perry, Ga.
Reprint. Originally published: Garden City, N. Y.: Doubleday, 1969.
Includes index.
1. Cookery, American—Southern States. I. Title.

[TX715. W2897   1981]   641.597581-2903
ISBN: 0-517-34664-8   AACR2

9 8 7 6 5 4 3

Contents

Hors d'Oeuvres & Punches   11

Salads & Dressings   31

Vegetables   55

Meats   73

Poultry & Game   93

Seafood   111

Cheese & Egg Dishes   127

Breads   135

Cookies   147

Cakes   159

Pies   185

Desserts   207

Candy   223

Preserving & Pickling   233

Weights and Measures, Oven Chart   249

Items marked with an asterisk may be located by consulting the Index.

Foreword

Picking up one's pen and writing a cookbook presents problems, but we'll solve them as we go along. There is always a "reason and rhyme" for everything, and as for my cookbook, it's like Topsy, "it jes' grew." It all began with a column called "The Cook's Nook," which I have edited for the hometown paper, the Houston *Home Journal*, in Perry, Georgia. This particular paper has a circulation which extends beyond the boundaries of our town, to those places far and near, where former Perry-ites reside. I have received many nice letters and recipes from these former residents along with those from the "hometown folks." This book is dedicated to those friends whose recipes and encouragement have made this cookbook "possible and publishable." The recipes herein are those favorites I have collected, and from friends who have generously contributed to my Cook's Nook. I have tried to make them clear and concise and you will find little cooking hints tucked in here and there. You will note that these little hints sometimes make the difference between mediocre cooking and gourmet food.

I have a vivid recollection of my early cooking days, a young bride who could not "boil water without burning it." So if these extra bits of information help those of you who are just beginning your culinary efforts, they will be well worth the time and effort.

And so we begin our cooking saga.

Hors d'Oeuvres & Punches

Having grown up in the South as the daughter of a small-town doctor, it's only natural that Southern cooking is very dear to me.

Some of my readers may remember a long summer evening sitting on the porch, rocking and sipping a long, cool drink, listening to the crickets or maybe the wind as it moaned through the pines. Some may have heard the waves lapping gently on the beach. These casual, carefree days seem to be a thing of the past for many of us in these hectic, rushing times. I hope you will find a bit of this "relaxed" living as you turn the pages of my book.

Hors d'oeuvres become more and more the order of the day. May you find these little tidbits to "whet" your appetite appealing. Among the tidbits to nibble on, you will find a little Cheese Corn Flake Cooky to be a favorite. You'll find spreads for sandwiches, dips for "that hour," and punches to quench your thirst. I have included the traditional Southern Egg Nog for the holiday season.

AVOCADO FINGERS

Preheat broiler. Mash pulp of 1 ripe avocado and season with dash of salt, paprika, and 1 teaspoon lemon juice. Spread on narrow toast strips. Place narrow strips of bacon over avocado and broil until bacon crisps. This makes about 20.

AVOCADO SANDWICHES

Slice a peeled avocado thin and marinate slices in lemon juice for at least an hour. Trim crust from a loaf of white bread (thin) or use unsliced bread sliced very thin. Spread bread with butter and season lightly with salt and pepper. Drain the avocado slices and sandwich them between the buttered slices of bread. If you prefer you may use mayonnaise for these. A bit of watercress in small pieces is good sprinkled on the buttered slices along with the avocado. Cut each sandwich in 4 triangles and chill before serving. Makes 8 to 10 whole sandwiches, 32 to 40 triangles.

CHEESE CORN FLAKE COOKY

This recipe is a "must," cheesy and crisp; good to nibble on anytime!

1 package (8 ounce) sharp	¼ teaspoon salt
Cheddar cheese	¼ teaspoon paprika
½ cup margarine	¼ teaspoon Tabasco sauce
1 cup flour	1½ cups corn flakes

Preheat oven to 350 degrees F. Have cheese at room temperature; grate. Cream with margarine. Mix with flour, salt, paprika, and Tabasco. Drop in corn flakes last. Mix with fork so as not to crush the flakes. Pinch off piece of dough, roll marble size, press down on un-greased cooky sheet. Do not roll out, press down on sheet to keep from crushing corn flakes. Bake. Makes about 50 cookies.

CHEESE DIP OR SPREAD

1½ pounds cottage cheese
1 tablespoon grated onion
¾ teaspoon salt

2 tablespoons chopped parsley
½ teaspoon sage
Dash red pepper

Combine all ingredients and mix well. Makes 1½ cups.

CHEESE PUFFS

These little Cheese Puffs are easy to do.

Preheat broiler. Blend 1 package (8 ounce) pimento cheese with 1 well-beaten egg. Season to taste. Toast small strips of toast on one side. Spread other side with butter and pimento cheese mix. Broil until brown and puffed. Makes about 30 to 35.

CHEESE STRAWS

Nothing is better to nibble on than a bit of cheese; try these Cheese Straws.

2 cups grated sharp Cheddar
  cheese
½ cup butter

2 cups sifted flour
Dash salt
⅛ teaspoon red pepper

Preheat oven to 350 degrees F. Have cheese and butter at room temperature. Cream together. Add flour, salt, and red pepper. Mix until creamy. Use the small star or the 1½-inch ribbon disk on a cooky press to make straws. Bake 10 to 15 minutes, on ungreased cooky sheet, watch closely. For a change, sprinkle a few caraway seeds over straws before baking. Makes about 50 cheese straws.

CRAB DIP

This Crab Dip is good for that hour which calls for dips and such.

1 package (8 ounce) cream
  cheese
1 can (6½ ounce) crab meat,
  drained
3 tablespoons mayonnaise

1 tablespoon horseradish
1 teaspoon grated onion
Dash spicy steak sauce
2 dashes Worcestershire sauce
Paprika (optional)

Soften cheese, add other ingredients. Mix well. Garnish with paprika if desired. Makes approximately 2 cups.

CRAB MEAT AND BACON ROLLS

Nice for the cocktail hour.

½ can (6½ ounce can) tomato
  paste
1 egg, well beaten
1 cup dry bread crumbs
Dash salt
Dash pepper

½ teaspoon parsley flakes
½ teaspoon minced celery leaves
1 can (6½ ounce) crab meat,
  drained and flaked
12 slices bacon

Preheat broiler. Mix tomato paste and egg. Add crumbs, seasoning, parsley, celery, and crab meat. Mix well, roll in finger lengths. Wrap each roll with half slice bacon and fasten with toothpick. Broil, turn often to brown evenly. Makes 24 rolls.

CREAM CHEESE AND GINGER SPREAD

This is a favorite for a little rolled sandwich.

Blend 1 package (8 ounce) cream cheese with cream or milk to spreading consistency. Add 1 teaspoon finely chopped candied ginger, or to suit your taste. Add a dash of salt and use for a rolled sandwich spread or make a bit softer for a tangy sweet dip. Spreads 25 to 30 sandwiches, tiny or rolled.

DAFFODIL DIP

This Dip is one of the best; it is firmer than most dips and the anchovy flavor, delightful!

1 package (8 ounce) cream cheese
½ cup mayonnaise
½ cup chopped parsley
2 tablespoons chopped onion

1 clove garlic, minced
1 tablespoon anchovy paste
Dash pepper
1 hard-cooked egg yolk

Soften cheese and add mayonnaise. Blend well. Add parsley and remaining ingredients, except egg yolk. Mix well. Sprinkle egg yolk on top. Serve with vegetable dippers such as cauliflowerets, celery, radish roses, cherry tomatoes, carrot sticks. This is also good to serve with crackers. Makes 1½ cups dip.

FRENCH FRIED OLIVES

Use large stuffed olives. Roll olives in fine seasoned cracker crumbs. Dip in beaten egg with dash of salt added, now in crumbs again. Fry in deep, hot fat. Drain and serve hot.

GARLIC CROUTONS

2 tablespoons butter
¼ teaspoon garlic powder
4 slices bread, cubed

Melt butter in medium-size frying pan. Stir in garlic powder. Sauté bread cubes in pan, stirring often in melted butter until bread cubes are toasted on all sides. Drain on paper towels. Store in screw-top jar. Delicious with a green salad, also good tossed in or floated on soup. This is a nice idea for the pieces of bread left from sandwich making. Makes about 40 croutons, depending on size cut.

NOTE: These will keep 3 to 4 weeks.

JUDY'S GUACAMOLE

1 large ripe avocado
1 tablespoon lemon juice
½ teaspoon grated onion
Dash cayenne

Salt to taste
Pepper to taste
1 medium tomato, diced fine

Mash avocado with a silver fork. Add lemon juice, onion, cayenne, salt, and pepper. Add the tomato last so it will not be soggy. Chill mix 2 or 3 hours in refrigerator. Serve with tortilla chips or crackers. Makes a medium-size bowl of dip.

HAM DELIGHTS

2 cups finely chopped cooked
  ham
1 teaspoon prepared mustard
1 tablespoon mayonnaise

5 to 6 tablespoons melted butter
3 tablespoons shortening
2 cups self-rising flour
⅔ cup milk

Preheat oven to 375 degrees F. Mix ham, mustard, mayonnaise, and butter. Mix shortening with flour, gradually add milk. Knead a bit and roll out on floured board. Roll thin, approximately ⅛ inch thick. Cut in tiny rounds and spread with bit of ham mixture; cover with another pastry round and press edges together with tines of fork. Bake until lightly browned. Makes 24 small rounds.

HAM SPREAD

1 pound cooked ham
4 tablespoons prepared mustard
½ cup mayonnaise

½ teaspoon Worcestershire sauce
Dash horseradish
Dash Tabasco sauce

Grind ham through meat chopper using medium blade. There should be 3 cups of ham. If not quite this much, cut down on your seasonings. Add other ingredients and mix well. Makes 3 cups.

LITTLE CHEESE BISCUIT

This is my favorite Cheese Biscuit; make them tiny to serve as an hors d'oeuvre.

1 cup grated sharp Cheddar
    cheese
½ cup butter

1¼ cups flour
Dash red pepper

Mix ingredients together and form into a long roll about 1 inch in diameter. Wrap in buttered or wax paper and store in refrigerator until ready to bake. Preheat oven to 400 degrees F. Slice cheese roll in ¼-inch rounds and bake for 5 minutes. If you wish, an almond or pecan may be added to top of biscuit before baking. Makes about 30 to 35 tiny biscuits.

NIPPY ROLLS

Blend 1 package (8 ounce) cream cheese and 2 to 3 teaspoons drained horseradish. Spread thinly on dried beef slices. Roll firmly and fasten with cocktail picks. Chill and slice. Makes 15 to 20 rolls.

PARTY CORNUCOPIAS

This makes a nice shell for your tea-table "goodies."

Preheat oven to 250 degrees F. Cut thin slices of bread in small rounds. Roll thin as paper with rolling pin. These should be tiny biscuit size when finished. Now butter both sides with melted butter, using pastry brush. Fold over in cornucopia shape and fasten with small pick. Brown lightly on greased cooky sheet in oven for short time. Watch closely. Fill shells with following mixture:

3 cans (2½ ounces each) deviled ham
2 tablespoons pickle relish or to taste
4 hard-cooked eggs, finely chopped

Mix to hold together. Fill shells with teaspoon, pressing filling in
with handle of spoon. Makes about 40.

SALTED NUTS

*Salted Nuts are nice for nibbling. Pecans toasted in this manner
will keep a longer time. No butter in these, they are done with
corn oil.*

Preheat oven to 375 degrees F. Place shelled pecans (or other nuts)
in shallow pan and bake 12 minutes. Stir one time. After removing
from oven sprinkle with corn oil and salt. Place on paper toweling
to drain.

SALTED PECANS

Preheat oven to 300 degrees F. Place the nut meats in pan in oven.
Let remain in oven turning occasionally until they are light brown
and toasted. Now pour a little salted, melted butter over nuts and
stir well.

SAUSAGE PINWHEELS

These Sausage Pinwheels are a nice addition to your canapé tray.

3 tablespoons shortening   ½ to 1 pound hot ground
2 cups self-rising flour   sausage
⅔ cup milk

Mix shortening with flour, gradually add milk. Knead a minute or
so and roll out on floured board in rectangle shape. Roll thin, approxi-

mately ⅛ inch thick. Spread sausage on dough and roll as for jelly roll. Refrigerate several hours. When ready to bake preheat oven to 350 degrees F. Slice dough in thin slices and place on ungreased baking sheet. Bake 15 to 20 minutes or until lightly browned. Remove from sheet and place on paper toweling to drain. Serve hot. Makes about 24.

NOTE: These may be placed in refrigerator or freezer before baking for several days.

SHRIMP CANAPES

These little Canapés are among my favorites.

Boil 1 pound shrimp approximately 15 minutes in salted water to which a little pickle vinegar has been added. Drain and shell. Chill. Put the shrimp and 2 stalks of celery through food chopper (medium blade). Mix with mayonnaise to which a dash of grated onion juice has been added. Now add dash of salt and paprika. Mix to spreading consistency and spread on little rounds or fancy shapes of thinly sliced bread. Place a bit of parsley, pimento, or a slice of olive in center for decoration. These will keep well if covered with wax paper or foil and not dry out for 1 or 2 hours. I like my shrimp dishes very fresh so when I make my party food I usually prepare these last. This will spread 40 small canapes.

SHRIMP SPREAD

2 pounds cleaned fresh or canned shrimp	¾ cup mayonnaise
Juice 1 lemon	½ teaspoon salt
1 small onion, grated	Dash pepper
1 teaspoon curry powder	Dash paprika

Grind cleaned cooked or canned shrimp, using fine blade. Add juice of lemon, onion, curry powder, mayonnaise, salt, pepper, and paprika. Makes approximately 2 cups.

SWEET-SOUR SAUSAGE BALLS

Hot hors d'oeuvres that are good (and different) are high on any hostess's list.

4 pounds hot ground sausage	¾ cup brown sugar
4 eggs, slightly beaten	6 tablespoons white wine
1½ cups bread crumbs	6 tablespoons soy sauce
3 cups catsup	

Combine sausage with beaten eggs and bread crumbs. Roll into marble-size balls and brown in skillet. Drain. In medium-size bowl combine catsup, sugar, wine and soy sauce. Pour over sausage balls, cover and simmer for 30 minutes; stir occasionally. Serve hot in chafing dish. Serves 15 to 20.

TOASTED DELIGHT

Here are some little party morsels to nibble on.

Blend together:

¼ cup melted butter or margarine	¼ teaspoon garlic salt
½ to 1 teaspoon Worcestershire sauce	¼ teaspoon celery seed
	Dash caraway seed (optional)

Combine in large flat ungreased pan the following:

1½ cups bite-size corn cereal	1 cup bite-size rice cereal
1 cup bite-size wheat cereal	2 cups (1 inch) pretzel sticks
1 cup bite-size oat cereal	½ pound pecans and peanuts

Preheat oven to 250 or 300 degrees F. Pour butter mixture over combined cereals, pretzels, and nuts. Stir and salt lightly to taste.

Bake about an hour. Stir carefully every 10 to 15 minutes. Makes 8 cups.

NOTE: You may choose to vary the cereals in your party mix.

CHAMPAGNE CUP

4 ounces champagne
¼ ounce Benedectine
¼ ounce brandy

Place a cube or two of ice in glass, add above ingredients. Stir. Add slice of orange and cherry or strawberry. Top with sprig of mint if desired. Serves one.

CHAMPAGNE PUNCH

Champagne Punch is not only for weddings but for any festive occasion. This one is simple to prepare, even for a large number.

3 cups sugar
3 cans (5½ ounces each) pure lemon juice
1½ quarts ice water

2 bottles (⅘ quart each) champagne
1 bottle (⅘ quart) dry white wine

Dissolve the sugar in the lemon juice, add water and pour in the punch bowl. Stir in champagne and wine. Be sure you have plenty of ice in bowl. Garnish with fresh strawberries or scoops of lemon ice if desired. This makes 6 quarts, serves about 35.

NOTE: Place the champagne in refrigerator for 2 hours or in an ice bucket for 30 minutes before adding to punch.

CITRIC ACID PUNCH

This Citric Acid Punch is good; try it for your next children's party, or for grown-ups.

1 quart boiling water
2 ounces citric acid (you may buy this at the drugstore)
6 oranges, peeled and juiced
4 cups sugar

2 cups hot water
2 quarts cold water
6 cups canned pineapple juice
1 quart ginger ale (optional)

Pour water over citric acid. Cut orange peel in small pieces, add to water and acid mixture. Let stand 2 hours. Strain and add orange juice. Add sugar dissolved in hot water. Use 1 quart of this mixture to 2 quarts of water and add the pineapple juice. If desired add ginger ale when ready to serve. Serves 40.

COFFEE PUNCH

1 pound coffee, tied in cheesecloth bag
3 quarts water
1½ cups sugar

1 can (5½ ounce) chocolate syrup
2 tablespoons vanilla

Put coffee and water in deep pot and boil for 20 minutes. Remove coffee bag and add other ingredients. Place in refrigerator overnight. When ready to serve add the following:

3 quarts cold milk
3 quarts vanilla ice cream

A bit of the ice cream should float in each cup of punch. Serves 40 to 50.

COFFEE ROYAL

2 quarts chilled coffee
½ cup rum
2 quarts vanilla ice cream

Just before serving combine the coffee, rum, and ice cream in a large punch bowl. Stir until most of the ice cream is blended into coffee and rum. Small bits of ice cream will "float" and serve as a garnish. This makes 30 punch cups.

NOTE: If you wish serve in small or after dinner coffee cups after a meal.

CRANBERRY PUNCH

This Cranberry Punch is a pretty one, nice for holiday time.

2 bottles (1 pint each) cranberry juice
1 can (12 ounce) frozen orange juice, diluted with 1 can water

1 can (12 ounce) frozen lemonade, diluted with 2 cans water
1 quart ginger ale

Mix ingredients except ginger ale and pour over crushed or cracked ice. Add ginger ale before serving. Makes 30 punch cups.

DELIGHT PUNCH

2 cups lemon juice
6 cups orange juice
6 cups apple juice

2 cups sugar or to taste
1 pint ginger ale
1 quart orange sherbet (optional)

Combine ingredients and chill. Add ginger ale and orange sherbet just before serving. This is a golden punch and would be nice for a golden wedding day. Serves 30.

EASY FRUIT PUNCH

6 cups canned pineapple-grapefruit drink
1 can (12 ounce) frozen lemonade, diluted as directed
1 quart ginger ale

Mix and pour over ice. If desired, stick a sprig of mint on top of each glass. Makes 30 cups.

FROSTED FRUIT SHRUB

This Frosted Fruit Shrub was served to me in Williamsburg, Virginia. Serve it for breakfast or for a luncheon.

Mix equal parts of apricot nectar, orange juice, and grapefruit juice. Stir a spoonful of orange sherbet in each glass. Serve in parfait or fruit juice glasses.

FRUIT SHERBET PUNCH

2 cups fresh orange juice, or frozen
2 cups canned pineapple juice
2 cups fresh lime juice, or frozen

2 quarts ginger ale
1 quart orange ice
Mint sprigs
Orange slices

Mix fruit juices, pour over block of ice. Add ginger ale and orange ice. Garnish with mint and slices of orange. Serves 40 to 50.
For a variation, use lime sherbet.

HOT BUTTERED RUM

Pour about ⅓ cup of rum in heavy mug. Add a sliver of lemon peel, a cinnamon stick, a whole clove, and enough boiling cider to fill mug. Put a pat of butter on top and stir well with the cinnamon stick. Serve hot. The amount of rum may be "added to" if you wish. Serves 1.

HOT NECTAR PUNCH

4 cups unsweetened canned
    pineapple juice
1 cup apricot nectar
2 cups apple cider

1 cup orange juice
¾ cup brown sugar
6 whole cloves
1 stick (2 inch) cinnamon

Combine ingredients. Heat to boiling, simmer 8 to 10 minutes. Remove cloves and cinnamon, serve in heated mugs. Makes 2 quarts.

IRISH COFFEE

This Irish Coffee is easy "to do" and nice to serve when having those special guests. Nice for after dinner, might double for dessert.

Preheat a 6-ounce goblet with very hot water. Fill and let stand a few seconds, then empty. Fill glass three-quarters full of good hot black coffee before glass has cooled. Add 1 to 2 teaspoons sugar to coffee. Stir until completely dissolved, now add jigger of Irish whiskey. Top with a scoop of whipped cream and serve hot. Drink through the cream. Serves one.

LEMON GRAPE PUNCH

1 cup lemon juice
4 bottles (1 quart each) grape
    juice

4 quarts ginger ale
¼ cup sugar
Slices orange and lemon

Blend fruit juices and ginger ale, add sugar, and stir well. Pour over ice and float slices of orange and lemon in punch. This punch is delicious served over scoops of lemon sherbet. Serves 30.

MILK PUNCH

Milk Punch is a must in your files.

To 1 pint of milk add sugar enough to make quite sweet. Add whisky, brandy, or rum to taste; mix or shake in cocktail shaker. Grate nutmeg over top and serve. With hot milk it makes a good "night cap" if you are catching cold. If you substitute an egg for the liquor it makes a good nourishing drink. Serves 2 to 3.

MINTY PUNCH

1½ dozen lemons, rinds and juice
4 cups water
3 cups sugar

6 cups canned pineapple juice
Green food coloring
1 drop peppermint flavoring
1 quart ginger ale

Simmer rinds with water and sugar 5 minutes. Cool and squeeze rinds, discard. Add lemon and pineapple juice, color as needed, add flavoring. Mix. Add ginger ale just before serving. Serves 40.

NINA'S PUNCH

Get out that gallon jug for this one, nice for a picnic.

1 cup sugar
1 cup hot water
2 cans (6 ounces each) frozen lemonade
1 can (6 ounce) frozen limeade

½ can (6 ounce can) frozen orange juice
1 pint ginger ale
1 gallon jug

Dissolve sugar in hot water in gallon jug. Add the undiluted cans of lemonade, limeade, and orange juice. Fill jug with cold water, leave room for the bottle of ginger ale to be added when ready to serve. Makes 1 gallon.

PEACH PUNCH

1 pint and 12 ounces Peach Juice
Drink
1 can (6 ounce) frozen lemonade
(diluted with half amount of
water as called for in directions)

1 can (6 ounce) orange juice
6 ounces pineapple juice
1 bottle (10 ounce) ginger ale

Mix fruit juices. Chill, and when ready to serve add ginger ale. Garnish with cherries and sprigs of mint. Serves 16.

RUSSIAN TEA

This Russian Tea is a spicy hot cup for that colder day.

2 lemons
12 cloves
1 quart water

2 cups sugar
2 quarts strong tea
Juice 3 oranges

Boil lemon rind with cloves and water 5 minutes. Add sugar and tea. Stir in lemon and orange juice. Serve hot. Serves 16.

NOTE: You may use frozen orange juice for this recipe. It takes one-half of the 6-ounce can of juice diluted as directed.

SHOWER PUNCH

1 can (12 ounce) frozen orange
juice
1 can (6 ounce) frozen
lemonade

1 quart vanilla ice cream
1 quart pineapple sherbet

Mix fruit juice as directed. Serve in glasses with one scoop each of vanilla ice cream and pineapple sherbet. Or if you prefer, just the pineapple sherbet. Serves 24.

SOUTHERN EGG NOG

No Southern cookbook would be complete without an egg nog recipe. Here is one which was given to me, and I think one of the best as it does not separate easily. Serve in tall glasses—for "holiday time," the traditional Southern Egg Nog to serve your most discriminating guests.

5 eggs	½ pint whipping cream
6 tablespoons whisky or brandy, and maybe a little more	5 rounded tablespoons sugar

The night before, or hours before you wish to serve the nog, separate the eggs. Beat yolks and add the whisky gradually, cover tightly and refrigerate. This will be a jelly-like mass. Refrigerate the whites also, covered. When ready to serve the egg nog, remove egg whites from refrigerator to bring to room temperature. Whip cream stiff and refrigerate. Now beat egg whites, adding sugar gradually, a tablespoon at a time. Continue to whip until meringue consistency. Quickly remove the whisky-yolk mixture from refrigerator and fold into whipped cream gently; stir no more than necessary. Now pour this mixture over whites and fold in. Serves 4 to 6.

SOUTHERN MINT JULEP

A recipe for "Southern gentlemen." Opinions differ as to the proper way to mix a Julep. One school says to crush the mint leaves with the sugar and the other says the mint should be smelled, not tasted. The crushed mint seems to be preferred. Note: Each julep should be made separately.

1 teaspoon granulated sugar	1 tablespoon water
10 to 12 tender mint leaves	1 to 2 ounces bourbon

Put sugar and mint in glasses, slightly crush mint with sugar and water. Stir well to dissolve sugar. Now add bourbon and lastly pack glasses with shaved or crushed ice. Stick a piece of fresh mint in ice and set in refrigerator to frost. When "frosted" insert a straw in ice and sip, relax and cool, cool, cool. This recipe is for 1 julep.

TWIN-BERRY PUNCH

A cool, summertime Berry Punch from frozen fruits.

2 packages (10 ounces each) frozen strawberries, thawed

2 packages (10 ounces each) frozen raspberries, thawed

1 can (6 ounce) frozen lemonade, slightly thawed

2 quarts ginger ale or soda, cold

Combine fruits, simmer about 5 minutes. Strain, cool, and chill. Blend lemonade and soda into fruit liquid. Serve over ice cubes. Serves 12.

WASSAIL BOWL

I think that you will welcome this Wassail Bowl for the holiday season. Serve it from your prettiest punch bowl.

1 gallon apple cider or apple juice

1 cup packed brown sugar

1 can (6 ounce) frozen lemonade

1 can (6 ounce) frozen orange juice

1 tablespoon whole cloves

1 tablespoon whole allspice

Cinnamon sticks, optional

Mix cider, sugar, and undiluted lemonade and orange juice and pour in large pot. Tie cloves and allspice in cheese cloth, add to cider mixture, and simmer covered for about 15 minutes. Remove and discard spice bag. Serve hot in punch cups. Serve a cinnamon stick in each cup if you wish. Makes 24 punch cup servings.

Salads & Dressings

Salad making is an art itself. Because so many and varied ingredients go into salad making, it appeals to many tastes. Salads should be planned and prepared in relation to the other foods served.

Some salads are hearty and may be served cold as an entree, such as Pressed Chicken Salad. Green salads should be crisp and may be varied to suit individual tastes with an assortment of ingredients and dressings. Toss your green salads with the finesse and care of an artist. I could not resist including an Old-fashioned Lettuce Salad. I remember as a small child that a neighbor always planted a small row of this garden lettuce for me. You might like to try my Molded Potato Salad with Baked Ham*, or perhaps a cranberry or mincemeat salad for your holiday table. There is a Dessert Salad, which is delicious and party-like.

Vegetables and fruits frozen or congealed will give you a variety to choose from. Shrimp Salad served with aspic is a grand summer idea. Whatever your choice, I hope you will enjoy my salads as they should be a focal point in your meals.

Sauces and dressings are here for you to select from. There is an Old-fashioned Barbecue Sauce which I especially dedicate to my men readers.

APPLE SALAD

4 to 5 stalks celery, chopped
4 to 5 apples, peeled and diced
Juice ½ lemon
½ cup broken pecans
3 to 4 tablespoons mayonnaise
Dash salt
Dash paprika
Raisins (optional)

Mix celery and apples. Add lemon juice. Mix with pecans and add mayonnaise to hold together. Add salt, paprika, and a few raisins if desired. Serves 6.

ASHEVILLE SALAD

1 can (10½ ounce) tomato
   soup, undiluted
1 tablespoon unflavored gelatin
2 cups cold water
3 packages (3 ounces each)
   cream cheese, softened
1 cup mayonnaise
¼ cup chopped cucumber
¼ cup chopped green pepper
½ cup chopped celery
Dash grated onion
Dash salt
½ cup chopped pecans

Bring soup to boil and add the gelatin which has been softened in ½ cup water. Allow mixture to cool. Mix the cheese with a small amount of mayonnaise and beat smooth. Now add the gelatin mixture with remaining ingredients. Pour into individual molds and chill until firm. Serves 10 to 12.

NOTE: If you prefer, omit cucumber.

AVOCADO-GRAPEFRUIT SALAD

1 can (8 ounce) grapefruit
  sections or 1 large grapefruit
2 packages (3 ounces each)
  orange pineapple-flavored
  gelatin
1 cup boiling water

1 cup grapefruit juice
1 bottle (7 ounce) ginger ale
  (1 cup)
2 avocados, halved, peeled, and
  sliced crosswise

Drain grapefruit and dice sections. Dissolve gelatin in water. Add fruit juice and cool. Add ginger ale, gently. Chill until partially set. Fold in grapefruit and avocados. Pour in mold or individual molds and chill until set. Makes 8 to 10 servings.

CALICO SALAD

This mixed vegetable salad keeps well covered tightly in your refrigerator.

1 can (15½ ounce) cut tender green beans
1 can (15½ ounce) cut tender yellow beans
1 can (16 ounce) red kidney beans

Wash and drain beans.

1 small green pepper, seeded
2 medium purple onions
2 medium-size carrots

1½ stalks celery
½ small package radishes

Slice pepper, onions, carrots, celery, and radishes. Add to beans. Mix with following:

2½ cups sugar
2 cups vinegar

½ teaspoon white pepper
½ teaspoon salt, or to taste

Mix sugar, vinegar, pepper, and salt. Stir well until all sugar is dissolved. Pour this over vegetables. Cover tightly and refrigerate for several hours or overnight. Drain and serve. Serves 12.

CHICKEN SALAD

3 to 4 cups chopped cooked
chicken
2 cups chopped celery
1 cup chopped sweet cucumber
pickles, or as desired
5 to 6 finely chopped hard-
cooked eggs

1 tablespoon lemon juice
½ teaspoon salt, or to taste
Dash red pepper
½ cup mayonnaise or cooked
salad dressing, more if needed
Pickle vinegar as needed

Place chicken in large bowl and add celery, pickles, and eggs. Season with lemon juice, salt, and red pepper. Add mayonnaise and a bit of pickle vinegar to moisten. Some like to add a few nut meats to their salad. Serves 12 to 14.

COLESLAW

2 pounds shredded white cabbage
⅔ cup vinegar
⅔ cup dairy sour cream

1 teaspoon grated onion
Salt to taste

Mix all together and chill. Grated carrot may be added if desired. Serves 8 to 10.

CREAMY CRANBERRY SALAD

1 can (1 pound) whole
cranberry sauce
1 cup boiling water
1 package (3 ounce) strawberry-
flavored gelatin

1 tablespoon lemon juice
½ cup mayonnaise
1 apple, diced
¼ cup chopped pecans

Heat cranberry sauce, strain out juice. Mix juice, water, and gelatin, stir until dissolved. Add lemon juice. Chill until slightly thickened. Add mayonnaise and beat with rotary beater until fluffy. Fold in cranberries, apple, and pecans. Stir and pour into individual molds. Chill until firm. Serves 6.

CUCUMBER ASPIC

This Cucumber Aspic is a pretty green salad. Shrimp or tuna fish go well with this one.

1 package (3 ounce) lime-
flavored gelatin
1 cup hot water
1 cup grated or diced cucumber,
drained
1 tablespoon lemon juice or
vinegar

4 drops Tabasco sauce
½ teaspoon salt
1 small seeded green pepper,
chopped
1 pimento, chopped (optional)

Dissolve gelatin in hot water. Add ingredients as listed. Turn into mold and chill until firm. If made in ring mold, fill center with Shrimp Salad*. Serve with mayonnaise. Serves 6.

CUCUMBER COTTAGE CHEESE SALAD

1 large unpeeled cucumber
½ tablespoon unflavored gelatin
1 cup liquid (cucumber juice
plus water)
1 package (3 ounce) lime-
flavored gelatin

1 cup cottage cheese
2 tablespoons grated onion
½ cup mayonnaise
½ cup slivered almonds
¼ teaspoon salt
Dash pepper.

Grate and drain cucumber. Soak unflavored gelatin in ¼ cup liquid. Heat the rest of liquid and dissolve lime gelatin. Cool. Mix cucumber well with cottage cheese. Add other ingredients. Mix with gelatin mixtures, pour into individual molds, and chill until firm. Serves 6 to 8.

DESSERT SALAD

This Dessert Salad may double as a salad and dessert. Nice for a bridal party.

2 tablespoons unflavored gelatin
1 cup canned pineapple juice
⅓ cup sugar
¼ teaspoon salt
¼ teaspoon paprika
1 pint mayonnaise
1 large grapefruit, cut in small segments

1½ cups white cherries, pitted and drained (17 ounce jar)
2½ cups drained canned crushed pineapple
¾ cup chopped almonds or pecans
1 pint cream, whipped

Sprinkle gelatin over ½ cup cold pineapple juice to soften. Heat remaining pineapple juice and dissolve gelatin-pineapple mixture in it. Add sugar, salt, and paprika and dissolve. Cool slightly and add all ingredients except cream. Set in refrigerator until cool and fold in whipped cream. Pour into individual molds and chill until firm. Makes 24 or more molds.

ELEANOR'S BING CHERRY SALAD

1 package (6 ounce) black cherry-flavored gelatin
3 cups hot water, no more
2 cups drained canned crushed pineapple
2 cups Bing or Dark Sweet pitted cherries

1½ cups drained and pitted white cherries (17 ounce jar)
½ cup cherry juice
Juice 1 small lemon
3 tablespoons sherry
1 cup chopped celery
1 cup chopped nuts

Mix gelatin with water according to directions. Add remaining ingredients. Pour into individual molds and chill until firm. Makes 20 molds.

ENGLISH PEA SALAD

*This English Pea Salad is good for most any meal. The first time
I ate it was at a brunch; it is particularly nice for this.*

2 cans (17 ounces each) very
  young small early green peas
½ pound grated sharp Cheddar
  cheese
1 jar (4 ounce) chopped
  pimento

1 cup finely chopped celery
1½ tablespoons grated onion
Salt to taste
Your favorite mayonnaise to
  moisten (homemade is best)

Drain peas thoroughly and dry on paper towels. It is most important
to dry peas. Mix the peas with other ingredients lightly. Chill and
serve. This salad will keep several days in refrigerator; the flavor
improves. This is pretty served in tomato aspic rings. Serves 10 to
12.

NOTE: Green peas are called English peas in some localities.

FROZEN FRUIT SALAD

*This Frozen Fruit Salad is a bit different and a grand summer
party salad.*

1 teaspoon unflavored gelatin
2 tablespoons cold water
2 tablespoons grapefruit juice
¼ cup mayonnaise
1 cup diced fruit, fresh or
  canned, drained

⅓ cup grapefruit pulp
Dash salt
Dash paprika
Sugar
½ cup cream, whipped

Soak gelatin in water. Dissolve over hot water, add grapefruit juice
slowly, and add to mayonnaise. Fold in diced fruit and grapefruit
pulp and season to taste with salt, paprika, and sugar. Carefully fold
in cream, mix lightly. Freeze in refrigerator tray. Serves 8 to 10.

FROZEN PINEAPPLE SALAD

This Frozen Pineapple Salad is good. It makes a cooling salad in the summertime.

1 package (3 ounce) cream
  cheese
¼ cup mayonnaise

½ pint heavy cream
½ pound cut marshmallows
1 cup canned crushed pineapple

Cream cheese and mayonnaise until smooth. Whip cream and add cut marshmallows. Combine cheese mixture with cream mixture. Add pineapple and freeze. Serves 8.

GINGER ALE SALAD

1 package (3 ounce) lemon-
  flavored gelatin
½ cup hot water
1½ cups ginger ale
2 tablespoons chopped
  crystallized ginger

1 cup chopped peeled apple
1 cup chopped dates
¼ cup chopped nuts
8 strawberries (optional)

Dissolve gelatin in water. Add ginger ale, blend thoroughly. Cool. When mixture begins to thicken, add ginger, apple, dates, and nuts. Drop a strawberry in bottom of individual molds and pour a bit of mixture over. Let harden a bit and pour remainder over. Chill and serve on lettuce. Makes 8 molds.

GREENGAGE PLUM SALAD

2½ cups greengage plums
  (canned)
2 packages (3 ounces each)
  lime-flavored gelatin
3½ cups hot water and plum
  syrup

Juice 1 lemon
1 package (8 ounce) cream
  cheese
1 cup chopped pecans

Drain plums. Dissolve gelatin in hot water using plum syrup as part of water. Cool. Remove plum seeds and run pulp through sieve or food mill. Add lemon juice. Cream the pulp and cheese until smooth. When gelatin is cool, add to plum mixture. Add nuts and pour into individual molds. Makes about 18 molds.

HARRIET'S SALAD

This is a grand vegetable salad; it comes from down in Alabama.

1 package (3 ounce) lemon-flavored gelatin
½ cup boiling water
1 can (8½ ounce) tiny early green peas, drained
½ cup liquid from peas
1¼ cups chopped celery
1¼ cups grated carrot
1 tablespoon chopped onion

1 tablespoon chopped green pepper
¼ cup vinegar
1 teaspoon dry or prepared mustard
1 tablespoon sugar
1 teaspoon salt
1 cup mayonnaise

Dissolve gelatin in water. Add remaining ingredients. Pour into individual molds. Makes 15 molds.

JELLIED BING CHERRY SALAD

1 tablespoon unflavored gelatin
¼ cup cold water
1 package (3 ounce) cherry gelatin
1½ cups hot water

1 can (1 pound) Bing or Dark Sweet pitted cherries
2 cups juice from cherries
½ cup sherry

Place unflavored gelatin in cold water. Combine cherry gelatin with hot water and dissolve unflavored gelatin in this. Drain canned cherries and add 2 cups cherry juice and sherry to gelatin. Place cherries in mold and fill with liquid. Put in refrigerator to set. Pecan halves may be placed in mold if you wish. Serves 6 to 8.

JELLIED CRANBERRY SALAD

1 package (3 ounce) lemon-
flavored gelatin
1 cup hot water
1 cup jellied cranberry sauce

1 cup diced celery
½ cup drained canned crushed
pineapple

Dissolve gelatin in water. Add cranberry sauce and beat until smooth with hand beater or electric at low speed. Chill. When slightly thickened fold in celery and pineapple. Makes 8 molds.

MOLDED EGG SALAD

This Molded Egg Salad is an Easter idea.

2 tablespoons unflavored gelatin
½ cup cold water
1 cup hot water
Clove garlic
12 large hard-cooked eggs
1 cup mayonnaise

2 teaspoons salt
¼ teaspoon pepper
1 tablespoon lemon juice
2 tablespoons chopped green
pepper
2 tablespoons chopped pimento

Sprinkle gelatin over cold water. Let stand for about 10 minutes and dissolve in cup of hot water. Rub mixing bowl with a cut clove of garlic. Discard garlic. Now sieve the eggs in bowl. If yolks are large or very yellow omit yolks of 3 or 4 eggs as the salad should be pale, not too yellow. Mix mayonnaise, salt, pepper, lemon juice, green pepper, and pimento. Add eggs and gelatin mixture. Grease individual molds with salad oil. Pour egg mixture in molds and chill thoroughly; when congealed unmold and serve on lettuce. Makes 10 to 12 servings.

MOLDED POTATO SALAD

This congealed Potato Salad is a nice change from regular potato salad. More party-like. I dreamed this one up one day when having smörgåsbord.

1 can (10½ ounce) cream of potato soup diluted with ½ cup water
1 tablespoon unflavored gelatin
¼ cup cold water
1 cup drained canned tiny green peas
1 cup chopped celery

¼ cup chopped pickles
2 tablespoons chopped pimento
1 tablespoon chopped green pepper
2 tablespoons mayonnaise
½ teaspoon salt
Dash paprika

Heat soup to boiling point. In the meantime sprinkle gelatin in water, let stand 5 minutes. Add gelatin to hot soup and stir until dissolved. Cool. Fold in peas, celery, pickles, pimento, pepper, and mayonnaise. Add salt and paprika. Pour into individual molds and chill until congealed. Unmold and garnish if desired with tomatoes and hard-cooked eggs. Makes 8 small molds.

MOON SALAD

2 packages (3 ounces each) cream cheese
1 package (3 ounce) lime-flavored gelatin
1 cup hot water

½ cup pineapple juice
1 cup drained canned crushed pineapple
1 cup chopped nuts

Cream cheese and gelatin in bowl, add water and juice; stir until gelatin is dissolved. Add pineapple and nuts. Pour into individual molds and chill in refrigerator until congealed. You may substitute lemon for lime-flavored gelatin in making this salad. Makes 8 molds.

OLD-FASHIONED LETTUCE SALAD

This next recipe will bring a feeling of nostalgia to many.

1 medium head leaf lettuce
½ cup chopped onions, green
  ones if you have them
½ cup light cream

1 teaspoon sugar
¼ cup vinegar
Dash salt

Tear lettuce into bite-size pieces. Add onions. Mix cream, sugar, vinegar, and salt. Pour over lettuce and onions. Toss and serve at once. Serves 4.

PERFECTION SALAD

1 package (3 ounce) lemon-
  flavored gelatin
2 cups hot water
½ cup finely shredded cabbage
1 cup finely chopped celery

2 to 3 teaspoons finely chopped
  pimento
½ teaspoon salt
1 tablespoon vinegar

Dissolve gelatin in water. Chill. When mixture begins to thicken, add remaining ingredients. Mold in individual molds if desired. Serve on lettuce with a bit of mayonnaise. (I sometimes substitute ½ cup canned green peas (drained) for the cabbage in this.) Makes 6 molds.

PICKLED PEACH SALAD

1 jar (1 pound, 13 ounce)
  pickled peaches
Water
5 to 6 cloves

1 package (3 ounce) lemon-
  flavored gelatin
½ cup chopped pecans

Drain juice from peaches, add water to make 2 cups juice. Bring to boil. Add cloves, boil 3 to 4 minutes. Remove cloves, add gelatin and dissolve. Cut peaches fine, add nuts, and place in molds. Pour gelatin mixture over and divide among individual molds. Place in refrigerator to congeal. Makes 6 to 8 molds.

PINEAPPLE AND CUCUMBER SALAD

2 tablespoons unflavored gelatin
¼ cup cold water
1 cup boiling water
¼ cup sugar
½ teaspoon salt
¼ cup vinegar
Juice ½ lemon

1 cup diced cucumber
1 cup drained canned crushed
  pineapple
½ cup mayonnaise
¼ cup cream, whipped
Dash paprika

Soak gelatin in cold water 5 minutes, then dissolve in boiling water. Add sugar, salt, vinegar, and lemon juice. Cool. When mixture begins to thicken stir in cucumber and pineapple and pour into individual molds. Chill until congealed. Unmold and garnish with mayonnaise to which the whipped cream has been added. Sprinkle with paprika. Serves 12 to 15.

PRESSED CHICKEN SALAD

5 cups finely chopped cooked
  chicken
2 tablespoons unflavored gelatin
¼ cup cold water
4 cups hot chicken broth
3 to 4 hard-cooked eggs, finely
  chopped
1 cup finely chopped celery

1 jar (2 ounce) chopped
  pimentos
½ cup mayonnaise or cooked
  salad dressing
Juice 2 lemons
Salt to taste
Pepper to taste
Dash paprika

Cut chicken smaller for this than for regular Chicken Salad. Soak gelatin in water. Dissolve in hot broth. Cool and mix in other ingredients. Mold. Serves 24.

RICE SALAD

1 cup rice
½ cup mayonnaise
1 tablespoon prepared mustard
Dash salt
Dash Worcestershire sauce
1 cup cooked green peas

½ cup diced celery
½ cup chopped pickles
1 tablespoon chopped pimento
1 tablespoon chopped green
pepper

Cook rice according to directions. Drain and cool. Combine mayonnaise, mustard, salt, and Worcestershire sauce. Toss with peas, celery, pickles, pimento, and pepper. Mix with rice. Arrange salad on lettuce. Serves 6 to 8.

RUTH'S MINCEMEAT SALAD

2 packages (3 ounces each)
cherry-flavored gelatin
2½ cups hot water
1 package (9 ounce) mincemeat

Juice and rind 1 lemon
½ cup sherry
½ cup chopped pecans

Dissolve gelatin in water. Add mincemeat, lemon juice, grated rind, sherry, and pecans. Pour into individual molds and chill until set. Makes 12 to 15 molds.

SAUERKRAUT SLAW

3 cups drained sauerkraut
1 to 2 cloves garlic, minced, or 1
tablespoon onion juice

1 cup dairy sour cream
1 teaspoon caraway seed
(optional)

Combine kraut and garlic in large bowl. Chill about 2 or 3 hours. Just before serving, stir in sour cream. For extra flavor, add caraway seed if desired. Serves 6.

SHRIMP ASPIC

This Shrimp Aspic is a "goody" for one of those hot, summer days. This is a good tomato aspic recipe; just omit shrimp.

2 tablespoons unflavored gelatin
½ cup cold water
2½ cups tomato juice
1 teaspoon prepared horseradish
¼ teaspoon red pepper
1 teaspoon salt
1 teaspoon Worcestershire sauce

2 tablespoons lemon juice
1 tablespoon onion juice
1½ cups cleaned and cooked shrimp
¼ cup diced celery
¼ cup finely chopped green pepper

Soften gelatin in water. Heat 1 cup of tomato juice, pour over gelatin, and stir until dissolved. Add remaining tomato juice, horseradish, pepper, salt, and Worcestershire. Chill until mixture begins to thicken and stir in rest of ingredients. Pour into oiled molds and chill until set. Serve with mayonnaise. Serves 10 to 12.

NOTE: This may be molded in a 2-quart ring mold.

SHRIMP SALAD

A Shrimp Salad is one of the best luncheon ideas of all, nice to serve with cucumber or tomato aspic.

4 pounds shrimp, cleaned and cooked
1½ cups finely chopped celery
Approximately 25 small chunks cucumber pickle, chopped
5 to 6 hard-cooked eggs, finely chopped

Salt to taste
Dash pepper
Dash paprika
Dash cayenne
Juice ½ lemon, or as needed
½ cup mayonnaise, or more as needed

Cut shrimp in medium-size pieces. Add other ingredients and season to taste. Serve on lettuce. Serves 8 to 10.

TOMATO ASPIC

1 package (3 ounce) lemon-
  flavored gelatin
1½ cups boiling water
1 tablespoon unflavored gelatin
¼ cup cold water
1 can (15 ounce) tomato sauce
1½ teaspoons vinegar

3 tablespoons lemon juice
½ teaspoon salt
Dash black pepper
1 to 2 drops Tabasco sauce
Chopped celery (optional)
Green pepper (optional)
Olives (optional)

Dissolve lemon gelatin in water. Sprinkle unflavored gelatin in cold water and dissolve over heat; add to lemon gelatin with other ingredients. Chill and mold plain or if desired add chopped celery, green pepper, and olives. Makes 10 to 12 individual molds.

NOTE: This is nice to make in 1½-quart ring mold and fill with Chicken* or Shrimp Salad*.

TROPICAL SALAD

One of the salads I serve often is this Tropical Salad. It is refreshing and goes well with meats. It is also a grand salad to serve with a meat sandwich. Simple and always good.

2 packages (3 ounces each)
  lemon-flavored gelatin, or lime
1 cup boiling water
Pineapple and grapefruit juice to
  equal 3 cups
2 cups drained canned crushed
  pineapple

Segments 1 fresh grapefruit
1 cup chopped pecans (optional)
1 tablespoon finely chopped
  green pepper (optional)

Dissolve gelatin in water. Add pineapple and grapefruit juice. When mixture begins to thicken, add pineapple, grapefruit, pecans, and pepper. Pour into individual molds and chill. Makes 12 to 15 molds.

YELLOW CHEESE SALAD

2 cups canned crushed pineapple
Juice 1 lemon
1 cup sugar
2 tablespoons unflavored gelatin
½ cup cold water
1 cup grated Cheddar cheese

½ pint heavy cream, whipped
2 tablespoons finely chopped
pimento
2 tablespoons finely chopped
green pepper

Heat pineapple, lemon juice, and sugar. Sprinkle gelatin in water, let stand 5 minutes. Dissolve in hot pineapple mixture. When cool add cheese, whipped cream, pimento, and pepper. Pour into molds and chill to congeal. Makes 12 to 14 molds.

BARBECUE SAUCE

Here is a Southern Barbecue Sauce for barbecued chicken. Set on a table by the grill and each time you turn the meat "mop" it with sauce. The chicken must cook slowly and be well done to be good.

2 medium-size onions, finely
chopped
2 medium-size green peppers,
finely chopped
1 hot pepper or cayenne to taste
2 cloves garlic

¼ cup Worcestershire sauce
½ pint vinegar
1 cup water
¼ cup sugar, or to taste
1 teaspoon salt

Mix all ingredients and let simmer covered about 15 minutes or until onions and peppers are done. Now "set back" for about an hour. Have sauce hot when you put it on the meat. Makes 2½ cups.

COOKED SALAD DRESSING

4 tablespoons flour
½ teaspoon salt
¼ teaspoon paprika
2 tablespoons sugar

½ teaspoon dry mustard
1½ cups boiling water
2 eggs
⅓ cup lemon juice

Mix and sift dry ingredients. Add water gradually, stirring constantly. Cook in top of double boiler until thick and smooth. Beat eggs slightly, pour cooked mixture slowly over them. When well blended, return to double boiler; cook 2 minutes. Add lemon juice, remove from stove and beat well. Makes 2 cups.

NOTE: This will keep about a week in refrigerator.

FRENCH DRESSING I

1 can (10½ ounce) tomato soup
1 cup salad oil
½ cup sugar
1 cup vinegar

2½ teaspoons salt
1¼ teaspoons dry mustard
1½ teaspoons black pepper
2 medium onions, grated

Mix all ingredients in a large bowl. Keeps indefinitely in refrigerator. Makes 1 quart.

NOTE: The mustard gives this an unusual flavor.

FRENCH DRESSING II

This is "extra special" French Dressing, a family favorite.

1 cup salad oil
½ cup sugar
1 medium onion, grated
½ cup apple cider vinegar
½ cup chili sauce

Juice 1 lemon
2 teaspoons salt
1 tablespoon pepper
2 teaspoons paprika

Mix all ingredients and serve on vegetable, green, or fruit salad. Store in jar in refrigerator; keeps indefinitely. Makes 2½ cups.

GREEN GODDESS DRESSING

1 cup mayonnaise
½ cup dairy sour cream
⅓ cup chopped parsley
3 tablespoons minced chives or
  green onions
2 tablespoons anchovy paste

3 tablespoons tarragon vinegar
1 teaspoon Worcestershire sauce
Dash dry mustard
¼ teaspoon pepper
1 clove garlic, minced

Combine all ingredients in bowl. Chill and allow flavors to blend and dressing to thicken, about 2 hours. This will keep about 2 weeks in refrigerator. Makes about 2 cups.

HARD SAUCE

½ cup butter
1½ cups sugar
2 tablespoons brandy

Cream butter; slowly work in sugar and beat until mixture is light and smooth. Slowly blend in brandy and chill. Serve with any hot pudding, fruit cake, mince or pumpkin pie. Makes 2 cups.

HOLLANDAISE SAUCE

A friend gave me this recipe; it's easy and good.

½ cup dairy sour cream
½ cup mayonnaise

1 teaspoon prepared mustard
2 teaspoons lemon juice

Mix and heat over very low heat. Makes 1 cup.

JIMPY'S SALAD DRESSING

2 cups sugar
2 cups salad oil
2 teaspoons grated onion
3 teaspoons salt

2 cups minced celery
1½ cups vinegar
2 teaspoons Worcestershire sauce
1 cup catsup or chili

Mix all ingredients in bowl. Keeps indefinitely. It is grand for green salads and particularly good on tomatoes. Makes 2½ cups dressing.

MOSS OAKS FRENCH DRESSING

½ cup sugar
½ cup salad oil
⅓ cup vinegar
½ cup catsup

2 teaspoons paprika
¼ teaspoon salt
Clove garlic
1 small onion, grated

Measure sugar first, then other ingredients. Put in glass jar and shake to mix. If placed in refrigerator it keeps indefinitely. Makes 2 cups.

OLD-FASHIONED BARBECUE SAUCE

This Barbecue Sauce was given to me a long time ago by some-one who was famous for his barbecue and barbecue sauce. He cooked his barbecue over a long pit in the ground, as they barbecue down South. This is the sauce he put on his meat with a "mop" as it slowly cooked over a hickory wood fire. We keep a bottle in our house today to pour over the barbecue that we buy.

3 tablespoons prepared mustard
2 tablespoons black pepper
2 tablespoons red pepper
⅓ cup catsup

⅓ cup Worcestershire sauce
1 quart vinegar
1 tablespoon sugar

Mix mustard, black and red pepper well. Mix in catsup, Worcestershire sauce, vinegar, and sugar. (For hotter sauce add a tablespoon of Tabasco.) Simmer sauce about 10 minutes. Store in bottle. Keeps well, not necessary to refrigerate. Makes 1 quart.

PINEAPPLE-LIME FRENCH DRESSING

This Pineapple-Lime French Dressing is grand for a fruit plate.

1 cup salad oil
¼ cup canned pineapple juice
¼ cup lime juice
1 tablespoon lemon juice

⅓ cup sugar
1 teaspoon paprika
½ teaspoon salt

Combine ingredients in jar, cover and shake. Chill. Shake before serving. This will keep a week or more. Makes 1½ cups.

POPPY-SEED DRESSING

½ cup sugar
Dash salt
Dash dry mustard

¼ cup salad vinegar
1 cup salad oil
½ teaspoon poppy seed

Combine sugar, salt, mustard, and vinegar; heat to boiling. Cool. Add oil slowly; beat constantly with electric or rotary beater. Stir in poppy seed. Keeps indefinitely if refrigerated. Makes 1½ cups.

SANFORD HOUSE DRESSING

1 teaspoon salt
1 teaspoon paprika
1 teaspoon dry mustard
1 teaspoon celery seed

½ cup sugar
1 cup salad oil
¼ cup tarragon vinegar
½ teaspoon grated onion

Combine dry ingredients in bowl of electric mixer. Add oil and vinegar alternately. Do this thoroughly. Beat well after each addition;

add onion last. Store at medium temperature. This dressing may be stored in refrigerator. Keeps indefinitely. If it separates, stir it together again. Makes about 2 cups.

SAUCE FOR TOMATO SALAD

1 cup sugar	¾ cup vinegar
1 tablespoon finely chopped onion	½ cup catsup
1½ teaspoons salt	1 tablespoon Worcestershire sauce
1 cup salad oil	1 cup chopped celery

Combine all ingredients except celery; beat with egg beater until mixed well. Add celery and stir with spoon. This will keep for several weeks in refrigerator. Makes 2 cups.

SOUR CREAM DRESSING

This Dressing is good on slaw as well as green salads.

1 cup dairy sour cream	1 tablespoon sugar
2 tablespoons vinegar	1 tablespoon salt
1 tablespoon lemon juice	

Combine ingredients and mix well. This dressing will keep a week in refrigerator. Makes 1½ cups.

THOUSAND ISLAND DRESSING

1 cup mayonnaise	1 teaspoon chopped pimento
3 tablespoons catsup	1 teaspoon finely chopped onion or chives
1 tablespoon chopped green pepper	

Blend thoroughly. Chill and serve on lettuce wedges. This will keep a week or more in refrigerator. Makes about 1½ cups.

VINAIGRETTE FOR ASPARAGUS

*This Vinaigrette dressing for asparagus is good not only for this,
but for beans or other vegetables as well.*

¼ cup wine or cider vinegar
½ cup salad oil
3 teaspoons prepared mustard
Dash salt
Dash paprika
Dash pepper

1 teaspoon chopped parsley
2 teaspoons finely chopped
   pimento
½ teaspoon grated onion
2 teaspoons sugar

Mix and serve over asparagus. This makes about 1 cup.

Vegetables

The vegetables you find in Southern cooking are usually prepared with a piece of bacon or ham in the water in which they are cooked. Black-eyed peas, green beans, and turnip greens are favorites in the Southland.

Fried Corn is mouth-watering, and gumbo made from fresh okra and tomatoes and seasoned to taste is something to rave about. You'll find casseroles the order of the day for today's cooks. These along with Candied Sweet Potatoes and Sweet Potato Soufflé are fare for any gentleman, Southern or otherwise. You'll be thinking as one man has so aptly put it, "all this and heaven too!"

Southern cooking is a home art; it's food flavored with the artist's blends of the particular family and served with a bit of courtesy and pride for this or that special recipe. There is a variety of vegetable recipes herein, among which I hope you will find your very own favorite.

ASPARAGUS CASSEROLE

1 can (14½ ounce) asparagus, with liquid	¼ cup water
2 tablespoons flour	1 cup bread crumbs
1 tablespoon butter	¼ to ½ cup slivered almonds
1 teaspoon salt	½ cup grated cheese
	2 hard-cooked eggs, sliced

Preheat oven to 325 degrees F. Drain asparagus, save liquid. Blend flour, butter, asparagus liquid, salt, and water. Cook until mixture is thickened. Line 1½-quart casserole with bread crumbs, reserve some for top. Place asparagus, almonds, cheese, and eggs in layers. Pour sauce over this. Cover with remaining crumbs. Bake until golden brown. Serves 6.

ASPARAGUS PIMENTO CASSEROLE

2 cups canned asparagus cut in 2-inch pieces	1 cup grated Cheddar cheese
1 teaspoon salt	1½ cups finely rolled cracker crumbs
Dash paprika	1 cup milk
1 pimento, cut in small pieces	½ cup margarine, melted
3 eggs, beaten	

Preheat oven to 350 degrees F. Mix all ingredients except margarine. Pour into buttered 2-quart casserole. Pour margarine over top. Bake uncovered about 20 to 30 minutes. Serves 6.

BLACK-EYED PEAS

It's an old Southern custom to serve Black-eyed Peas and hog jowl on New Year's Day. This is supposed to bring good luck throughout the year. I'll eat the peas, you may have the jowl. For everyday eating cook the peas with bacon or ham. For "Hopping John," serve peas with a little of the liquid from peas with boiled rice.

¼ to ½ pound hog jowl or ¼ pound streak lean bacon
5 cups water, add more if necessary during cooking

1 teaspoon salt or to taste
2 cups shelled fresh or dried black-eyed peas

Add hog jowl (or other meat) to water, add salt and bring to boil. Cook slowly a few minutes and add peas. Simmer until meat and peas are done. Serves 6.

NOTE: If you use dried peas, wash and boil for 10 or 15 minutes in enough water to cover. Drain off this water as it will be dark. Now add these peas to pot with hog jowl and cook until done.

BROCCOLI CASSEROLE

2 packages (10 ounces each) frozen chopped broccoli, cooked as directed
3 to 4 tablespoons butter or margarine
3 tablespoons flour

Dash salt
2 cups milk
½ cup grated Cheddar cheese
1 teaspoon grated onion
¼ cup bread crumbs

Preheat oven to 350 degrees F. Place broccoli in 2-quart casserole. Melt butter over low heat, stir in flour and salt until well blended. Slowly stir in 2 cups milk. Mix well. Add cheese to sauce as it cooks. Let cheese melt, add grated onion. Pour cheese sauce over broccoli. Top with bread crumbs and place in oven. Bake 10 to 15 minutes to heat through and brown lightly. Serves 8.

BROWN RICE CASSEROLE

This Brown Rice Casserole is a grand dish to serve with chicken, ham, or turkey.

½ cup margarine
1 cup white long grain rice
1 can (10½ ounce) condensed onion soup
1 can (10½ ounce) condensed consommé

Dash Worcestershire sauce
Dash black pepper
1 can (2 ounce) mushrooms, drained

Preheat oven to 375 degrees F. Place margarine in pan, add rice. Brown until rice "crackles." Pour onion soup and consommé in 2-quart casserole. Stir. Add rice to mixture and season with Worcestershire and pepper. Add mushrooms. Bake covered for 1 hour. Serves 6 to 8.

CABBAGE CASSEROLE

This is a dish the men enjoy, a nice way with cabbage.

3 pounds cabbage, chopped or shredded
1 pound onions, sliced
2½ cups rolled cheese crackers, reserve ½ cup
½ cup butter or margarine

4 tablespoons butter or margarine
4 tablespoons flour
1 tablespoon salt
2 cups milk
1 can (10½ ounce) condensed cream of mushroom soup

Preheat oven to 375 degrees F. Cook cabbage in boiling water for 7 minutes. Cook onion slices in boiling salted water until tender. Place layer of cabbage in 2-quart casserole, a layer of onions, and layer of cheese cracker crumbs. Dot ½ cup butter over top. Make sauce of remaining butter, flour, salt, and milk. Combine with mushroom soup and pour over top. Sprinkle with ½ cup reserved cracker crumbs. Bake 30 minutes. Serves 12.

CANDIED SWEET POTATOES

Mother's cook, Malissa, used to serve the best Candied Sweet Potatoes I've ever eaten. I think that once you cook potatoes in this manner you will agree that they are the "best."

1½ cups sugar, plus 2 to 3 teaspoons
½ cup water
Dash salt

3 to 4 medium sweet potatoes
2 tablespoons butter
⅛ teaspoon vanilla

Mix 1½ cups sugar, water, and salt. Stir until sugar is almost dissolved. Place on top of stove on high heat. Peel potatoes, slice in half, then slice in 3 or 4 long pieces. (I cut my potatoes on a bread board; they are easy to slice in this manner, and it saves slicing your hand.) As you cut potatoes drop them in the water and sugar mixture. Cook on high heat about 10 minutes and then on medium heat for about 20 minutes or until potatoes are tender. Cook these uncovered, the juice will boil down and thicken. (Do not worry if the syrup mixture does not cover potatoes when put in pot. They will soon "cook down" into the syrup.) Add butter and when syrup has cooked down about half, add flavoring and pour into shallow baking dish, 11½×7½ inches. Sprinkle 2 or 3 teaspoons of sugar over potatoes and run under broiler about 5 to 10 minutes to glaze and brown a bit. Serves 4 to 6.

NOTE: For variation you may use dash of cinnamon, nutmeg, or allspice for flavor, add drained crushed pineapple to the syrup, or sprinkle with 1 teaspoon grated lemon rind.

NOTE: This dish may be made ahead and reheated. It seems to improve in flavor.

CASSEROLE OF PEAS AND ONIONS

Easy-to-do casseroles are popular these days when so many of us are working gals. This one for peas and onions is good; you may substitute green beans for the peas as a change.

2 to 2½ cups drained canned early green peas, reserve liquid
1 can (10½ ounce) condensed cream of mushroom soup
Dash salt

Dash paprika
1 can (3½ ounce) French fried onions
1 to 2 tablespoons butter

Preheat oven to 350 degrees F. Add ¼ cup of the liquid from peas to soup. Pour half the peas in 1½-quart casserole and add dash of salt and paprika. Pour half of the soup over this and sprinkle on half the onions. Again a layer of peas, season with dots of butter, now remaining soup, top with onions. Bake for 20 to 30 minutes or until hot and bubbly. Serves 6 to 8.

CAULIFLOWER CASSEROLE

1 medium cauliflower, broken in flowerets
1 package (10 ounce) frozen green peas
Salt
1 to 2 tablespoons butter
¼ teaspoon salt

Dash paprika
1 cup bread crumbs
2 cups Medium Cream Sauce (as below)
½ cup grated sharp Cheddar cheese
½ cup bread crumbs

Cook cauliflower and peas separately in a small amount of salted water about 5 minutes. Drain and place a layer of each in 2-quart casserole. Dot with butter, add salt, paprika, and layer of bread crumbs. Pour over sauce to which cheese has been added. Repeat layers. When casserole is filled top with ½ cup bread crumbs. Preheat oven to 400 degrees F. Bake about 15 to 20 minutes. Serves 6 to 8.

MEDIUM CREAM SAUCE

4 tablespoons butter or margarine	Dash salt
3 tablespoons flour	2 cups milk or cream

Melt butter over low heat, remove from heat. Add flour and salt, stir until smooth. Slowly stir in milk. Return to heat, bring to boil stirring constantly. Simmer 1 minute. Makes 2 cups.

CELERY CASSEROLE

These Celery Casseroles will be a change for your vegetable list.

2 cups sliced celery	1 cup buttered bread crumbs
1 can (10 ounce) condensed cream of chicken soup	Salt to taste
	Pepper to taste
½ cup blanched almonds	
1 to 2 tablespoons chopped pimento	

Preheat oven to 350 degrees F. Mix ingredients, reserving a few bread crumbs for top of casserole. Place in 1½-quart casserole and bake about 15 minutes or until bubbly. Serves 6.

CELERY AND MUSHROOMS

3 cups celery cut in ¼-inch crosswise pieces	1 to 2 tablespoons butter
1 cup boiling water	Dash salt
1 cube chicken bouillon	⅛ teaspoon pepper
1 can (4 ounce) drained mushrooms	1 teaspoon soy sauce
	½ cup slivered, toasted almonds

Preheat oven to 350 degrees F. Cook celery in water with bouillon cube until tender. Drain. Sauté mushrooms in butter for 3 to 5 minutes. Season with salt, pepper, and soy sauce. Add to cooked celery. Pour into 1½-quart casserole and top with almonds. Bake until it is heated through and bubbly. Serves 8.

CORN AND TOMATO PIE

1 cup sliced tomatoes
2 cups fresh corn cut from the cob or 1 can (1 pound, 1 ounce) cream-style corn
½ cup sliced green peppers
2 to 3 pieces bacon, fried crisp and crumbled

1 teaspoon salt
1 teaspoon sugar
2 tablespoons butter
1 cup bread crumbs

Preheat oven to 350 degrees F. Fill greased 2-quart casserole with ingredients, alternating layers of tomatoes, corn, peppers, and bacon. Sprinkle each layer with dash of salt and sugar. Top with layer of corn. Dot with butter and cover with crumbs. Bake about 30 minutes. Serves 8.

DEVILED CORN CUSTARD

Here is a "quickie" casserole using two delicious canned items, corn and deviled ham.

3 eggs, separated
½ cup scalded milk
1 tablespoon margarine or butter
1 can (1 pound, 1 ounce) cream-style corn

2 cans (2½ ounces each) deviled ham
½ teaspoon dry mustard
⅛ teaspoon pepper
Dash paprika

Preheat oven to 300 degrees F. Beat egg yolks. Mix in milk, cook over medium heat, stirring constantly. Add butter and allow to melt in mixture. Now add corn, ham, mustard, and seasonings. Beat egg whites until stiff but not dry; fold into corn mixture. Bake in 1½-quart casserole about 1 hour or until firm. Serves 6.

FRIED ASPARAGUS

This Fried Asparagus is another idea to try with asparagus.

1 can (14½ ounce) asparagus   Fat for frying
1 egg diluted with 2 tablespoons   Paprika
  water   Salt
Cracker crumbs

Drain asparagus and dip in beaten egg. Roll in cracker crumbs, dip in egg again. Fry in deep fat, drain on paper toweling. Dust with paprika and salt. Serve hot. Serves 6.

FRIED CORN

Nothing is better in the summertime "down South" than Fried Corn.

8 ears tender corn   Salt to taste
3 to 4 tablespoons bacon   Pepper to taste
  drippings   ½ to 1 teaspoon sugar
1 cup milk   3 to 4 tablespoons butter

Cut corn close to outer edge, cutting twice around ear. Now scrape the ear to remove all the milk. Have skillet warm, add drippings and corn. Sometimes I add a bit of water to corn if it seems too dry. Stir constantly for a minute or so and add milk, salt, pepper, and sugar. Let simmer for about 15 minutes or until thickened. Watch and stir often as corn burns and sticks easily. Add butter the last few minutes of cooking. Serves 4 to 6.

NOTE: If you have no bacon drippings, fry 5 or 6 pieces of bacon and use drippings. Discard bacon.

FRIED GREEN TOMATOES

Slice firm, green tomatoes in slices about a quarter or half inch thick. Dip each slice in corn meal to which you have added a generous amount of salt, and a dash of sugar. Fry in bacon drippings or salad oil until brown; turn once during cooking. One tomato makes 3 to 4 slices. Serve 3 or 4 slices per serving.

GREEN BEANS AND CHESTNUTS

2 cups celery cut in 1-inch pieces
2 tablespoons butter
1 can (5 ounce) water chestnuts, drained
2 packages (10 ounces each) frozen French-style green beans, cooked and drained

Salt to taste
Pepper to taste

Place celery and butter in saucepan. Cover and cook over medium heat 2 minutes. Reduce heat to low. Cook about 5 minutes or until celery is tender and crisp, adding a little water if necessary. Combine chestnuts, celery, and beans. Add salt and pepper. Heat together before serving. Serves 8.

GREEN (SNAP) BEANS, SOUTHERN STYLE

While writing my column I had many requests for recipes for cooking vegetables. This was a special one requested for cooking Green (Snap) Beans, Southern Style, like "mother used to cook." Turnip greens may be cooked in this manner.

1½ pounds (fresh) green beans
1½ to 2 quarts water
¼ pound salt pork (wash), or ham hock

1 teaspoon salt, or to taste
Pinch sugar

String beans and break into 1½-inch pieces. Wash. Fill a 3-quart saucepan half full of water and add meat. Cook (covered) approximately 20 minutes. Add beans, salt, and sugar. Cook about 45 minutes to an hour or until beans are tender and liquid is cooked down. Serves 4 to 6.

NOTE: I string my beans by cutting the string down each side with a sharp knife; this takes time, but is well worth the effort.

Butter beans may be cooked as above; I usually add a little butter just before serving.

GUMBO GEORGIA STYLE

Okra and tomatoes go together like "bread and butter." A favorite recipe is Gumbo Georgia Style. Serve it with ham— add a corn muffin, yum, yum.

2 to 3 tablespoons bacon drippings	Salt to taste
1 medium onion, chopped	Pepper to taste
2 cups canned tomatoes or 5 to 6 fresh ones, peeled and sliced	Dash celery seed
2 cups sliced okra	1 teaspoon chopped green pepper (optional)

Place drippings in heavy frying pan. Add onion and fry until light brown; add tomatoes, okra, and other ingredients. Cook covered for about 10 minutes; uncover and cook slowly until thick enough to eat with fork. Stir often to prevent sticking. Serves 6.

HAM AND ASPARAGUS CASSEROLE

Here is another variation of an Asparagus Casserole. This is a good way to use leftover ham and a grand company casserole.

3 to 4 tablespoons butter
1 teaspoon grated onion
Dash garlic salt (optional)
1 teaspoon paprika
½ teaspoon salt
⅛ teaspoon pepper
2 tablespoons flour

3 cups milk
2 cups grated sharp Cheddar
cheese
2 packages (10 ounces each)
frozen asparagus
1 cup poultry stuffing crumbs
2 cups sliced cooked ham

Melt 2 tablespoons butter and blend in grated onion and seasonings along with flour. Slowly add milk and heat, stirring constantly until thickened. Add cheese and stir until melted. Cook asparagus according to directions and cut into 1-inch lengths. Preheat oven to 375 degrees F. In the bottom of 2-quart buttered casserole sprinkle a layer of stuffing crumbs. Add layer of ham and one of asparagus. Now pour part of cheese sauce over and repeat layer of ham, asparagus, and sauce until ingredients are used. Top with remaining crumbs and butter. Bake for 45 minutes or until bubbly and browned. Serves 6.

HARVARD BEETS

Harvard Beets are a nice addition to your menu, colorful and with a sweet, tangy taste.

½ cup sugar, scant
½ tablespoon cornstarch
¼ cup vinegar
¼ cup water

2 tablespoons butter
Dash salt
1 (1 pound) jar small beets,
drained

Mix sugar and cornstarch. Add vinegar, water, butter, and salt. Boil 5 minutes. Add beets and let cook over low fire 25 to 30 minutes. Serves 6.

ITALIAN EGGPLANT

This is my favorite way to cook eggplant. I usually serve it in the eggplant shell as it looks pretty, but your casserole will do as well.

1 medium eggplant	⅔ cup water
Salt	½ teaspoon salt
½ cup chopped onion	⅛ teaspoon pepper
3 tablespoons bacon fat or salad	1 bay leaf or pinch oregano
oil	Parmesan cheese
1 can (6 ounce) tomato paste	

Pare eggplant, cut in large pieces, and cook in boiling salted water for about 10 minutes. Drain. Sauté onion in fat, add tomato paste and water, season with salt and pepper, and add bay leaf. Cook a few minutes and add eggplant. Check seasoning and remove bay leaf. Preheat oven to 350 degrees F. Place in 2-quart casserole or eggplant shells and sprinkle Parmesan cheese over top.

NOTE: To make the shells, scoop and cut out the eggplant after cutting in half lengthwise. Be careful not to cut through shell. Bake 10 to 15 minutes. Serves 6.

POTATOES AND ONIONS AU GRATIN

2 tablespoons butter or	Dash paprika
margarine	2½ cups diced or sliced cooked
2 tablespoons flour	potatoes
1 cup milk	1 jar (1 pound) onions
½ teaspoon salt	¾ cup grated Cheddar cheese
Dash pepper	

Melt butter or margarine in pan, blend in flour. Gradually add milk. Cook stirring constantly until thick. Add salt, pepper, and paprika. Preheat oven to 325 degrees F. Arrange alternate layers of potatoes, onions, sauce, and cheese in greased 2-quart baking dish. Bake 20 to 25 minutes. You may use a little of the onion liquid in your sauce if you wish, it will give a bit of flavor. Serves 6 to 8.

QUICK BAKED BEANS

These Quick Baked Beans are a nice addition to a picnic supper or for any other time. Easy and quick to do.

3 tablespoons catsup	1 teaspoon minced onion
1 tablespoon prepared mustard	1 can (1 pound) baked beans
2 tablespoons brown sugar or molasses	3 to 4 strips bacon

Preheat oven to 350 degrees F. Mix catsup, mustard, sugar, and onion; mix this with beans. Place in 1½-quart casserole. Place 3 to 4 strips bacon over top of casserole and bake 25 to 30 minutes. Serves 6 to 8.

SHREDDED YAMS

2 pounds sweet potatoes	½ cup white corn syrup
1 gallon water	½ cup water
1 tablespoon salt	¼ cup margarine
1 cup sugar	1 cup pineapple juice

Preheat oven to 350 degrees F. Peel and shred potatoes (yams) in gallon of water. Add salt. Drain and wash well. Place in baking dish, 11½×7½ inches. Mix sugar, syrup, and ½ cup water; cook until simple syrup. Add margarine. Pour pineapple juice over potatoes, then syrup. Cook 35 minutes or until they are transparent. Serves 12. (This is a famous recipe at the New Perry Hotel Dining Room in Perry, Georgia.)

SOUR CREAM SCALLOPED POTATOES

1 medium onion, chopped
1 can (3 ounce) mushrooms, drained
2 to 3 tablespoons margarine
8 medium potatoes, peeled, boiled and sliced
Bit parsley
1 teaspoon seasoned salt
Bit herb seasoning
⅛ teaspoon pepper
⅛ teaspoon paprika
1½ pints dairy sour cream

Preheat oven to 350 degrees F. Sauté onion and mushrooms in margarine. Place a layer of potatoes, onions and mushrooms, parsley, and seasonings in 2-quart casserole. Cover with sour cream. Bake 20 minutes. Serves 6.

SPINACH CASSEROLE

2 packages (10 ounces each) frozen spinach
1 can (10½ ounce) condensed cream of mushroom soup
1 to 2 bouillon cubes
3 tablespoons hot water
¾ cup grated sharp Cheddar cheese, and a bit more
1 egg, beaten
Herb crumbs

Preheat oven to 350 degrees F. Cook spinach and drain. Add soup and bouillon cubes, which have been dissolved in water. Add cheese and egg. Place in 1½-quart casserole and top with more cheese. Add a few herb crumbs to topping. Bake until bubbly. Serves 6.

SQUASH CASSEROLE

This is one of the best casseroles of its kind, a Squash Casserole with cheese.

4 to 5 strips bacon
1 large onion, chopped
1 pound shredded raw squash
1 cup fine bread crumbs
¾ cup milk
1 teaspoon salt
⅛ teaspoon pepper
1 cup grated sharp Cheddar cheese

Preheat oven to 350 degrees F. Fry bacon and drain. Sauté onion in small amount of bacon drippings. Crumble bacon and mix with onion, squash, bread crumbs, milk, and seasonings. Add cheese, saving a bit to sprinkle on top. Put in buttered 2-quart casserole and bake about 1 hour. Serves 6.

SQUASH CASSEROLE WITH PIMENTO

3 tablespoons butter
1 carton sour cream
1 cup dry bread crumbs
2 cups mashed cooked squash
1 tablespoon grated onion
1 pimento cut fine, or 1
  tablespoon canned

1 teaspoon salt
⅛ teaspoon pepper
2 eggs
½ cup buttered bread crumbs

Preheat oven to 350 degrees F. Melt butter, add crumbs and sour cream. Mix well and add squash, onion, pimento, and seasonings. Beat eggs and add to mixture. Pour into greased 2-quart casserole and cover with buttered bread crumbs. Bake 20 to 30 minutes. Serves 6.

SWEET POTATO SOUFFLE

6 medium-size sweet potatoes
¼ cup butter or margarine
½ cup brown sugar
½ cup orange juice or more if
  needed

1 tablespoon grated orange rind
10 to 12 marshmallows

Wash and boil potatoes in salted water until soft or bake in oven until done. Peel and mash or put through ricer. Add butter, sugar, juice and rind to hot potatoes. Beat until light (as creamed potatoes). Preheat oven to 350 degrees F. Place in 2-quart casserole and bake about 20 minutes. Remove from oven and cover with a topping of marshmallows. If you do not like marshmallows, try shredded coconut. Run back in oven to brown topping a bit. Serves 8.

NOTE: You may mix this dish with cream or milk in place of orange juice and rind. Our mothers did this, added a bit of nutmeg or cinnamon, and sometimes added a few raisins or pineapple to the potatoes. They topped them with marshmallows. It is versatile, so use your own ingenuity. You may use canned sweet potatoes if you cannot find good ones out of season at your grocery.

Meats

You will find pork high on the list of your Southern meats. Baked ham, Stuffed Pork Chops along with a sausage casserole, made with hot bulk sausage and combined with rice, all add up to mouth-watering dishes. Steak may be smothered with onions and let me say to those of you who have not eaten it prepared in this manner, that you have missed something. Stroganoff is here, along with other casserole dishes, for today's busy cooks. You'll find something nostalgic in the recipes for salt pork and gravy.

It may be a ham baking or ribs barbecuing on the grill. In either case, the seasoning may be your secret. And nothing will ever have the aroma of barbecue cooking over an open pit—barbecue at its best!

ROAST BEEF

Some like beef rare, some like it well done, but either way it should be cooked slowly.

Rub roast with salt and pepper. Place in roaster or baking dish and put a bit of fat on top of roast. Your butcher will give you some fat if you ask him. Roast (uncovered) at 300 to 325 degrees F. Using meat thermometer cook 28 to 30 minutes per pound for rare, 32 to 35 minutes per pound for medium, and 37 to 40 minutes per pound for well done.

NOTE: For standing rib roast count on about ¾ pound (including bone) for a serving. Let roast stand a few minutes before carving.

BEEF GRAVY: Skim off all but about 2 or 3 tablespoons fat by tipping roaster. Blend in 2 or 3 tablespoons flour, stir in 1½ to 2 cups water. Cook, stirring and scraping drippings in bottom of roaster until gravy is slightly thick. Season to taste. Add a bit of Worcestershire sauce if desired. Makes about 2 cups.

BEEF STROGANOFF

This Beef Stroganoff is nice to serve with your favorite green salad.

1 pound lean sirloin of beef
2 tablespoons flour
½ teaspoon salt
⅛ teaspoon pepper
2 tablespoons butter
½ cup chopped onion
1 clove garlic, minced
1 can (3 ounce) mushrooms, drained

1 tablespoon tomato paste (optional)
1 can (10½ ounce) condensed beef broth
1 cup dairy sour cream
2 tablespoons sherry

Trim fat from beef and cut beef in strips about ¼ inch wide and 2 or 3 inches long. Combine flour, salt, and pepper, dredge meat in mixture. Heat skillet, add butter. When melted add beef and brown quickly. Add onion, garlic, and mushrooms and cook until onion is barely tender. Now slowly add tomato paste and beef broth. Cook covered approximately 30 minutes or until meat is tender. Stir in sour cream and sherry; heat slightly. Serve over rice or noodles. Serves 4 to 6.

BRAISED SHORT RIBS

These Braised Short Ribs are delicious and may be prepared casserole style. Serve with rice and a green salad. This dish may be made ahead and reheated.

3 pounds short ribs of beef
Flour to dredge meat, about ½ cup
3 to 4 tablespoons salad oil or fat
3 tablespoons flour
2 cups water

½ cup tomato sauce
¼ cup chopped carrots
¼ cup chopped onions
¼ cup chopped celery tops
½ clove garlic
1½ teaspoons salt
⅛ teaspoon pepper

Preheat oven to 350 degrees F. Have ribs cut in individual portions. If very fat trim off some of the fat. Dredge in flour and brown on both sides in hot salad oil or fat. Place ribs in 3-quart baking dish. Blend flour into pan drippings, gradually add water. Add tomato sauce, carrots, onions, celery tops, garlic, salt, and pepper. Pour over ribs. Cover and cook in oven about 1½ hours or until tender. When done remove garlic. Serves 8.

CHILI

2 medium onions, chopped
2 to 3 tablespoons bacon drippings
1 to 1½ pounds ground beef
4 cups canned tomatoes
4 cups red kidney beans, drained
¾ teaspoon salt, or more
⅛ teaspoon pepper

1 teaspoon sugar
2 bay leaves
2 green peppers, seeded and chopped
1 cup chopped celery
1 teaspoon oregano
1 clove garlic
2 tablespoons chili powder

Sauté onions in hot bacon drippings. When tender add beef and brown. Add tomatoes and other ingredients. Simmer covered until thickened, about 2 hours. Remove bay leaves before serving. Serves 6 to 8.

CREOLE SPAGHETTI

2 large onions, chopped
1 green pepper, seeded and chopped
1 cup diced celery
3 to 4 tablespoons bacon drippings
4 cups canned tomatoes

Salt to taste
1 teaspoon Tabasco sauce
3 tablespoons Worcestershire sauce
2 cans (15¼ ounces each) spaghetti

Sauté onions, pepper, and celery in hot bacon drippings until tender. Add the tomatoes, salt, Tabasco, and Worcestershire; cook about 45 minutes. Add the spaghetti to mixture and cook covered 30 minutes. Serve hot with ham or chops. Serves 6 to 8.

GOURMET POT ROAST

Here is a Gourmet Pot Roast for you to try.

3 to 5 pounds chuck roast
2 tablespoons flour
Salt to taste
Pepper to taste
Fat if needed
1 cup sliced onions
½ cup water

⅓ cup dry red wine
4 tablespoons catsup
Pinch garlic powder
¼ teaspoon dry mustard
Generous pinch oregano
1 can (3 ounce) sliced mushrooms

Dredge meat in flour seasoned with salt and pepper to taste. Brown in hot fat (if meat is lean use bacon drippings) in deep pan or skillet; if meat has excess fat it will not be necessary to add fat to pan. Drain off excess drippings. Blend onions with water, wine, catsup, garlic powder, mustard, and oregano; add to meat. Cover and simmer for 2½ to 3 hours, or until meat is tender, adding more liquid if needed; I use liquid from mushrooms. Turn meat a time or two. A few minutes before meat is done add mushrooms. Serves 6 to 8.

HAMBURGER CASSEROLE

This Hamburger Casserole is from the mother of teen-agers; and you know she will know what they like!

1 pound ground beef
1 can (10½ ounce) condensed vegetable soup

1 can (10¾ ounce) condensed minestrone soup
1 to 2 cups mashed potatoes

Preheat oven to 350 degrees F. Brown beef lightly in frying pan, drain off drippings. Pour vegetable and minestrone soups into 3-quart casserole. Pour beef over soups, cover with desired thickness of mashed potatoes. (Instant potatoes are good for this and quicker.) Bake for about 1 hour. Serve with salad and rolls. Serves 6.

HAM AND CHEESE CASSEROLE

¼ cup milk
1 can (10½ ounce) condensed cream of mushroom soup
4 hard-cooked eggs, quartered or sliced
1 cup cubed cooked ham

1 cup grated Cheddar cheese
½ teaspoon salt
⅛ teaspoon paprika
1 package (10 ounce) frozen asparagus, prepared as directed
1 cup buttered bread crumbs

Preheat oven to 350 degrees F. Mix milk with soup. Add eggs, ham, cheese, salt, and paprika. Reserve ¼ cup of mixture for top and place the remainder in buttered 2-quart casserole. Arrange asparagus over top near center and mound reserved ham mixture in center. Border casserole with bread crumbs. Bake uncovered for 30 minutes. Serves 6.

HAWAIIAN HAM CONES

This is the nicest way to use leftover ham you will ever find; it makes a grand luncheon dish.

1 can (1 pound, 4 ounce) sliced pineapple (10 slices)	1 tablespoon parsley flakes
	1 tablespoon prepared mustard
1 pound ground cooked ham or chicken	1 egg, slightly beaten
	1 cup bran flakes or other cereal
1 tablespoon finely chopped onion	½ cup brown sugar
	1 tablespoon vinegar

Preheat oven to 350 degrees F. Drain pineapple reserving ⅓ cup syrup. Arrange slices in buttered shallow baking dish, 13×9½ inches. Combine ham, onion, parsley, mustard, 2 tablespoons pineapple syrup, egg, and cereal. Mix well and shape into 10 cones. Place one on each slice of pineapple. Bake for 15 minutes. Combine sugar, remaining reserved syrup, and vinegar. Pour 1 tablespoon over each cone—return to oven and bake 15 minutes longer. Serves 10.

HAWAIIAN "HOT DOGS"

Another version of the favorite hot dog.

12 wieners	12 slices bacon
1 jar (11¼ ounce) hot dog relish	Wiener buns or long buns
1 can (8¼ ounce) sliced pineapple, cut in tiny pieces	

Preheat broiler. Split wienie and fill with hot dog relish and 5 to 6 bits of pineapple. Wrap a slice of bacon around wienie, securing at each end with toothpick. Place these in pan and broil about 5 minutes or until bacon browns on one side; turn and brown bacon on other side. These have a tangy taste and are so good. Serves 12.

HUNGARIAN GOULASH

A friend in Baltimore gave this Hungarian Goulash recipe to me a long, long time ago. It is a grand cold weather dish.

3 tablespoons butter or
  margarine
2 pounds steak, cut in cubes
1 pound onions, sliced
1½ teaspoons paprika
1 clove garlic
Peel from 1 slice lemon
Pinch caraway seed

1 teaspoon salt
Dash pepper
1 cup stewed tomatoes, not too
  much juice
Beef stock
¼ cup flour
2 tablespoons butter

Melt butter in heavy skillet or large pot. Put in meat, onions, and paprika. Simmer until onions are soft and "disintegrated." Chop garlic and lemon peel very fine. Add with caraway seed. Season with salt and pepper, add tomatoes and beef stock to cover. Simmer covered until meat is tender, about 2 hours. Thicken gravy with a paste of flour and butter. (You may use bouillon cubes to make your beef stock.) Serves 4 to 6.

ITALIAN SPAGHETTI

1 pound ground beef
1 onion, chopped fine
2 to 3 tablespoons bacon
  drippings or salad oil
2 cups canned tomatoes
1 can (8 ounce) tomato paste
1 cup water or more if needed
  as sauce cooks

1 bay leaf or pinch oregano
1 small clove garlic
Salt to taste
Pepper to taste
1 pound thin spaghetti
Parmesan cheese

Brown meat and onion in hot bacon drippings. Add other ingredients except spaghetti and cheese and simmer uncovered 1 hour, or until sauce is thick. "Fish out" bay leaf and garlic clove, discard.

Cook spaghetti as directed. Drain, pour meat sauce over spaghetti, and sprinkle with Parmesan cheese. Serves 6.

NOTE: If you prefer, you may make small meat balls with the ground meat and brown in hot bacon drippings. Remove when well browned, add chopped onion to skillet, and brown. Return meat balls to skillet and add sauce ingredients. Simmer about 1 hour, as above.

LAMB CHOPS ORIENTAL

6 lamb chops, cut ½ inch thick	1 clove garlic, minced
½ cup soy sauce	6 canned peach halves
½ cup water	Mint jelly

Score fat edges of chops. Place in shallow baking dish. Combine soy sauce, water, and garlic; pour over chops and let stand in refrigerator for several hours. Preheat broiler. Arrange the marinated chops on broiler rack. Broil 3 inches from heat about 10 minutes on first side, turn chops. Broil 5 to 8 minutes longer, adding drained peach halves filled with mint jelly toward end of broiling time. Arrange halves around chops. Serves 6.

LASAGNE

1 pound ground beef	1 teaspoon chopped parsley
1 clove garlic, minced	½ pound lasagne or wide
2 tablespoons salad oil	noodles
1 can (8 ounce) tomato paste	4 to 5 quarts boiling water
¼ cup water	1½ tablespoons salt
2 cups canned tomatoes	1 pound ricotta or cottage cheese
1 teaspoon salt	½ cup Parmesan cheese
⅛ teaspoon pepper	½ pound mozzarella or Swiss
½ teaspoon oregano	cheese

Brown beef and minced garlic in salad oil over medium heat. Add tomato paste, water, tomatoes, seasonings, and parsley; simmer uncovered about 30 minutes. Cook noodles in boiling water with 1½ tablespoons salt added, leaving them slightly underdone. Drain. Preheat oven to 350 degrees F. Arrange 1½ cups of the beef-tomato mixture in the bottom of a greased shallow baking dish, 13×9½ inches. Lay half the noodles one at a time on top of the beef-tomato mixture until it is entirely covered. Spread half the ricotta cheese on the noodles. Sprinkle with half of the Parmesan cheese and top with one-third of the sliced mozzarella cheese. Repeat layers. Top with remaining beef-tomato mixture and sliced mozzarella cheese. Bake for 45 minutes. Let stand about 15 minutes after removing from oven so it will cut easily. Serves 8.

NOTE: You may add a small chopped onion and brown with the beef and garlic if you wish.

LEE'S ROLLED CUBE STEAKS

Buy a cube steak per person. On the cubed side put short strip of bacon, a slice of dill pickle and cut lengthwise. Add a sprinkling of chopped onion. Roll steaks (as jelly roll) and fasten with thin thread. Fry these rolls quickly on all sides in a little bacon drippings; dust lightly with flour and add water, just enough to cover bottom of pan. Add 1 bay leaf and a few peppercorns. Salt to taste. Cook slowly about 2 hours or until tender in covered pan on top of stove.

LONDON BROIL

This London Broil is dedicated to the men who love rare meat, meat not ruined by overcooking.

1 flank steak

Marinate in the following:

3 to 4 tablespoons cooking oil	1 teaspoon salt
2 tablespoons Worcestershire sauce	½ teaspoon cracked pepper
	Dash garlic powder

Marinate steak from 1 to 6 hours. Preheat broiler. Drain and broil very quickly until brown on each side. This is best cooked over charcoal. Center should be rare. Slice diagonally, this is very important. Serves 6 to 8.

LOUIE'S SPARERIBS

Buy a bag of charcoal, get set for a "cookout," and I'll guarantee this will be a favorite.

Use pork ribs, a pound per person. Leave in slab and cut after cooking; this keeps meat from drying out during cooking process. Trim excess fat from ribs. Now pick your favorite sausage seasoning and apply fairly heavy and rub in well on ribs. Place on grill and sear on one side, turn and sear on other side. Continue cooking, turning frequently until done, approximately 30 to 45 minutes. (Be sure and coat rib slab well with seasoning as it is only applied before cooking.) Immediately after cooking cut ribs as desired and serve.

MEAT LOAF

Meat Loaf is a grand way to use ground meat—also an easy dish on the budget. The secret of this loaf is the sweet milk.

1½ pounds ground beef
1 cup soft bread crumbs, or herb
  seasoned crumbs
¾ cup milk
1 teaspoon salt

⅛ teaspoon black pepper
2 teaspoons Worcestershire sauce
1 teaspoon grated onion
½ teaspoon parsley flakes
3 hard-cooked eggs (optional)

Preheat oven to 350 degrees F. Combine beef, crumbs, and milk; add seasonings, Worcestershire, onion, and parsley flakes. Mix well. If you wish to dress up your loaf slice the ends off of eggs, fit together and place in middle of loaf. (The slices look pretty when cut with this egg center.) Shape meat in loaf around eggs and place in baking pan. Bake 45 minutes to 1 hour, depending on how well done you wish your beef. Serves 6 to 8.

MY BAKED HAM

This is my favorite way to cook Baked Ham. It is first simmered on the top of the stove and left standing in stock for a while. It is then dressed up with a brown sugar and mustard mixture to finish baking in the oven.

6-pound piece cured ham, any good brand, there are many
½ cup vinegar
5 to 6 cloves
1 small onion, sliced
1 teaspoon salt
¼ teaspoon pepper

6 to 8 tablespoons prepared mustard
6 to 8 tablespoons brown sugar, plus 1 to 2 tablespoons
Cloves
1 can (6 ounce) orange juice
½ to 1 cup ham stock

Place ham in a vessel of simmering water. Add ½ cup vinegar, cloves, onion, salt, and pepper. Cover. Simmer slowly allowing 15 to 20 minutes per pound in cooking. (Cook until meat begins to recede from bone.) Remove from heat and let stand in stock for several hours. Preheat oven to 350 degrees F. when ready to bake ham. Remove ham from stock and remove any heavy skin from fat side. Place in baking dish. Score fat on ham and mix prepared mustard and 6 to 8 tablespoons brown sugar to make a paste. Pat and rub over ham, even on cut side. Now stick cloves in fat part about an inch apart. Add orange juice mixed with 1 cup ham stock. Stir in 1 or 2 tablespoons brown sugar. Pour around ham in baking dish. Bake 30 minutes to 1 hour or until ham begins to brown. Baste several times. Ham is easier to carve if cool. Serves 16 to 18.

PEPPER STEAK

1 medium onion, chopped coarsely
2 cloves garlic, crushed

1 tablespoon shortening
1¼ pounds lean tenderloin beef

Sauté onion and garlic in shortening. Add the beef, which has been cut in 1-inch cubes. Brown lightly on all sides.
Add:

1½ teaspoons crushed black pepper	1½ cups strips or 1-inch pieces green pepper
1 teaspoon salt	½ cup tomato paste
1½ cups sliced mushrooms	2 cups beef consommé

Heat to boiling, lower heat, and simmer until beef is tender and flavors blend.
Next step:

2 tablespoons flour
¼ cup water
½ cup dry wine

Thicken pepper steak sauce with flour mixed with water for desired consistency. Heat sauce to boil again and cook clear. Add wine and cook only long enough to blend well. Serves 6. Rice is served with this dish.

PORK CHOPS AND WINE

6 pork chops	½ cup dry wine
1 tablespoon shortening	½ bay leaf
3 tablespoons minced onion	½ teaspoon salt
1 tablespoon prepared mustard	⅛ teaspoon pepper
1 tablespoon Worcestershire sauce	1 tablespoon cornstarch
1 cup beef bouillon	Water

Brown chops in hot shortening. When well browned add onion, mustard, Worcestershire, bouillon, wine, bay leaf, salt, and pepper. Cover and simmer for 1 hour or until chops are tender. Discard bay leaf. Taste and adjust seasoning. Remove chops from pan. Add cornstarch mixed with a little water to liquid in pan and stir until smooth. Serve gravy over chops. Serves 6.

QUICK STEW

4 medium-sized potatoes
1 bunch carrots (8 to 10
    carrots)
Water
4 medium-sized onions
4 tablespoons flour

2 tablespoons cold water
1 can (10½ ounce) condensed
    onion soup
1 cup canned tomatoes
3 cups cooked beef or lamb,
    diced

Peel, dice vegetables, and cook together in water to cover until tender. Mix flour with 2 tablespoons water and add to soup. Add tomatoes. Cook, stirring constantly until thick. Add vegetables and meat. Simmer 10 minutes. Serves 6.

ROAST PORK

4 to 6 pounds loin or rib end
    of pork
1 clove garlic, cut
½ to 1 cup flour, sifted

1 teaspoon salt
Dash black pepper
¼ teaspoon paprika
⅛ teaspoon ginger

Preheat oven to 350 degrees F. Wipe roast with damp cloth. Dry. Rub well with garlic. Mix flour, salt, pepper, paprika, and ginger. Dredge or sprinkle mixture on roast. Place fat side up on rack in a pan in the oven. Bake covered for 30 minutes per pound. Uncover roast the last 30 to 40 minutes of cooking to brown.

GRAVY: Remove roast from pan. Pour off all but 2 or 3 tablespoons drippings. Blend in 1 to 2 tablespoons flour. Stir until flour has thickened and mixture is smooth. Add 1½ cups water (or stock mixed with water to make 1½ cups). Bring to boil. Stir and season gravy with salt and pepper. Serves 8 to 10.

NOTE: Baked sweet potatoes go nicely with pork roast.

SALT PORK AND GRAVY (BATTERED)

I could not resist including salt pork recipes in my cookbook. They are "Deep South," and methinks they will bring memories to a lot of folks.

1 pound salt pork
Milk
½ cup corn meal
2 to 3 tablespoons bacon
   drippings

2 tablespoons flour
2 tablespoons pan drippings
1½ cups milk

Slice salt pork very thin. Soak in milk a few minutes. Dip in meal. Now place bacon drippings in skillet or frying pan, heat, and fry pork on each side until brown. Drain on paper toweling. Serves 6 to 8.

GRAVY: Blend flour with 2 tablespoons of the pan drippings. Add 1½ cups milk and cook over low heat until thickened. Stir all the while. Salt and pepper to taste.

SALT PORK WITH GRAVY

1 pound salt pork, sliced thin
2 tablespoons flour
2 tablespoons pan drippings

1½ cups milk
Dash salt and pepper

Cook slices of pork slowly in frying pan over medium heat. Remove from heat and drain on paper. Make gravy as in above recipe. Serve hot with biscuits or grits. Serves 8.

SAUSAGE AND RICE CASSEROLE

This Sausage and Rice Casserole has been a favorite of all who have sampled it. It may be made with wild rice, but I have found that the half white and half wild rice makes a marvelous dish. It is my favorite smörgåsbord dish, the men "love" it. This goes well with ham or chicken.

1½ to 2 cups half white and half wild rice
1 pound hot ground sausage
1 large onion, chopped fine
1 can (8 ounce) mushrooms, drained
1½ cups chicken broth
2 tablespoons flour
¼ cup milk

1 teaspoon monosodium glutamate
½ teaspoon salt
Dash black pepper
Pinch oregano or Italian seasoning
Pinch parsley
¾ cup herb bread crumbs or slivered almonds

Cook rice as directed. Brown sausage and drain on paper toweling. Brown onion lightly in small amount of sausage drippings and add to sausage; mix with rice and mushrooms. Place in 3-quart casserole. Preheat oven to 350 degrees F. Thicken chicken broth with flour and milk, which have been mixed to a smooth paste. Add seasonings, oregano, and parsley and cook about 5 minutes to thicken slightly. Pour broth mixture over sausage and rice in casserole. Sprinkle crumbs or almonds over top. Bake 25 to 30 minutes. Serves 8 to 10.

NOTE: Some packages of white and wild rice have a package of herb seasoning enclosed. Use one-half of the seasoning in package for this recipe.

SAVORY SMOTHERED STEAK

¼ to ½ cup flour, or as needed
2½ pounds round steak, 1 inch thick
2 to 3 tablespoons bacon drippings
1 teaspoon salt
¼ teaspoon pepper
2 tablespoons catsup
½ teaspoon prepared mustard
1½ cups hot water
1 small onion, chopped
Pinch oregano (optional)

Pound as much flour as possible into steak. Brown steak in hot bacon drippings in heavy skillet. Season with salt and pepper. Add catsup and prepared mustard to water. Mix and pour over meat. Add onion. Cover tightly and simmer for about 1½ hours or until tender. Add pinch of oregano if desired while cooking. Serves 6.

STEAK EN CASSEROLE

This Steak en Casserole is an "easy to do."

2½ pounds round steak, cut 1 inch thick
¼ to ½ cup flour
2 tablespoons fat
1 teaspoon salt
¼ teaspoon pepper
1 to 2 cups tomato juice
1 can (6 ounce) mushrooms, drained
1 onion, chopped
Dash Worcestershire sauce

Preheat oven to 350 degrees F. Trim edges of steak and cut in pieces about 2 to 3 inches square. Pound flour into pieces and brown well on both sides in hot fat in frying pan. Now place browned steak in roaster and season with salt and pepper. Add tomato juice and mushrooms. Add onion and Worcestershire. Place cover on roaster and bake for about 2 hours. Serves 6.

STUFFED HAM ROLLS

¾ cup cooked rice
2 tablespoons chopped parsley
¼ cup slivered almonds
½ teaspoon salt
⅛ teaspoon pepper
Dash herb seasoning

3 tablespoons melted butter or
 margarine
6 or 8 thin slices cooked ham
1 or 2 cups Creamed Chicken
 (as below)

Mix the rice, parsley, almonds, salt and pepper, herb seasoning, and butter to make stuffing. Place some of this rice mixture on each ham slice and roll up carefully. Secure with a pick if necessary. Place on dish and pour Creamed Chicken (below) over. Serves 6 to 8.

CREAMED CHICKEN

3 tablespoons butter or
 margarine
3 tablespoons flour
½ teaspoon salt
Dash pepper
Dash paprika
1½ cups milk

½ cup chicken broth
1 tablespoon mayonnaise
1 to 2 tablespoons chopped
 pimento
¼ cup sliced mushrooms, or
 more
2 cups diced cooked chicken

Melt butter in skillet or saucepan over low heat. Add flour, salt, pepper, and paprika, blend well. Add milk and broth, stir constantly until mixture thickens. Add mayonnaise, pimento, and mushrooms. Add chicken, heat thoroughly. Serves 6 to 8.

NOTE: This chicken is good served over toast. Add ½ cup cooked green peas for color. This makes a nice luncheon or supper dish.

STUFFED PORK CHOPS

4 cups soft bread crumbs
½ cup melted margarine
1 onion, chopped fine
½ teaspoon salt
¼ teaspoon pepper
¼ teaspoon oregano
1 teaspoon sage

6 thick pork chops (about 2
   inches thick) with pockets cut
   in each
1½ cups water
¼ cup catsup
¼ teaspoon Worcestershire sauce

Preheat oven to 350 degrees F. Mix and make dressing of bread crumbs, margarine, onion, seasonings, oregano, and sage. Stuff chops with this and put in 2-quart baking dish. Mix together water, catsup, and Worcestershire and cover chops with this liquid. Bake covered for about 2 hours. Serves 6.

NOTE: Add a little water to your dressing mix if it is not moist enough to stuff chops.

SWEET-SOUR MEAT BALLS

1 pound ground beef, seasoned
   with salt
1 to 2 tablespoons salad oil
1 cup canned pineapple chunks,
   drained
2 green peppers, seeded and cut
   in strips

2 tablespoons soy sauce
½ cup canned pineapple juice
2 tablespoons cornstarch
¼ cup cold water

Make meat into bite-size balls. Brown in oil and drain. Mix pineapple, peppers, soy sauce, pineapple juice, and cornstarch, which has been mixed with the water. Cook about 10 minutes and add meat balls. Simmer covered about 15 minutes. Serve over cooked rice. Serves 6.

SWEET-SOUR PORK

2 pounds lean pork shoulder, cut in 1-inch pieces
2 to 3 tablespoons fat
1 can (1 pound, 4 ounce) pineapple chunks
1 can (4 ounce) mushrooms
¼ cup dark brown sugar
2 tablespoons soy sauce
½ teaspoon salt
¼ cup vinegar
1 small green pepper, seeded and cut in strips
¼ cup thinly sliced onions
1½ tablespoons cornstarch
Water

Brown pork in hot fat in large skillet. Drain pineapple and mushrooms, reserving juice. Add enough water to juice to make 2 cups. Add to pork in skillet and simmer covered for about 1 hour. Stir in brown sugar, soy sauce, salt, and vinegar. Add pineapple chunks, green pepper, and onions. Cook 15 minutes longer. Mix cornstarch with small amount of water, stir into hot mixture. Cook stirring until slightly thickened. Serve with hot rice. Serves 6.

TAMALE PIE

Try this Tamale Pie the night you wish a bit of Mexican-flavored food.

½ cup chopped onion
¼ cup chopped green pepper
3 to 4 tablespoons bacon drippings or shortening
1 pound ground beef
1 teaspoon salt
¼ teaspoon pepper
1 teaspoon chili powder
2 cups canned corn
2 cups canned tomatoes
½ cup corn meal
¼ teaspoon salt
2 cups boiling water

Sauté onion and pepper in hot drippings until tender; add beef and brown. Add salt, pepper, chili powder, corn, and tomatoes. Cook about 20 to 30 minutes. Add the meal and salt to water and cook until thickened. Preheat oven to 400 degrees F. Pour the meat mixture in casserole and pour corn meal mush over top. Bake for about 25 to 30 minutes or until crust is a bit brown. Serves 6.

VEAL CUTLET (BREADED)

1½-pound slice round veal steak cut 1 inch thick
1 teaspoon salt
⅛ teaspoon pepper
1 egg, beaten
Cracker crumbs
3 to 4 tablespoons shortening, or as needed

3 small onions, chopped
2 tablespoons flour
2 cups strained tomatoes
1 tablespoon Worcestershire sauce
Salt to taste
Pepper to taste

Preheat oven to 325 degrees F. Cut veal into suitable pieces for serving. Sprinkle with salt and pepper. Bread, using egg and crumbs, dip in egg then in crumbs. Brown in generous amount of hot shortening. Remove to heavy baking dish, 13×9½ inches. Add onions to remaining shortening, brown lightly. Add flour and cook to smooth paste. Add tomatoes. Add Worcestershire, salt and pepper to taste. Pour over cutlets and cover tightly. Bake for 1 hour or until steaks are very tender. Serve on platter with sauce. Serves 6.

Poultry & Game

Poultry and game are favored foods in the Southland and you'll find many recipes for these in my book. Fried Chicken served with rice and gravy, old-fashioned Georgia Chicken Pie, Roast Turkey with Giblet Gravy and Southern Corn Bread Dressing are a few of my favorites. There is a Brunswick stew with butterbeans, yummy served over split corn muffins. A Soy Sauce Chicken is broiled chicken at its best, and so easy to do. Chicken Julie is a must. You'll find game recipes dear to a hunter's heart. Those for quail, fried doves, and pheasant are here for your culinary efforts. May the hunter in your family be lucky!

BARBECUED CHICKEN IN PAPER BAG

1 medium-size parchment paper bag and string
1 broiler (2½ pounds), cleaned and dressed
¾ cup vinegar
½ cup water
1 teaspoon each steak sauce and mustard

Generous dash chili powder
1 teaspoon salt
1 teaspoon pepper
1 teaspoon red pepper
1 teaspoon Tabasco sauce
½ teaspoon ground cloves
⅓ cup butter or margarine

Grease a string and paper bag inside and out. Place chicken cut in half in bag, skin side down. Mix other ingredients into a sauce. Pour over chicken, tie bag with string, place in pan, and bake 2 hours at 350 degrees F. Begin cooking with cold oven. Serves 4.

BUENA'S ROAST TURKEY

For your Thanksgiving or Christmas dinner—Roast Turkey with Giblet Gravy and Southern Corn Bread Dressing.

1 turkey (12 to 16 pounds, ready-to-cook weight)
½ cup margarine
5 to 6 tablespoons self-rising flour

1 tablespoon salt
1½ teaspoons black pepper

Preheat oven to 225 degrees F. Wash turkey and dry thoroughly. (It is important to have turkey dry.) Melt margarine over low heat, do not brown. Make paste with margarine, flour, salt, and pepper; rub paste well over turkey (use your hands!). Place in open roaster and cook in oven. Baste often. Have breast up until last hour of cooking, then turn bird over. When turkey is brown, cover with foil and finish cooking. To test for doneness, pull leg back; if it is not pink between leg and body the turkey is done. This takes about 5 to 6 hours cooking in this slow oven. Remove turkey from pan and make Giblet Gravy from drippings and stock. Serves 10 to 12.

Some prefer to stuff their turkey but others make the dressing and cook it in another pan. The recipe for the gravy and dressing follows.

GIBLET GRAVY

1 stalk celery, chopped	Turkey neck, gizzard, and liver
½ small onion (optional)	4 cups water
½ teaspoon salt	Turkey drippings and ½ cup fat
Dash pepper	½ cup flour

Simmer celery, onion, salt, pepper, and turkey pieces in water, covered, for about an hour. Strain, measure, add water to make 4 cups. Chop giblets from turkey pieces and add to stock. After removing turkey from roaster, pour fat off, leaving brown drippings in pan. Put about ½ cup of fat back into pan. Blend in flour and cook stirring all the while until mixture bubbles. Add the stock and turkey giblets and continue cooking until the gravy thickens; boil a minute or two. Makes about 3 to 4 cups.

When Mother served turkey or baked chicken she made the dressing. The cook could never make it as she did, so she prepared this part of our holiday dinner. This is the type of dressing she made as near as I can make it; she baked it separately in a pan, and when it was done cut it in squares to serve, or "spooned" it from the pan.

SOUTHERN CORN BREAD DRESSING

3 cups crumbled corn bread	1 onion, chopped fine
2 to 3 eggs	¼ cup finely chopped celery
2 to 2½ cups crumbled dry bread, use day-old light bread	½ teaspoon pepper
	½ tablespoon salt
4 to 5 cups turkey or chicken stock	½ tablespoon sage or poultry seasoning
½ cup melted butter	

Preheat oven to 425 degrees F. Mix bread, add raw eggs and other ingredients. Mix well. Have dressing soft, about consistency of cake batter or thick soup (really soupy, this is secret of good dressing, it will cook dry); this degree of consistency was the hardest for me to learn. Bake in greased baking dish 13×9½ inches for about 40 minutes. Serves 10 to 12. If you wish you may stuff your bird with this dressing. If bird is stuffed, allow 5 minutes more cooking per pound.

For Chestnut Dressing: Follow recipe for Southern Corn Bread Dressing, adding 1 cup chopped cooked chestnuts.

For Oyster Dressing: Follow recipe for Southern Corn Bread Dressing, adding 1 cup chopped oysters.

CHICKEN BREASTS SUPREME

This recipe for Chicken Breasts Supreme is one I "dreamed up" one night when I came home very weary and hungry.

3 whole chicken breasts, cut in half
Salt
2 tablespoons bacon drippings or cooking oil
1 can (10½ ounce) condensed cream of mushroom soup

¾ to 1 can water to dilute soup
Salt to taste
1 teaspoon dried parsley flakes
Pinch Italian seasoning
Pinch sage

Wipe chicken breasts dry and salt. Place chicken in skillet and brown breasts slightly in bacon drippings (do not flour). Remove when brown to paper toweling. Add mushroom soup diluted with water to pan drippings in skillet. Stir a minute and place chicken breasts in skillet. Add salt, parsley flakes, Italian seasoning, and sage. Cover and simmer on low for about 45 minutes. Uncover and cook about 10 to 15 minutes longer to cook gravy down a bit. Serve with rice. Serves 6.

CHICKEN BURGUNDY

1 frying-size chicken (3 pounds), cut in pieces
5 to 6 tablespoons shortening
3 onions, chopped
½ cup sliced mushrooms
1 can (1 pound) Bing or Dark Sweet pitted cherries in heavy syrup

2 carrots, sliced
1 cup burgundy
½ teaspoon salt
⅛ teaspoon pepper
1 tablespoon cornstarch
Water

Brown chicken in hot shortening. Add other ingredients except cornstarch and water. Cover and simmer 30 to 40 minutes or until tender. Mix cornstarch with a little water. Add to mixture and stir until thickened. Serve hot over rice. Serves 6.

CHICKEN CASSEROLE
(with Beans and Pimentos)

2 cans (1 pound each) French-style beans
3 whole chicken breasts, split in 2 pieces and deboned
Butter or fat
1 tablespoon salt
1 jar (4 ounce) pimentos
1 package (8 ounce) cream cheese

½ cup milk
½ teaspoon garlic salt
½ teaspoon onion salt
Black pepper to taste
1 can (3½ ounce) French fried onions

Steam beans ½ hour and drain. Cook chicken breasts in small amount of butter until done. Salt. Preheat oven to 350 degrees F. Place cooked chicken breasts in 2-quart casserole. Add a layer of steamed beans, then a layer of pimentos. Spread over this a mixture of the cheese, milk, and seasonings blended together well. Bake for 30 minutes; top with onions and bake 10 minutes longer. Cut in squares to serve. Serves 10 to 12.

NOTE: Try decorating your casserole with pimento bells or other Christmas toppings cut from the peppers.

CHICKEN JOYCE

6 to 8 pieces dried beef
3 to 4 whole chicken breasts, cut in half
6 to 8 pieces bacon

1 can (10½ ounce) condensed cream of mushroom soup
½ pint dairy sour cream
Slivered almonds (optional)

Place slices of dried beef in 2-quart casserole. Atop each piece place a piece of unseasoned chicken wrapped in a strip of bacon. Cover with mixture of mushroom soup and sour cream. Add slivered almonds if desired. Cover with casserole top or foil and bake in preheated oven at 300 degrees for 2 hours or 350 degrees for about 1 hour. Serves 6 to 8.

CHICKEN JULIE

This is a delicious and unusual chicken casserole.

2 frying-size chickens (2½ pounds each), cut in serving pieces
Shortening
4 cloves garlic
3 to 4 onions, chopped
2½ tablespoons flour
1 can (10½ ounce) beef bouillon

1 chicken bouillon cube
1 cup warm water
½ teaspoon thyme
¼ teaspoon salt
2 to 3 bay leaves
½ cup diced, ripe olives
¼ cup sherry

Preheat oven to 350 degrees F. Brown chicken, unfloured, in shortening. Add flour to garlic and onions, brown slightly. Add beef bouillon, the chicken bouillon cube dissolved in warm water, thyme, salt, and bay leaves. Combine all in 3-quart casserole and cook slowly 1 hour or more in oven. Near end of cooking time, add olives and sherry. At this time remove garlic cloves and bay leaves if you wish. Serves 6 to 8.

CHICKEN PARMESAN

1 frying-size chicken (3 pounds),
   cut in serving pieces
¾ cup dry bread crumbs
1 can (3 ounce) Parmesan
   cheese
1 clove garlic, minced

1 tablespoon salt
½ tablespoon oregano
¼ tablespoon black pepper
¼ cup melted butter
1 tablespoon butter

Preheat oven to 350 degrees F. Remove skin from chicken. Combine bread crumbs, cheese, garlic, salt, oregano, and pepper. Blend well. Dip chicken in melted butter, then into crumb mixture, coating evenly. Arrange chicken in shallow buttered baking dish. Dot with butter. Bake until tender, about 1 to 1½ hours. Serves 4 to 6.

CHICKEN TETRAZZINI

Chicken Tetrazzini makes a nice casserole dish for a luncheon, or just for guests.

½ pound spaghetti
Salt
1 small onion, chopped fine
½ cup sliced mushrooms
3 tablespoons butter
1 tablespoon flour
¾ to 1 cup consommé
¾ cup white wine
½ cup evaporated milk

½ teaspoon salt
Dash pepper
Dash cayenne
1½ cups cubed cooked chicken
   or turkey
Buttered bread crumbs
2 to 3 tablespoons Parmesan
   cheese

Preheat oven to 450 degrees F. Cook spaghetti in salted water until tender. Drain and rinse. Cook onion and sliced mushrooms 5 minutes in butter. Sprinkle with flour, stir as smooth as possible, add consommé and wine. Cook stirring until smooth and add milk. Season to taste. In greased baking dish, 11½×7½ inches, place layers of spaghetti, chicken, and sauce. Repeat and end with spaghetti. Top with buttered crumbs and cheese. Bake about 15 minutes or until brown. Serves 6.

CHLOE'S BRUNSWICK STEW

Here is a Brunswick Stew recipe given to me a long time ago. Corn and butterbeans go into this along with chicken, a combination hard to beat.

1 boiled hen (4 to 5 pounds), cut up as for salad
2 cups canned corn
1 cup canned butterbeans, drained
½ cup canned green peas, drained

½ cup Worcestershire sauce
1 bottle (14 ounce) catsup
Salt to taste
Pepper to taste
2 cups broth, or more if needed

Mix ingredients and simmer, covered, cooking slowly about 30 minutes. It should be thick enough to eat with a fork. Serves 8.

NOTE: This is good to serve over split corn meal muffins.

CURRIED CHICKEN

1 frying-size chicken (2½ to 3 pounds), cut in serving pieces
Flour
½ teaspoon salt
¼ teaspoon pepper
Dash paprika
Shortening
1 medium onion, chopped

½ cup minced celery
1 medium apple, chopped
¼ cup pan drippings
¼ cup melted butter
2 tablespoons flour
1 to 2 tablespoons curry powder
1½ cups chicken stock

Roll each piece of chicken in flour seasoned with salt, pepper, and paprika. Cook in hot shortening until golden brown, remove from pan as it browns. Mix the onion, celery, and apple with the pan drippings and butter; cook until light brown and add the 2 tablespoons flour, curry powder, and cook for a minute. Add the chicken stock. Check seasoning and adjust. Cook until thick. Replace chicken and simmer until tender, about 30 to 40 minutes. Cook covered. Serve with plain boiled rice. Serves 6.

NOTE: Chutney, salted peanuts, and sieved boiled eggs are relishes served with curry dishes. Watermelon rind pickles are excellent with this dish.

FRIED CHICKEN

This or any other Southern cookbook would not be complete without Fried Chicken. This is the way most of us fry it down in Georgia.

Disjoint a frying-size chicken (from 1½ to 2 pounds), season with salt and pepper, and thoroughly coat with flour. Heat about 1 pound of shortening in skillet on top of stove until smoking hot. Place pieces of chicken in hot fat, reduce heat and cover. Cook slowly until chicken is brown and tender, turning during cooking until each piece is brown. Drain on paper toweling and place on serving dish. Serves 6.

GRAVY: Cream gravy goes with fried chicken. To make this pour off all but about 2½ tablespoons of the fat in which chicken was fried. Add to this 1 heaping tablespoon flour, let brown, stirring constantly. Now slowly add 1 cup of milk. Stir constantly until gravy is of desired thickness. Season with salt and pepper to taste.

GEORGIA CHICKEN PIE

1 chicken (5 to 6 pounds), cleaned and dressed	1½ teaspoons salt
4 tablespoons butter	⅛ teaspoon pepper
4 tablespoons flour	2 or 3 hard-cooked eggs
2 cups hot chicken stock	Pastry for 1-crust pie

Disjoint chicken and cook in small amount of water with a few stalks of celery and a carrot or two. Keep covered and simmer until meat is ready to fall from bone. Remove skin and bones and cut fowl into good-sized pieces, alternating white and dark meat in 2-quart baking dish. Pour over sauce made from the butter melted and blended with the flour. Add chicken stock, salt, and pepper and cook until thickened. Note: Add seasonings according to richness of stock. Chop or slice the eggs and add to the pie mix. Preheat oven to 450 degrees F. Cover pie mix with pastry crust and bake until crust is brown and sauce is bubbling. Serves 6 to 8.

NOTE: Our Southern grandmothers made chicken pie without vegetables. Over the years, chicken pies have varied to such a degree that vegetables have been added by some cooks. If you wish, add ¾ cup cooked green peas and ¼ cup cooked, diced carrots to your pie ingredients.

HARRIET'S BARBECUE CHICKEN WITH RICE PILAF

3 (2 pounds each) broiling-size   Pepper
    chickens, cleaned and dressed   2 to 3 tablespoons butter
Salt

Cook as directed below.
Mix following ingredients for barbecue sauce:

1½ cups catsup   4 tablespoons brown sugar
1½ cups wine vinegar   2 teaspoons Worcestershire sauce
1 teaspoon dry mustard   6 to 7 onions, diced

Split chickens in half and salt and pepper. Dot with butter and place skin side up in covered roaster. Place in oven. Bake for 20 minutes. Now cover with sauce and cook slowly for an hour or more, or until tender, in preheated 300-degree F. oven. Uncover chicken the last few minutes of cooking to brown a bit. If sauce cooks out and you need more to serve, add liquid. Serves 6 to 8.

RICE PILAF

The "go along" dish with the Barbecue Chicken.

1½ cups raw long-grain white   1½ cans (10½ ounces each)
    rice   condensed consommé
1 large onion, chopped   1 cup water
½ cup butter   ½ to 1 cup shelled pine nuts or
2 tablespoons chopped parsley   toasted pecans

Preheat over to 350 degrees F. Sauté rice and chopped onion in butter in skillet until rice is golden. Combine with parsley, consommé, and water. Pour in 2-quart greased casserole. Cover, bake for 30 minutes or until rice is tender and water absorbed. Uncover, fluff with fork, sprinkle with nuts. Serves 6 or 8.

NOTE: This may be cooked in electric fry pan or skillet.

SOY SAUCE CHICKEN

One of the best and my favorite chicken recipe follows. It's grand when you are pressed for time and company drops in for dinner. It will cook in an hour, good to serve a crowd. Serve with a vegetable casserole, salad, toasted French bread, and you have it made!

1 broiling-size chicken (2½ pounds), cleaned and dressed
Salad oil
½ teaspoon salt
⅛ teaspoon pepper
1 tablespoon lemon juice, or more

1 teaspoon Worcestershire sauce
Bit chopped parsley
1 can (3 ounce) sliced mushrooms, drained
Soy sauce to taste

Preheat oven to 350 degrees F. In a shallow pan lined with foil place broiler, split in half. Rub both sides of chicken with oil. Add salt, pepper, lemon juice, Worcestershire, parsley, mushrooms, and soy sauce to taste. Cover pan with foil and bake for 1 hour. Remove foil and brown a bit. Thicken gravy if you wish; add a little flour as for other gravies. You may cook as many chickens as you need, allow ½ chicken per person. Serves 2.

NOTE: Increase the other amounts in recipe to cook more chickens.

TURKEY WITH HERB BARBECUE SAUCE

This is an easy way to have your husband help with the cooking of your Thanksgiving bird. It is cooked on the grill. (Must be grill with cover.)

1 turkey (10 to 12 pounds, ready-to-cook weight)	¾ cup tarragon vinegar
	Fresh ground black pepper
4 or 5 cups packaged bread stuffing (optional)	2 teaspoons dried minced herbs for salad
¼ pound butter or margarine	1 teaspoon salt
1 clove garlic, minced	3 tablespoons brown sugar
1 onion, minced	

Prepare the turkey for cooking, stuffing or not as desired, and truss as usual. Fold a sheet of heavy-duty foil, double thick, and turn up edges all around about 1 inch to make a shallow pan. Place the turkey on the grill in this pan, brush with barbecue sauce made from remaining ingredients, which have been combined. Simmer 3 to 4 minutes. Cover the turkey loosely with a single sheet of foil—just draping it over the bird. (Note again, you must use covered grill for this.) Close oven, adjust vents about half open, and roast 3½ to 4½ hours. One hour before roasting is finished remove the foil cover and baste with the herb sauce or add damp hickory and continue cooking, basting once or twice more. Completely covering the turkey inside and out with this sauce before beginning to cook makes it better. Serves 10 to 12.

NOTE: Allow about 25 minutes for unstuffed bird and 30 minutes for a stuffed one.

DOVES "A LA TOTSIE"

I think you will be pleased with the recipes for cooking doves.

12 doves, prepared as below	½ teaspoon sugar
Salt	½ stick butter
Pepper	Dash Worcestershire sauce
Shortening	Parsley flakes
Chopped celery	1 clove garlic if desired
Sliced onions	½ cup burgundy or any good
Juice 1 lemon, or more	red wine

Preheat oven to 350 degrees F. After birds are dressed split down back. Sprinkle birds with salt and pepper and brown unfloured in hot shortening. You may brown in deeper fat as this browns the birds evenly without turning to brown. Take roaster and cover bottom with water; add a bit of celery and sliced onions. Now place rack in roaster and put birds on rack after browning. Season with lemon juice (this is the secret for game); add sugar, more salt and pepper to taste, butter, Worcestershire, and parsley flakes. Some like a bit of garlic. Cover roaster and place in oven. Rotate birds in roaster while cooking and baste often. Before birds are entirely done add wine to basting liquid. I suggest you serve at least 2 birds per person.

GRAVY: Remove birds and brown flour in pan fat as for other gravies; add liquid from roaster to desired thickness. Add mushrooms if you wish. Serve with plain or wild rice; down "South" we serve grits.

JO'S FRIED DOVES

Cover cleaned and dressed birds with cold water, add salt to taste. You may add a little onion to the water. Parboil until tender. Drain birds, reserving liquid for gravy. For the following mix, use 10 to 12 birds:
Beat 2 whole eggs in mixing bowl. Dip birds in eggs, lay on paper towels, sift flour over birds on both sides. In deep, hot shortening that covers birds fry until they are brown. Drain on paper towels.

Pour off grease, leaving just enough to make gravy. Add flour enough to thicken, let flour brown, and add stock birds were parboiled in, amount needed for your gravy. Cook until thick. Season with salt and black pepper. Serves 5 to 6.

NOTE: Hot biscuits and grits are good with this, or a rice casserole if you prefer.

PHEASANT WITH RICE IN FOIL

2 pheasants (2½ to 3 pounds), cleaned and dressed	1 can (4 ounce) sliced mushrooms, drained
3 tablespoons bacon drippings	½ teaspoon salt
5 tablespoons butter or margarine	½ teaspoon seasoned salt
1 cup brown or wild rice	¼ teaspoon pepper
	¼ teaspoon ginger

Preheat oven to 350 degrees F. Cut pheasants into serving pieces, as for broiling chicken. Brown in bacon drippings and 3 tablespoons butter. Cook rice as directed on package. Brown mushrooms in remaining butter and add to rice. Mix in seasonings and ginger. Place a large piece of foil on cooky sheet, put rice mixture on it, and top with pheasant pieces. Seal foil. Bake in moderate oven for 1¾ hours. Open foil and bake 15 minutes longer to crisp pheasant. Serves 6 to 8.

GRAVY FOR PHEASANT

Pheasant back, wings, and neck	1 stalk celery, with leaves
3 cups water	Browned flour
1 chicken bouillon cube	Salt
1 large onion, quartered	Pepper

Simmer pieces of pheasant in water with bouillon cube, onion, and celery. To brown flour, place dry flour in dry skillet and stir until golden brown. Thicken broth with browned flour to make gravy. Add salt and pepper to taste. Serves 6.

QUAIL (BROILED)

Bobwhite quail are distinctly American. Down South we say a man loves his bird dog as well as his wife. Many famous personalities journey South each year to hunt quail on well-stocked plantations.

Clean quail thoroughly. Cut in halves and place cut side down on a well-buttered broiler. Season with salt and pepper. Brush with melted butter. Broil 25 to 30 minutes or until browned. Brush frequently with butter. Serve on toast.

QUAIL

Our cook Malissa used to cook quail in this manner.

6 quail, cleaned and dressed
½ cup flour, or as needed
½ teaspoon salt
⅛ teaspoon pepper
¼ cup butter plus 4 tablespoons

1 tablespoon shortening
1½ cups boiling water
1 tablespoon flour
1 cup water

Dredge birds in flour, salt, and pepper. Put ¼ cup butter and shortening in skillet. Heat without scorching. Add birds and brown quickly to seal in juices. Turn often. Now lower temperature and add 1½ cups water to birds and simmer until tender. Cook covered. Add more water if needed and when birds are tender and water gone, place breast side down in 4 tablespoons butter and brown over low heat. Remove birds and make gravy. For this stir in 1 tablespoon flour in butter dripping. Add 1 cup water and stir until thick. Serves 6.

ROAST DUCK WITH STUFFING

The mallard duck represents elegant dining in any gourmet restaurant as well as at home. They fly with great speed and are a challenge to a hunter's skill.

2 mallard ducks, cleaned and dressed
1½ teaspoons salt
⅜ teaspoon pepper

¼ cup melted butter or margarine
2 to 3 tablespoons lemon juice

Preheat oven to 325 degrees F. Dry ducks thoroughly inside and out. Rub salt and pepper on inside of ducks. Combine butter and lemon juice. Brush on inside and outside of ducks. Fill with Stuffing (as below) and truss. Wrap in aluminum foil and place in shallow pan. Bake in slow oven for 1½ hours. Uncover birds and baste with drippings. Continue basting and bake 30 minutes or until brown. Prepare gravy from drippings. Serves 4.

STUFFING

½ cup chopped onion
½ cup chopped celery
2 tablespoons chopped celery leaves
¼ cup butter or margarine
1 quart dry bread crumbs

½ cup chopped pecans
¾ cup giblet stock or chicken bouillon
½ teaspoon seasoned salt
Dash pepper
½ teaspoon thyme

Cook onions, celery, and celery leaves in butter until tender. Add to bread crumbs and pecans. Toss lightly. Add stock to moisten. Mix in seasonings.

VERNA'S PHEASANT OR QUAIL

This recipe came from North Carolina.

1 pheasant (2½ to 3 pounds), cleaned and dressed
¼ cup salad oil
1 medium onion, chopped
1 clove garlic, minced
1 teaspoon salt
¼ teaspoon pepper
1 tablespoon oregano
2 fresh tomatoes, diced
1 can (4 ounce) sliced mushrooms
Parsley

Coat pieces of fowl with salad oil. Now brown in heavy skillet over medium heat. Add onions and garlic, cook several minutes. Sprinkle with salt, pepper, and oregano. Add tomatoes and mushrooms with juice. Cover and cook over low heat 30 minutes or until tender. Garnish with parsley. Serves 4 to 6 people.

NOTE: Chicken is delicious prepared in this manner.

Seafood

Our Southern coastal waters abound in seafood for our enjoyment.
I can almost hear the cry of "shrimp boats a'coming," which you
hear chanted down Louisiana way. I do not have to remind those
of you who have seen the shrimp boats going out in the early dawn,
and coming in at dusk off the Golden Isles of Georgia, that this is
a beautiful sight!

Whether it is Shrimp Jambalaya, Deviled Crab, or a Florida Fish
Chowder, you may be sure it will be well seasoned and served with a
flourish by your hostess. You may be a lucky fisherman, or buy

your seafood fresh or frozen at the market. It may be broiled, baked, steamed, fried, or "en casserole" and served hot or cold. Whatever you choose from the list of "the deep's wonderful food store," serve it often, as it should be included in your daily fare.

AU GRATIN CRAB MEAT

2 tablespoons melted butter	Drop Worcestershire sauce
1½ tablespoons flour	¼ pound grated sharp Cheddar
½ teaspoon salt	cheese
½ pint milk	4 cups lump crab meat
⅛ teaspoon paprika	Bread crumbs

Preheat oven to 300 degrees F. Melt butter in saucepan. Slowly blend in flour and salt. Cook over low heat until mixture is smooth. Remove from heat and add milk. Stir constantly until smooth. Add paprika, Worcestershire, and cheese. Cook over low heat until smooth and thickened. Place 3 to 4 tablespoons of this sauce in bottom of 2-quart casserole; add crab meat and cover with remainder of sauce. Top with a sprinkling of bread crumbs and heat in oven about 15 minutes. Serve hot. Serves 4.

BAKED FISH

When friend husband catches a big fish we sometimes like to bake it. Here is your answer to that "big one."

Take a fish about 3, 4, or 5 pounds. Scrape and clean. Rub with salt and softened butter. Dredging with flour is optional. Dash on a bit of paprika. Cut two or three deep gashes in each side of your fish. Stuff fish with following stuffing and fasten together with toothpicks or skewers.

STUFFING FOR FISH

1½ cups bread crumbs
2 tablespoons finely chopped
  onion
2 tablespoons finely chopped
  celery
2 tablespoons finely chopped
  parsley

1 to 2 eggs, beaten
½ teaspoon salt, or to taste
⅛ teaspoon pepper
Stock or water to make a soft
  dressing

Mix ingredients. Makes 2 cups. After stuffing fish place in lightly greased baking dish and bake in preheated 350-degree F. oven about 15 minutes to the pound. Baste often with a mixture of butter, hot water, and juice of a lemon. Sprinkle with parsley and garnish with lemon slices if desired. Serves 6 to 8.

BAKED FLOUNDER AND SHRIMP

1 medium flounder
¼ pound cleaned shrimp
Dash cayenne
⅛ teaspoon salt
¼ teaspoon parsley flakes
1 teaspoon lemon juice
½ cup bread crumbs, or as
  needed

⅛ teaspoon grated onion
  (optional)
Milk (or stock, made with
  chicken bouillon cube)
Salad oil or butter
¼ cup buttered bread crumbs
1 to 2 tablespoons butter or
  salad oil

Preheat oven to 350 degrees F. Cut fish as for fillet and raise flesh as far back as possible on each side. Stuff with chopped shrimp mixed with cayenne, salt, parsley flakes, lemon juice, and bread crumbs. Add onion if desired. Add enough milk or stock to hold together. Flatten surface of fish and brush with oil or butter, sprinkle with buttered bread crumbs. Bake in shallow baking dish 20 to 25 minutes. Serves 4.

BAKED STUFFED SHRIMP

This Baked Stuffed Shrimp came from down New Orleans way.

1 pound fresh or frozen shrimp (larger ones, 12 to 15 count)
1 pound crab meat
2 slices fresh bread, crust removed, cubed
2 tablespoons mayonnaise
½ teaspoon pepper sauce
1 teaspoon Worcestershire sauce
1 teaspoon prepared mustard
½ teaspoon salt
1 small onion, minced
½ green pepper, finely chopped
½ cup melted butter or margarine

Preheat oven to 400 degrees F. Shell uncooked shrimp, leaving tails on. Split shrimp down the back and spread apart butterfly fashion. Combine crab meat, bread cubes, mayonnaise, pepper sauce, Worcestershire, mustard, and salt. Sauté onion and pepper in 2 tablespoons melted butter until soft and add to crab meat mixture. Stuff shrimp with crab mixture.

Place shrimp tail side up on greased shallow baking dish. Brush with remaining butter and bake about 15 to 20 minutes or until browned. Serves 4 to 6.

BOILED SHRIMP

¼ cup salt
2 to 3 slices lemon
1 onion, chopped
1 bay leaf
3 to 4 sprigs celery leaves
½ cup vinegar
1 pod red pepper (optional)
⅛ teaspoon black pepper
2 pounds green unshelled shrimp

Pour enough cold water in container to cover shrimp. To each 2 quarts water add above ingredients. (You may prefer to use one of the new commercial seasonings, there are several on the market.) Let water boil 5 to 10 minutes, then add shrimp and boil for about 15 minutes, until shells are bright red. Turn off heat, let stand in water 5 to 10 minutes. Drain, remove shell, and vein. Serve with your favorite cocktail sauce or in your favorite shrimp dish.

CHEESE AND SHRIMP CASSEROLE

1 can (4 ounce) mushrooms, drained
2 to 3 tablespoons butter
1 small onion, grated
1 pound shrimp, cleaned and cooked
2 cups cooked rice

1½ cups grated Cheddar cheese
½ cup cream
2 tablespoons catsup
1 teaspoon Worcestershire sauce
½ teaspoon salt
⅛ teaspoon pepper

Preheat oven to 350 degrees F. Slice mushrooms and sauté in butter. Add onion, shrimp, rice, and cheese; mix lightly. Combine cream, catsup, Worcestershire, salt, and pepper. Add to shrimp mixture. Pour in buttered 2-quart casserole and bake about 30 minutes. Serves 4 to 6 people.

COCKTAIL SAUCE

Here is a Cocktail Sauce worthy of any bowl of seafood.

⅔ cup catsup
2 to 3 tablespoons chili sauce
2 to 3 tablespoons lemon juice or more
2 to 3 tablespoons bottled horseradish

Dash cayenne
¼ teaspoon salt
Dash Tabasco sauce

Combine ingredients, mix. Serve over shrimp or oysters. Makes about 1 cup sauce.

CRAB MEAT CASSEROLE

This Crab Meat Casserole is a bit different as it uses rice rather than a cream sauce for its base.

6 ounces crab meat, frozen or canned, drained
½ cup mayonnaise
1 teaspoon lemon juice
1 teaspoon celery salt
¼ teaspoon paprika

½ teaspoon prepared mustard
1 tablespoon chili sauce (optional)
2 cups hot cooked rice
2 tablespoons grated Parmesan cheese

Preheat broiler. Mix together the first seven ingredients, blend well. Place hot rice in 2-quart casserole and spoon crab meat mixture over the rice. Sprinkle with cheese and broil under low heat until cheese is melted. Serves 6 to 8.

CREOLE SHRIMP

¼ cup chopped green pepper
½ cup chopped onion
1 cup finely chopped celery
1 clove garlic, minced
3 tablespoons bacon drippings or butter
2 cups canned tomatoes
1 can (8 ounce) tomato sauce
½ cup water

1 teaspoon prepared mustard
½ teaspoon sugar
Dash Tabasco sauce
1 teaspoon salt
⅛ teaspoon pepper
1 bay leaf
1 pound shrimp, cleaned and cooked
3 cups hot cooked rice

Sauté pepper, onion, celery, and garlic in bacon drippings. Add tomatoes, sauce, water, prepared mustard, sugar, Tabasco, seasonings, and bay leaf. Simmer 20 to 25 minutes, stirring often. Add shrimp and simmer 10 minutes longer. Remove bay leaf. Serve over rice. Serves 6.

NOTE: For a bit of color add the following to the rice: ½ green pepper chopped and cooked in a bit of butter a minute or two.

CURRIED SHRIMP

This is quick and easy Curried Shrimp.

1 can (10½ ounce) condensed
cream of chicken soup
1 can (4 ounce) mushrooms, not
drained
½ teaspoon Worcestershire sauce
¼ teaspoon dry mustard
½ to 1 teaspoon curry powder

⅛ teaspoon pepper
¾ pound shrimp, cleaned and
cooked
1 tablespoon melted butter
½ cup toasted almonds, slivered
2 to 3 cups hot cooked rice

Mix soup, mushrooms, Worcestershire, mustard, curry, and pepper.
Heat well and add shrimp and heat a bit longer. Add butter and
almonds. Serve over hot rice. Serves 4.

DEVILED CRAB

1 can (6 ounce) crab meat or
½ pound fresh crab meat
1 egg
½ cup milk
1 teaspoon mayonnaise
½ teaspoon prepared mustard
1 tablespoon Worcestershire
sauce
½ cup grated cheese

1 small onion, chopped or
grated
1 tablespoon finely chopped
green pepper
½ cup buttered cracker crumbs
Dash Tabasco sauce
½ teaspoon salt
⅛ teaspoon pepper
Cracker crumbs

Preheat oven to 325 degrees F. Pick over crab meat and mix with
remaining ingredients except unbuttered cracker crumbs. Pack mixture into ramekins or crab shells. Sprinkle top with the cracker
crumbs, and bake until brown. Serves 6.

DEVILED EGG AND SHRIMP CASSEROLE

This nice shrimp dish was given to me by the hostess who served it. Good!

10 to 12 Deviled Eggs*
4 tablespoons butter
4 tablespoons flour
1 teaspoon salt
4 cups milk
½ cup grated Cheddar cheese

Dash paprika
2 pounds shrimp, cleaned and cooked
1½ to 2 cups herb-seasoned stuffing or bread crumbs

Preheat oven to 350 degrees F. Devil eggs, be sure to cut lengthwise. Melt butter in saucepan. Slowly blend in flour and salt. Cook over low heat until mixture is smooth. Remove from heat, stir in milk. Add cheese and paprika. Return to heat, stir constantly until smooth and cheese is melted. Add shrimp to sauce. Fill 3-quart casserole or baking dish with a layer of eggs and shrimp sauce, alternating until ingredients are used. Crush stuffing crumbs a bit and sprinkle over top of dish. Bake approximately 30 minutes or until bubbly and lightly browned. Serves 10 to 12.

FLORIDA FISH CHOWDER

2 slices bacon
½ cup chopped onion
2 cups hot water
1 cup diced potatoes
1 pound fish fillets

2 cups half cream and milk
1 teaspoon salt
⅛ teaspoon pepper
⅛ teaspoon paprika

Fry bacon and remove. Add onions to drippings. Sauté until lightly browned. You may add chopped bacon to chowder if you desire. Add water and potatoes. Cook until potatoes are almost done. Cut fillets into pieces approximately 1 inch square. Add fish to mixture and cook until fish flakes when tested with fork. Pour in milk and seasonings. Heat and serve. Serves 6.

FLOUNDER BAKED IN SOUR CREAM

Try this Flounder Baked in Sour Cream for one of the most delicious ways to prepare flounder. A grand new company dish, delicately flavored. Serve with toasted French bread spread with herb butter.

4 tablespoons butter or margarine
2 pounds flounder fillets
1 teaspoon salt
½ teaspoon hot pepper sauce
1 tablespoon paprika
¼ cup grated Parmesan cheese
1 cup dairy sour cream
¼ cup fine dry bread crumbs

Preheat oven to 350 degrees F. Grease 2-quart baking dish with 1 tablespoon butter. Arrange fish fillets in baking dish. Blend salt, pepper sauce, paprika, and Parmesan cheese into sour cream. Spread over fish. Top with bread crumbs and dot with remaining 3 tablespoons butter. Bake uncovered for 30 minutes or until fish is easily flaked with fork. Serves 4 to 6.

FRIED OYSTERS

These Fried Oysters have an extra "bit of dash" due to the horseradish used in this recipe.

Select large oysters, drain well, and season with salt, pepper, and lemon juice. On each oyster spread a small bit of horseradish. Dip the oysters in fine crumbs, then in egg beaten slightly with a teaspoon of cold water. Dip again in crumbs and fry in deep hot fat. Drain and serve with catsup or chili sauce. Garnish with lemon slices.

LAURIE'S SEAFOOD CASSEROLE

2 tablespoons butter
2 tablespoons flour
1. pint light cream
1 teaspoon salt
⅛ teaspoon pepper
1 teaspoon Worcestershire sauce
1 teaspoon paprika
1 tablespoon lemon juice
2 tablespoons catsup

1 cup grated Cheddar cheese
1 tablespoon sherry
1 pound cooked or canned crab
meat
1 pound shrimp, cleaned and
cooked
1 jar (15 ounce) artichoke
hearts, halved
½ cup bread crumbs

Preheat oven to 400 degrees F. Melt butter over low heat in saucepan. Blend in flour, cook over low heat until blended. Remove from heat, add cream. Return to heat, add salt, pepper, Worcestershire, paprika, lemon juice, catsup, cheese, and sherry. Place layer of seafood, artichoke hearts, and sauce in 3-quart casserole. Repeat. Sprinkle bread crumbs over top. Bake for 20 minutes. Serves 8.

LOBSTER THERMIDOR

This is a prize Lobster Thermidor recipe.

4 large frozen lobster tails
(about 6 to 8 ounces each)
2 to 3 tablespoons butter
1 onion, grated
1 can sliced mushrooms, drained
4 tablespoons flour
1½ cups milk
1 cup cream
1 teaspoon dry mustard

1 teaspoon celery salt
½ teaspoon salt
⅛ teaspoon pepper
Dash cayenne
2 eggs, slightly beaten
1½ cups grated Cheddar cheese
4 tablespoons sherry
1 tablespoon lemon juice
½ cup bread crumbs

Cook lobster tails as directed; drain. When cool, cut through membranes lengthwise with kitchen shears. Discard membranes. Remove meat from shells and cube. Preheat oven to 350 degrees F. Heat butter and sauté onion and mushrooms. Blend in flour and add milk, stirring constantly over low heat until thickened. Add cream, mustard, celery salt, and seasonings. Add eggs, 1 cup cheese, lobster meat, sherry, and lemon juice. Cook for 5 to 10 minutes. Place in buttered 3-quart casserole, top with remaining cheese and crumbs. Brown in oven. Serves 8.

MARINATED SHRIMP

This Marinated Shrimp recipe will be most welcome I think, good party food.

1¼ cups salad oil	2½ tablespoons capers and juice
¾ cup vinegar, use sweet pickle vinegar if you have it	Dash Tabasco sauce
1½ teaspoons salt	2½ pounds shrimp, cleaned and cooked
2½ teaspoons celery seed	3 to 4 onions, thinly sliced

Bring oil, vinegar, salt, celery seed, capers, and Tabasco to boil. Place layer of shrimp, next a layer of onions in bowl. Pour marinade over. Let stand in refrigerator overnight. If marinade does not fully cover baste with mixture several times. A clove of garlic may be added if desired. Serves 12.

SALMON CROQUETTES

This recipe for Salmon Croquettes is a family recipe; from one of my favorite cooks! I think it is one of the best. The Sour Cream Mustard Sauce gives this a gourmet touch.

1 can (1 pound) red salmon	¼ teaspoon salt
Juice 1 lemon	¼ teaspoon pepper
1 egg, slightly beaten	½ cup corn meal
1 medium onion, grated	Deep fat for frying

Drain salmon. Remove backbone and any other larger bones along with skin. Mix by hand with other ingredients except fat. Roll into croquettes, shape as desired; they are nice in rolls about 2 inches long. Fry in deep hot fat until brown. Drain on paper toweling. Serve with Sour Cream Mustard Sauce. Makes 12.

NOTE: Pink salmon may also be used in this recipe.

SOUR CREAM MUSTARD SAUCE

½ cup mayonnaise	Juice ½ lemon
½ cup diary sour cream	½ teaspoon sugar
2 tablespoons drained sweet	½ teaspoon salt
pickle relish	½ teaspoon red pepper
1 tablespoon prepared mustard	

Mix ingredients. Serve hot or cold. Makes about 1½ cups.

SCALLOPED OYSTERS

Scalloped Oysters are almost a must in many households for holiday time.

1 quart oysters	1 egg
1 teaspoon salt	¾ to 1 cup milk, or more
¼ teaspoon pepper	½ cup buttered bread crumbs
3 tablespoon butter, or more	
2 cups coarse soda cracker crumbs	

Preheat oven to 350 degrees F. Remove any pieces of shell from oysters. Drain. Place layer of oysters in greased 2-quart casserole. Sprinkle with half the salt and pepper, dot with bits of butter, add layer of cracker crumbs. Put in another layer of oysters, repeat seasonings, butter, and cracker crumbs. Add layer of oysters on top. Break egg in milk and mix well. Pour over the dish of oysters and let it go into mixture. Cover top with buttered crumbs and bake about 30 minutes. If the dish seems to "dry out," add a bit more milk and butter. Serve at once if you want the oysters at best. Serves 6.

SHRIMP AND ASPARAGUS ELEGANT

1 pound grated sharp Cheddar
cheese
¾ cup milk
½ cup minced green onion
1 to 2 green peppers, chopped
fine
1 can (4 ounce) mushrooms,
drained

2 cups shrimp, cleaned and
cooked, or canned
½ teaspoon salt
1 tablespoon Worcestershire
sauce
2 cans (14½ ounces each)
asparagus, drained
Parsley

Make a cheese sauce by melting cheese in top of double boiler and adding milk. Stir until smooth. Cook the onion and pepper in boiling water 3 minutes. Drain. Add to cheese sauce with mushrooms and shrimp. Stir in salt and Worcestershire, check seasoning. Place 3 to 4 asparagus stalks on toast rounds and cover with shrimp-cheese sauce mixture. Garnish with parsley. Serves 8.

SHRIMP JAMBALAYA

This is another famous dish from down Louisiana way, Shrimp Jambalaya.

1 cup sliced celery
2 cups diced green pepper
2 medium onions, chopped fine
4 tablespoons butter, divided
1 clove garlic, minced
1 pound cooked cubed ham
2 pounds cleaned shrimp

1½ teaspoons salt
¼ teaspoon Tabasco sauce
2 teaspoons Worcestershire sauce
1 teaspoon sugar
4 cups canned tomatoes
3 cups hot cooked rice

Cook celery, pepper, and onions in half the butter until tender, not brown. Add garlic and ham, cook 5 minutes longer. Add remaining butter, shrimp, salt, Tabasco, Worcestershire, and sugar. Cook, tossing often with fork until shrimp are pink. Add tomatoes, simmer uncovered about 15 minutes. Stir in rice, serve. Serves 8.

SHRIMP MARINADE

4 to 5 pounds shrimp, cleaned and cooked

Mix together:

½ cup catsup
1 cup mayonnaise
1 cup tartar sauce

Stir in:

3 large onions, shredded
1 teaspoon seafood seasoning

Combine shrimp with all other ingredients. Chill in refrigerator 3 to 4 hours before serving time. Serves 20.

SHRIMP REMOULADE

I ate Shrimp Remoulade in New Orleans one hot summer day in a courtyard. Here is one that tastes as good I do believe.

½ cup tarragon vinegar
2 to 3 tablespoons tomato
    catsup or chili
3 to 4 tablespoons horseradish
    mustard
1 tablespoon paprika
1 teaspoon salt
½ teaspoon cayenne pepper

1 clove garlic, minced
1 cup salad oil
½ cup minced green onions,
    with tops
½ cup minced celery
4 pounds shrimp, cleaned and
    cooked
¼ head lettuce, shredded

Mix vinegar, catsup, mustard, paprika, salt, pepper, and garlic in small bowl. Add oil gradually. Stir in onions and celery. Pour sauce over shrimp and marinate in refrigerator 4 to 5 hours. For each serving place 6 to 8 marinated shrimp on shredded lettuce. Serves 12 to 14, depends on amount of shrimp on each serving.

SHRIMP REMOULADE GOURMET

Another version of Shrimp Remoulade.

4 pounds shrimp
1 pint mayonnaise
1 clove garlic, minced
1 tablespoon prepared mustard

1 tablespoon chopped capers
½ tablespoon minced parsley
½ tablespoon minced chives

Prepare and cook shrimp as for cocktail. Mix other ingredients and chill. Mix shrimp with sauce and serve on lettuce as a salad or mix and serve in a large bowl as an addition to your buffet meal. Serves 12.

SMOKED OYSTER AND CORN CASSEROLE

1 egg
½ cup undiluted evaporated
  milk
2 cups cream-style corn
⅛ teaspoon salt

2½ teaspoons soy sauce
1 tablespoon minced onion
1 can (3⅔ ounce) smoked
  oysters, drained
5 to 6 soda crackers

Preheat oven to 325 degrees F. In 2-quart casserole to be used for baking, beat egg lightly. Add milk, corn, salt, soy sauce, and onion. When mixed, scatter oysters over top. Now sprinkle with coarsely crushed crackers. Bake about 30 to 35 minutes until mixture is set. Serves 8.

SPANISH CRAB

1 medium onion, chopped
2 tablespoons margarine
1 tablespoon flour
2 cups canned tomatoes
½ pound sautéed fresh
  mushrooms, or 1 can (8
  ounce), drained
1 can black olives, drained and
  sliced

½ teaspoon salt, or to taste
¼ teaspoon pepper
1 teaspoon sugar
1 teaspoon Worcestershire sauce
2 pounds canned or cooked
  crab meat
3 cups hot cooked rice

Sauté onion in margarine until tender. Add flour and tomatoes, simmer about 30 minutes. Purée sauce. Add mushrooms, olives, seasonings, Worcestershire, and crab meat to sauce. Heat well and serve over rice for a luncheon dish. Serves 8.

SWEET AND SOUR SHRIMP

1 pound shrimp, cleaned and
    cooked
3 to 4 tablespoons butter
¼ cup brown sugar
2 tablespoons cornstarch
½ teaspoon salt
⅓ cup vinegar

1 cup canned pineapple juice
1 tablespoon soy sauce
1 green pepper, seeded and
    chopped
1 onion, sliced
3 slices canned pineapple, diced
3 cups hot cooked rice

Brown shrimp in butter. Combine brown sugar, cornstarch, salt, vinegar, pineapple juice, and soy sauce in bowl. Pour over shrimp and let cook until thick. Let stand for 10 minutes, covered. Add pepper, onion, and pineapple. Cook 2 to 3 minutes covered. Serve over rice. Serves 4.

Cheese & Egg Dishes

A bit of cheese is always a nice tidbit to nibble on. For a change we combine cheese with many ingredients. May I suggest that you sample the Grits Casserole and "methinks" it will make a grits fan of you. Cheese Pudding, a nice luncheon or supper dish, is always a welcome idea. You'll find ways with eggs—Creole Eggs make a tasty casserole. This is an excellent choice for a brunch or the Easter season. No picnic would be complete without Deviled Eggs, and the omelet has as many variations as some of our folk songs.

CHEESE GRITS

The friend who gave this one to me says it is particularly good with birds.

4 cups boiling water
1 teaspoon salt
1 cup instant grits
½ cup butter or margarine

1 roll (8 ounce) garlic cheese, crumbled
2 to 3 eggs
Milk

Preheat oven to 350 degrees F. Bring salted water to rolling boil and slowly stir in grits. Cook 3 minutes, stirring constantly. Remove from heat and stir in butter and garlic cheese. Put eggs in cup and add milk to make 1 cup. Beat well. Add to grits mixture. Bake in greased 2-quart casserole for 1 hour. Serves 6.

CHEESE PUDDING

This Cheese Pudding is so good and "will wait" to be served.

6 slices white bread
3 eggs
3 cups milk

1 teaspoon salt
2 cups grated sharp Cheddar cheese

Preheat oven to 400 degrees F. Cut crusts from bread and cut in small squares. Beat eggs, milk, and salt. Add cheese. Put bread in buttered 2-quart casserole. Pour egg mixture over it and bake for 20 minutes. Run under flame or broiler to brown before serving. Serves 6 to 8.

CHEESE AND RICE CROQUETTES

This is an idea to use that dish of "cold rice." You'll be surprised!

1 egg
2 tablespoons melted butter
½ teaspoon salt
⅛ teaspoon pepper

2 cups cold cooked rice
1 pound sharp Cheddar cheese, softened
Fine bread crumbs

Add egg, butter, salt, and pepper to rice; mix well. Form cheese into small balls. Cover these with rice mix on all sides so cheese will be inside rice covering. Dip in crumbs. Fry in deep hot fat. Serve with a cheese sauce if desired. Serves 6.

CHEESE SOUFFLE

This is a foolproof soufflé and so easy to do!

1 can (10½ ounce) condensed cream of mushroom soup
2 cups grated sharp Cheddar cheese

4 eggs
¼ teaspoon salt

Heat soup and cheese in top of double boiler until cheese melts and mixture is smooth. Add 4 egg yolks and salt. Cool, and fold in the stiffly beaten egg whites. Put in greased 1½-quart casserole and cook in pan of water on top of stove for 15 minutes and then in preheated 350-degree F. oven for 30 minutes. Serves 4 to 6.

CREOLE EGGS

Creole Eggs are for "home folks" or company; there isn't a better casserole than this one.

1 medium onion, chopped fine	1 teaspoon salt, or to taste
2 tablespoons bacon drippings	⅛ teaspoon pepper
2 cups canned tomatoes	Dash paprika
½ green pepper, chopped fine	10 hard-cooked eggs
½ cup finely chopped celery	Bread crumbs

Sauté onion in bacon drippings until lightly browned. Add tomatoes, pepper, and celery. Season to taste with salt, pepper, and paprika. Cook until thick. This is the tomato sauce for eggs. Make cream sauce as follows:

2 tablespoons butter or margarine	1 cup milk
2 tablespoons flour	½ teaspoon salt
	Few grains pepper

Melt butter, blend in flour, gradually add milk. Cook over hot water or low heat, stir constantly until thick. Add salt and pepper. Cook 5 minutes, stirring occasionally. Preheat oven to 350 degrees F. Slice eggs in thick slices. Layer eggs in 3-quart casserole. Pour a layer of tomato sauce over eggs, next over this a layer of cream sauce. It will run together. Repeat layers until ingredients are used. Sprinkle top with bread crumbs, brown in oven about 20 minutes. Serve hot. Serves 8.

DEVILED EGGS

No picnic is complete without Deviled Eggs.

6 hard-cooked eggs
Mayonnaise
Vinegar, use pickle vinegar if
   you have it
½ teaspoon salt, or to taste
⅛ teaspoon pepper

Dash paprika
¼ teaspoon prepared mustard,
   or to taste
Few finely chopped pickles
   (optional)
1 teaspoon chopped pimento

Cut eggs in halves lengthwise. Remove yolks and mash them. Moisten with mayonnaise and season to taste with vinegar, salt, pepper, paprika, and mustard. Mix well, add pickles. Mix again and pile lightly into the halved egg whites. Garnish with bits of pimento. Serves 6.

GRITS CASSEROLE

1 cup grits
3 cups boiling water
½ teaspoon salt
¼ cup butter or margarine

3 eggs, beaten
¾ to 1 cup milk
¼ cup grated Cheddar cheese

Preheat oven to 350 degrees F. Pour the grits into boiling salted water. Mix well and cook until thickened. Add butter, beaten eggs, milk, and cheese. Stir well and place in 2-quart casserole. Bake about 30 minutes. Serves 6.

HARD-COOKED EGGS

Place unshelled eggs in saucepan. Cover with cold water and place over medium heat. Bring to boil. Reduce heat and let eggs simmer for 8 to 10 minutes. Remove eggs and plunge in cold water. Peel and use as desired.

JOYE'S MUSHROOM EGGS AND POTATO BASKETS

This is a prize recipe; I suggest serving it for breakfast on toast, for lunch in Potato Baskets, or as a casserole for dinner.

4 tablespoons butter	⅛ teaspoon seasoning salt
5 tablespoons flour	1 teaspoon Worcestershire sauce
2 cups hot milk	⅛ teaspoon garlic salt
2 cups grated Cheddar cheese	½ teaspoon onion salt
1 can (4 ounce) sliced	6 hard-cooked eggs, sliced
mushrooms, drained	Bread crumbs
1 teaspoon dry mustard	Paprika

Preheat oven to 350 degrees F. Melt butter, add flour and milk, stir until blended. Cook on low heat until thick, stir constantly. Add next 7 ingredients, mix well. Place eggs in 2-quart casserole, pour mixture over eggs, top with bread crumbs. Bake for 15 minutes. Remove from oven and sprinkle with paprika. Serves 6 to 8.

POTATO BASKETS

Peel potatoes, wash and dry well. Shred on coarse shredder. Using two hand strainers, one slightly larger than the other, place shredded potatoes in larger strainer to about ¼ inch thickness, having potatoes high as possible. Fit smaller strainer into potatoes, turning gently to form a basket. Holding the two strainers firmly together, lower into deep hot fat and fry at 375 degrees F. until golden brown or crisp, about 1 to 1½ minutes. To remove potato baskets lift up top strainer and strike lower strainer with a knife to release the basket. Fill with creamed eggs or any other creamed food.

MACARONI AND CHEESE

1 cup uncooked macaroni
1½ cups scalded milk
1 cup bread crumbs
½ cup melted butter
1 chopped pimento (optional)
1 tablespoon parsley
1 tablespoon chopped fresh
  onion

1½ cups grated Cheddar cheese
½ teaspoon salt
¼ teaspoon pepper
⅛ teaspoon paprika
3 eggs, beaten well

Cook macaroni according to package directions. Preheat oven to 350 degrees F. Scald milk and add rest of ingredients, cooking and stirring constantly until cheese melts. Combine sauce with macaroni and sprinkle with additional paprika. Bake in unbuttered 2-quart baking dish for about 50 minutes. Serves 6.

MACARONI AND CHEESE QUICKIE

Mother's cook used to make quick macaroni with canned macaroni, nice when one is in a hurry.

1 can (15 ounce) macaroni with
  cheese sauce
1 egg, beaten
¼ to ½ cup milk

½ cup grated Cheddar cheese
¼ teaspoon salt
1 to 2 tablespoons butter

Preheat oven to 350 degrees F. Mix macaroni, egg, milk, cheese, and salt, reserving a bit of cheese for top of dish. Dot with butter, cover top with remaining cheese, and bake in 8-inch baking dish about 20 minutes. Serves 4 to 6.

PLAIN OMELET

This Omelet recipe is the one I've used for a long time. I like the Spanish Omelet. Take this foundation recipe and make any variation you desire.

Use 1 egg for each person served and 1 tablespoon of hot water for each egg. Separate yolks and whites. Season the yolks with salt and pepper to taste, add water, and beat well. Beat the whites until stiff and fold in the yolks. Pour gently into a well-greased ovenproof pan (skillet) and cook slowly until the underside is a delicate brown, this on top of stove on medium heat. Now place the pan in preheated oven keeping the temperature between 325 to 350 degrees. When the omelet responds to touch it is done. Make 2 cuts part of the way down the middle of omelet in pan, then tip pan, slide a spatula down under the omelet and fold it over as you slip it out onto a platter.

SPANISH OMELET: Use a tomato sauce as for spaghetti, sometimes adding a few drained canned green peas.
BACON OMELET: Add crisp bacon, broken, into egg mix before cooking; sprinkle a bit over when done.
CHEESE OMELET: Sprinkle grated Cheddar cheese over omelet before folding or cheese may be stirred into egg mixture before cooking.
HAM OMELET: Add chopped cooked ham over omelet as you fold; a bit may be added before cooking.
FRUIT OMELET: After omelet is cooked spread its surface with jam or fresh fruit.

Breads

Hot breads are really Southern fare, from Hot Biscuits to Hush Puppies.

Biscuits were a must in my home. My father had our cook bake them for breakfast to "go" with his grits and eggs. Biscuits hot and buttered and served with a dab of fig or strawberry preserves make one think of days gone by.

Hush Puppies, little puffed-up morsels of corn bread batter fried in deep fat, are delicious served with your fish. The story goes that they were first cooked to throw to the puppies to keep them from barking at outdoor fish fries. Hot Corn Bread is served with our vegetables. But please, no sweet corn bread.

ANGEL BISCUITS

These Angel Biscuits are nice to make and keep in refrigerator until needed.

6 cups self-rising flour
⅓ cup sugar
¼ teaspoon salt
1 teaspoon soda
1 cup shortening

2 packages (¼ ounce each) active dry yeast, dissolved in ¼ cup lukewarm water
2 cups buttermilk

Preheat oven to 450 degrees F. Sift flour, sugar, salt, and soda together. Cut in shortening. Add yeast and buttermilk. Knead well. It may be necessary to knead in more flour. Cut out biscuits and bake 10 to 12 minutes. Dough may be covered and refrigerated for a week. Makes 24 to 30 biscuits.

NOTE: This dough does not have to rise before baking. Biscuits may be baked immediately. If using plain flour, add 1 tablespoon baking powder.

BANANA BREAD

½ cup butter or margarine
1 cup sugar
2 eggs
1½ cups flour, sifted

1 teaspoon soda
¼ teaspoon salt
1 cup mashed ripe bananas
1 cup chopped pecans

Preheat oven to 350 degrees F. Mix butter, sugar, and eggs together. Fold in dry ingredients sifted together, add mashed bananas and nuts. Bake in loaf pan, 9×5 inches, 40 to 50 minutes. Makes 1 loaf.

BISCUIT PIZZA SNACKS

½ to ¾ pound ground pork
sausage
1 tablespoon crushed oregano
1 clove garlic, minced
1 package (8 ounce) refrigerated
biscuits

1 can (6 ounce) tomato paste
1 cup grated sharp Cheddar
cheese
¼ cup grated Parmesan cheese
⅛ teaspoon salt
Sliced stuffed olives

Preheat oven to 425 degrees F. Brown sausage, drain. Add oregano
and garlic. On a greased baking sheet flatten biscuits to 4-inch circles
with the bottom of a floured custard cup, leaving a rim around edges.
Fill with sausage and tomato paste. Sprinkle with grated cheeses
and salt. Bake about 10 to 12 minutes. Top with a slice of stuffed
olive. Makes 10 pizzas.

BUTTERMILK ROLLS

1½ cups buttermilk, scalded
2 packages (¼ ounce each)
active dry yeast
¼ cup warm water
¼ cup sugar

½ cup melted shortening
1 teaspoon salt
4½ cups flour
½ teaspoon soda
Melted butter, as needed

Scald milk in double boiler. Dissolve yeast in water. Add milk, cooled
to lukewarm. Add sugar, shortening, and salt, now flour and soda,
which have been sifted together. Mix well and let stand 10 minutes.
Roll out and cut or shape as desired. Brush tops with melted butter.
Allow to rise until double in bulk, about 30 minutes. Preheat oven
to 425 degrees F. Bake about 15 minutes. Makes 24.

For Clover Leaf Rolls, fill greased muffin tins about half full with
3 small balls. Brush tops with melted butter and let rise until double
in bulk. Bake as above.

BUTTERSCOTCH BREAD

2 eggs
2 cups brown sugar
3 tablespoons melted margarine
4 cups flour
1 teaspoon soda

1½ teaspoons baking powder
½ teaspoon salt
2 cups sour milk or buttermilk
1 cup chopped pecans or
    walnuts

Preheat oven to 350 degrees F. Beat eggs and add sugar gradually, mixing thoroughly. Add margarine. Sift flour, measure and sift again with soda, baking powder, and salt. Add to egg mixture alternately with the milk. Add nuts. Pour into 2 greased loaf pans, 9×5 inches, and bake for 45 minutes. This makes 2 loaves, 1 pound each.

CINNAMON BISCUITS

8 teaspoons ground cinnamon
2 cups granulated sugar
½ cup butter or margarine

2 cans (8 ounces each)
    refrigerated biscuits

Preheat oven to 375 degrees F. Mix the cinnamon and sugar together well. Melt the butter or margarine. Dip the biscuits in the butter, then roll them in the cinnamon mixture. (This makes a large batch of sugar and cinnamon mix; store the extra in jar for future use.) Place these on ungreased baking sheet and bake for 12 to 15 minutes, according to your oven. For party biscuits, cut with a small cutter. Makes 20.

CORN BREAD

This is a good Corn Bread to serve with those spring and summer vegetables.

2 eggs
1¼ cups milk
¼ cup melted shortening
1½ cups corn meal

¾ cup flour
1 teaspoon salt
2½ teaspoons baking powder

Preheat oven to 400 degrees F. Beat eggs, add milk and shortening. Sift remaining ingredients together, add to egg mixture, and beat well. Pour into greased shallow 9×9-inch pan and bake in hot oven until bread shrinks from sides of pan, about 20 to 25 minutes. This may also be baked in greased corn stick pans. Serves 6 to 8.

CORN MEAL MUFFINS

2 to 3 eggs	2 cups sifted corn meal
2 cups buttermilk	1 teaspoon soda
3 tablespoons melted shortening	Water
1 teaspoon salt	1½ teaspoons baking powder

Preheat oven to 450 degrees F. Beat eggs together, add milk, shortening, and salt. Add meal. Beat smooth and let batter rest while greasing pans; let pans heat. Add soda dissolved in a little water, now sift in baking powder. Mix and pour in greased muffin tins. Bake 20 to 25 minutes. Makes 12.

CRACKLING BREAD

This Crackling Bread came from Kentucky. For Pone Bread leave out the cracklings.

2 cups coarse corn meal	1 cup cracklings
1 cup boiling water	¼ teaspoon soda
1 teaspoon salt	¾ cup buttermilk

Preheat oven to 400 to 450 degrees F. Scald the meal with the boiling water. Add salt and cracklings. Put the soda in the buttermilk and add to meal mixture. Form into small oval pones with fingers and flatten slightly. Place on greased griddle and bake until done and brown. If necessary turn once during baking. Makes about 8 pones, depending on size you make pones.

DATE NUT BREAD

4 eggs
1 cup sugar
⅛ teaspoon salt
1½ tablespoons vanilla

2 tablespoons baking powder
2 cups flour
1 pound chopped pecans
1 pound chopped dates

Preheat oven to 300 degrees F. Beat eggs, add sugar, salt, vanilla. Sift baking powder with 1¾ cups flour and add to egg mixture. Add pecans and dates, which have been dredged with remaining flour. Bake in greased 9×5-inch loaf pan about 1 hour and 15 minutes. Serves 12 to 14.

DELUXE CORN BREAD

2 eggs
1 cup sour cream
½ cup salad oil
1 cup finely chopped fresh corn

1 cup corn meal
1 teaspoon salt
3 teaspoons baking powder

Preheat oven to 375 degrees F. Beat eggs, blend in sour cream, oil, and corn. Sift together the meal, salt, and baking powder and mix well with the egg mixture. Bake in 9×9-inch greased pan 30 to 45 minutes or until done. Serves 6.

EDNA'S BISCUITS

Here is a Biscuit recipe from a grand cook. Better get out the butter and jelly for these.

2 cups flour
½ teaspoon salt
3 teaspoons baking powder

3 heaping tablespoons
  shortening
⅔ cup milk

Preheat oven to 400 to 425 degrees F. Sift flour, salt, baking powder together. Cut in shortening, add milk, mix and roll out on floured board to about ½ inch thickness. Cut out biscuits and place on ungreased baking sheet. Bake about 10 minutes. Makes 12 to 15 biscuits.

GINGERBREAD

½ cup butter or margarine	2½ cups flour
½ cup sugar	1 cup molasses
2 eggs	1 teaspoon soda dissolved in 1
1 teaspoon cloves	cup boiling water
1 teaspoon ginger	

Preheat oven to 350 degrees F. Cream butter, add sugar gradually, creaming until light and fluffy. Add the well-beaten egg yolks. Sift spices and flour together and add alternately with the molasses and soda water. Fold in the stiffly beaten egg whites. Pour into greased 9×9×2½-inch pan and bake about 30 to 40 minutes. Serve with Lemon Sauce. Serves 10 to 12.

LEMON SAUCE

A friend gave me this Lemon Sauce recipe; it has been "handed down" in her family.

1 cup sugar	Juice 1 lemon
1 egg	1 tablespoon butter

Mix ingredients well. Cook over medium heat until thick. Makes 1 cup.

HUSH PUPPIES

This Hush Puppies recipe hails from Mississippi. Fish and hush puppies go together, as bread and butter.

1 cup corn meal	1 egg
½ cup flour	1 cup buttermilk
1½ teaspoons soda	1 medium onion, chopped fine
½ teaspoon salt	Deep fat for frying

Mix and sift dry ingredients. Add beaten egg, buttermilk, and onion. Mix well. Drop by spoonfuls into deep, hot fat. Fry to golden brown. Drain on paper towels. Makes 10 to 12, depending on spoon size.

HUSH PUPPIES ELOISE

1 cup pancake flour
1 cup corn meal
½ teaspoon salt
1 egg

1 cup milk, or as needed
1 small onion, chopped
Deep fat for frying

Mix and sift dry ingredients. Add beaten egg and milk to make batter thick enough to drop from spoon. Add onion, mix well. Drop by spoonfuls into deep hot fat and fry until brown. Drain on paper toweling. Makes 15 to 20, according to spoon size.

JEWEL'S ROLLS

1 package (¼ ounce) active dry
  yeast
1 cup lukewarm water
½ cup sugar

3 eggs, beaten
5 cups flour
⅛ teaspoon salt
¼ cup melted butter or salad oil

Dissolve yeast in water, add sugar. Beat in eggs. Add flour and salt sifted together. Place in greased bowl, brush top with shortening and let rise until doubled in bulk. Preheat oven to 375 degrees F. Knead dough. Roll about ¼ inch thick and cut into rounds with floured biscuit cutter; or make into desired shape. Bake about 20 minutes. Makes 24.

MEXICAN CORN BREAD

2 eggs
1 cup dairy sour cream
⅔ cup salad oil
1 teaspoon salt
3 teaspoons baking powder
1½ cups plain corn meal

1 cup cream-style canned corn
2 jalapeño peppers, chopped
2 tablespoons chopped green
  pepper
1 cup grated sharp Cheddar
  cheese

Preheat oven to 350 degrees F. Beat eggs and add cream, oil, and salt. Sift baking powder with meal; add to egg mixture. Add corn and peppers. Mix, pour half of the mixture into hot greased skillet. Sprinkle with half of the cheese. Add remaining mixture and sprinkle with remainder of cheese. Bake for 30 to 35 minutes. Serves 6 to 8.

ONION CHEESE SUPPER BREAD

½ cup chopped onion
2 tablespoons fat
1 egg, beaten
½ cup milk
1½ cups biscuit mix

1 cup grated sharp Cheddar cheese
2 tablespoons snipped parsley
2 tablespoons melted butter

Preheat oven to 400 degrees F. Cook onion in hot fat until tender but not brown. Combine egg and milk, add to biscuit mix (stir until moistened). Add onion, half of cheese and parsley. Spread dough in greased 8-inch round cake pan. Sprinkle with remaining cheese and parsley. Drizzle butter over. Bake 20 minutes or until toothpick comes out clean. Makes 6 to 8 servings.

PUFFY FRENCH TOAST

This Puffy French Toast is a bit different. It makes a grand breakfast or brunch dish. A goody for your supper with scrambled eggs and bacon.

1 egg
1 cup milk
1 cup flour, or more if needed
1 teaspoon baking powder

¼ teaspoon salt
4 to 5 slices white bread
Deep fat for frying
1 to 2 teaspoons sugar

Beat egg and milk together in shallow bowl. (A soup bowl will do nicely.) Sift in flour, baking powder, and salt. Batter should be slightly thicker than for pancakes. Dip bread in thick batter and fry in deep fat. Fry one side until lightly browned, turn and brown other side. Have deep fat hot, as for frying potatoes. Drain on paper toweling and serve sprinkled with a little granulated sugar. Serve with marmalade. Makes batter for 4 to 5 pieces of bread.

SESAME SEED STRIPS

Serve these Sesame Seed Strips with spaghetti. They will be a hit!

2¼ cups sifted flour, plus	1 cup milk
1 tablespoon	⅓ cup melted butter
3½ teaspoons baking powder	Sesame seed
1½ teaspoons salt	

Preheat oven to 450 degrees F. Sift dry ingredients into bowl. Add milk. Mix with fork. Turn out on board, knead 10 times. Roll out and cut in strips with floured knife. Put strips in melted butter. Sprinkle sesame seed over strips. Bake on ungreased pan for 15 minutes. Will make about 25 to 30 strips.

SIXTY-MINUTE ROLLS

1 cup milk	3 cups sifted flour
1 package (¼ ounce) active dry yeast	4 tablespoons soft butter
	¾ teaspoon salt
1 tablespoon sugar	1 tablespoon melted butter

Scald milk and cool to lukewarm. Dissolve yeast and sugar in milk, add 1 cup flour. Beat with electric mixer on low speed for 5 minutes; add soft butter, beat 1 minute, add ½ cup flour and salt. Turn out on bread board with remainder of flour and knead well. Cover and allow to rise 30 minutes. Roll to ¼ inch thickness. Cut into rounds with biscuit cutter. Dip knife handle in flour, crease across middle of each roll. Fold rolls over and press edges together. Brush tops with melted butter. Place on greased pan and let rise in warm place about 15 minutes or until double in bulk. Bake in preheated 400-degree F. oven about 15 to 20 minutes. Makes 30.

SPOON BREAD

This Spoon Bread came from Kentucky.

½ teaspoon salt
1 cup corn meal
1½ cups boiling water
1½ tablespoons melted
   shortening

3 eggs
1 cup milk
1 tablespoon baking powder

Preheat oven to 350 degrees F. Add salt to meal and add this mixture to water. Add shortening. Beat eggs, add to milk. Add to meal mixture, add baking powder. Mix well and pour into greased 1½-quart casserole. Bake for 30 to 40 minutes or until firm. Serve in baking dish with melted butter poured over it. Serves 6.

SWEET POTATO BISCUITS

This recipe is Deep South. I'm sure it will be welcome as it is not in many cookbooks. These Sweet Potato Biscuits will bring back memories to many of you.

6 medium sweet potatoes
4 tablespoons butter or
   margarine
2 cups plain flour
1 teaspoon salt

½ cup sugar
4 teaspoons baking powder
6 tablespoons milk, more or
   less as needed

Preheat oven to 400 degrees F. Boil or bake potatoes. Peel. Mash well; you should have 3 cups. Mix in butter. Sift flour and salt along with sugar and baking powder. Add to potatoes alternately with milk. Dough should be moist but not sticky. Turn out on floured board, use as little flour as possible. Work about a minute, now roll and cut biscuits. Brush tops of biscuits with milk before placing in oven. Placed in greased pan and bake about 15 minutes. Makes 24.

Cookies

Remember the visits to Grandmother's house in years gone by? The cooky jar held a special appeal for many of us. I hope that the cookies in my book will remind you of this pleasure of childhood and home . . . and be worthy of Grandmother's cooky jar.

The Tea Cakes, a Date Cooky, and Lemon Sours are a few of the treats in store for you. The Date Cooky is so easy, and has been served often at church suppers and teas. The Lemon Sours are worth all the effort involved in making them. So open your cooky jar and if you do not have one, buy one, and proceed to fill it. Your grandchildren will be happy in your kitchen, you'll see.

ALMA'S COOKY

1 cup sugar
1 cup butter
1 egg
1 teaspoon vanilla
¼ teaspoon salt

½ teaspoon almond extract
2 cups plain flour
1 tablespoon sugar
2 cups finely slivered almonds
  or pecans

Preheat oven to 250 degrees F. Cream together sugar and butter. Add egg yolk, vanilla, salt, almond extract, and sifted flour. Grease shallow 16×11-inch pan and press the cooky dough flat. Beat egg white with sugar until frothy. Spread on batter. Sprinkle slivered almonds on top, press down a little. Bake 1½ hours and cut while warm. Remove from pan. Makes about 24.

BECK'S DATE COOKY

Among all the recipes published in my newspaper column, this Date Cooky has been one of the most popular.

½ cup butter or margarine
1 cup dark brown sugar
1 package (7½ ounce) dates, cut in small pieces

Mix all together in pan. Cook over low heat until mixture bubbles. Simmer 5 minutes longer. Remove from stove and add the following except the sugar:

1 cup chopped pecans
1 cup canned coconut
2 cups dry rice cereal
  (crispies)

1 teaspoon vanilla
⅛ teaspoon salt
Powdered sugar

This mixture will be thick. Roll into small walnut-size balls and roll in powdered sugar. Makes about 40 to 50.

BROWNIES WITH GLAZE

½ cup shortening
1 cup brown sugar
2 eggs
½ cup flour
⅛ teaspoon salt

2 squares (1 ounce each)
　unsweetened chocolate,
　melted
½ cup chopped pecans
1 teaspoon vanilla

Preheat oven to 350 degrees F. Cream shortening, add sugar and eggs. Beat mixture well. Sift flour with salt. Fold in mixture. Add chocolate and pecans. Flavor with vanilla. Spread about ½ inch thick in square pan, 9×9 inches. Bake about 30 minutes. Cut in squares while warm. Spread with Confectioners' Glaze. Makes 12 to 15.

CONFECTIONERS' GLAZE

1 cup sifted confectioners' sugar
2 tablespoons white corn syrup

1 tablespoon sweet milk
⅛ teaspoon vanilla

Combine and stir ingredients until well blended. Spread on cooled brownies.

NOTE: If you wish you may add 1 to 2 drops of green food coloring to your glaze for a bit of color.

CHOCOLATE-DROP COOKY

This Chocolate-Drop Cooky is a delicate chocolate cooky, nice for a party.

¼ cup butter
¼ cup margarine
¾ cup sugar
1 egg
2 squares (1 ounce each)
　unsweetened chocolate,
　melted

1¾ cups flour
½ teaspoon soda
½ teaspoon salt
½ cup sweet milk
1 teaspoon vanilla
½ cup chopped pecans
Pecan halves (optional)

Preheat oven to 350 to 375 degrees F. Cream butter and margarine, and add sugar gradually. Beat well and add egg. Stir in chocolate. Add the flour sifted with soda and salt alternately with the sweet milk. Mix this and stir in vanilla and pecans. Drop cooky dough by teaspoons on ungreased baking sheet, leaving about 1 inch between as cookies will spread. An easy way to get cookies the same size is to push dough off teaspoon with another spoon. Bake 7 to 8 minutes. Remove at once. Makes 25 to 30.

NOTE: Watch carefully as chocolate has a tendency to burn easily.

While they cool on rack, make the following icing for topping:

Milk or cream
2 cups confectioners' sugar
⅛ teaspoon salt

1 teaspoon vanilla
Pecan halves (optional)

Add enough milk or cream to sugar to make an easy spreading frosting. Add salt and vanilla. Drop 1 teaspoon frosting onto center of cooky; it will drip down cooky or you may swirl with spatula. Top each cookie with pecan half.

CORN FLAKE MACAROONS

This is an easy cooky, and good.

4 egg whites
⅛ teaspoon salt
1 cup sugar
1 cup shredded coconut

1 cup chopped nuts
½ teaspoon vanilla
3 cups corn flakes

Preheat oven to 250 degrees F. Beat egg whites with salt until stiff, gradually add sugar. Add coconut, nuts, vanilla, and corn flakes. Drop from a spoon on greased pan. Bake 15 to 20 minutes. Makes about 30.

CRESCENTS

These Crescents are a nice tea sweet.

1 cup butter
1 tablespoon sugar
2 cups flour
2 teaspoons vanilla

1 cup finely chopped pecans or
   almonds
Confectioners' sugar

Preheat oven to 350 degrees F. Cream butter, sugar, and flour. Add vanilla and nuts. Roll about ¼ inch thick on bread board. Cut in crescent shapes, place on ungreased cooky sheet, and bake for about 20 minutes. While still warm roll crescents in confectioners' sugar. Makes about 3 dozen.

DATE COOKIES

½ cup butter
½ cup white sugar
¼ cup brown sugar
1 egg
1½ cups flour

½ teaspoon soda
1 teaspoon vanilla
¾ cup chopped nuts
1 cup chopped dates

Preheat oven to 350 degrees F. Cream butter and sugars, add egg and mix. Sift flour and soda, add along with remainder of ingredients. Drop from teaspoon on ungreased baking pan and bake for about 12 minutes. Makes 2 dozen.

DROP PECAN COOKIES

2 tablespoons butter
¼ cup sugar
1 egg, beaten
½ cup chopped pecans
½ teaspoon lemon juice

½ cup flour
1 teaspoon baking powder
⅛ teaspoon salt
2 tablespoons milk
16 to 18 pecan halves

Preheat oven to 400 degrees F. Cream butter and sugar. Add egg, pecans, and lemon juice. Sift flour, baking powder, and salt. Add alternately with milk to egg mixture. Mix well. Drop from teaspoon on greased baking sheet about 2 inches apart to allow for spreading. Press flat. Place 1 pecan half on each. Bake 10 to 15 minutes. Makes 16 to 18.

ENGLISH TOFFEE COOKY

1 cup soft butter
1 cup light brown sugar, firmly
    packed
1 egg
1 teaspoon vanilla

2 cups sifted flour
1 bar (9 ounce) chocolate
    candy
½ to 1 cup finely chopped
    pecans

Preheat oven to 350 degrees F. Cream butter and sugar in small bowl. Add egg, vanilla, and flour. Grease a 12×18-inch pan with oil. Warm pan in oven and wipe out excess grease. Put dough, which will be stiff, in 12 portions over pan and spread out evenly with silver knife. Bake at least 30 minutes. Spread cookies with the following topping:
Melt the candy bar over hot water in top of double boiler. Spread evenly over hot cookies. Now sprinkle with chopped pecans. Cut in 1½-inch squares immediately. Cool. Store in tight cans. Makes 24.

FRUIT COOKIES

This is a marvelous Christmas cooky. It is a fruit cooky and similar to fruit cake.

1 cup butter
1 cup brown sugar
3 eggs, well beaten
3 cups flour
1 teaspoon soda
1 teaspoon cinnamon
½ cup milk

¾ pound raisins
6 slices candied pineapple, cut
    in small pieces
2 cups chopped dates
2 cups candied cherries
7 cups chopped pecans

Preheat oven to 300 degrees F. Cream butter and sugar. Add eggs. Sift flour, soda, and cinnamon together. Add alternately with milk to egg mixture. Fold in fruits and nuts. Drop from spoon onto greased shallow pan and bake 20 to 30 minutes. Makes 50 to 60.

JELLY-FILLED SWEDISH COOKIES

½ cup brown sugar	1¼ to 1½ cups flour
¼ cup butter	⅛ teaspoon salt
¼ cup shortening	½ cup finely chopped nuts
1 egg	Jelly

Preheat oven to 350 degrees F. Mix sugar, butter, and shortening. Add egg yolk. Fold in flour sifted with salt. Mix well. Make sure batter is stiff enough to roll in ball the size of a walnut. Add more flour if needed. Dip one side in slightly beaten egg white, then dip in finely chopped nuts. Place on greased baking sheet. Press center of cooky with thumb to make a slight indentation before baking. Bake until slightly browned. Fill center with jelly when done. Makes 20 to 30.

LEMON SOURS

This is a must on your cooky list; these Lemon Sours are unusual and delicious.

STEP 1:

½ cup butter
½ cup dark brown sugar, sifted
1 cup self-rising flour

Preheat oven to 350 degrees F. Cream butter and sugar. Add flour and mix well. Press in a greased pan, spreading batter evenly into corners. Bake for 10 minutes.

NOTE: Have second step ready when the 10-minute cooking is up and pour immediately on top of first mixture.

STEP 2:

2 eggs
1 cup brown sugar, sifted
1 cup chopped pecans
1 cup shredded coconut

2 tablespoons flour
1 teaspoon vanilla
⅛ teaspoon salt

Beat eggs until frothy. Add sugar and beat until thick. Add pecans and coconut, which have been tossed with flour. Flavor with vanilla, and salt. Spread over first mixture. Bake 20 minutes at 350 degrees F. (Part of the secret in making these is the sifting of the sugar and using self-rising flour.)

NOTE: Have third step ready when cookies have baked the 20 minutes and spread it over hot cookies.

STEP 3: Icing

1½ teaspoons grated lemon rind
2½ tablespoons lemon juice
1 cup confectioners' sugar

Mix rind, juice, and sugar. Spread icing on top of cooky mix, cool and cut. Makes 24 to 28.

MARY'S TEA CAKES

A Tea Cakes recipe is a must for a Southern cookbook. I think you will like the one you find here.

1½ cups sugar
1 cup butter or margarine
1 egg

1 teaspoon vanilla
2½ cups self-rising flour

Preheat oven to 350 degrees F. Mix sugar, butter, and egg. Add to this vanilla and sifted flour. Roll out on floured bread board as for biscuit dough (about ¼ inch thick) and cut into desired shapes. If using a biscuit cutter, use a smaller one as these tea cakes tend to be a little larger when baked. Place on ungreased cooky sheet and bake for 10 to 12 minutes. Take up at once. Makes about 90.

PECAN WAFERS

2 tablespoons shortening
¼ cup sugar
1 egg
½ cup chopped pecans
½ teaspoon lemon juice

½ cup pastry flour
1 teaspoon baking powder
⅛ teaspoon salt
2 tablespoons milk
16 to 20 pecan halves

Preheat oven to 350 degrees F. Cream shortening and sugar. Add beaten egg, pecans, and lemon juice. Sift flour, baking powder, and salt. Add alternately with milk to sugar-egg mixture. Mix well. Drop onto greased cooky sheet. Press flat and place a pecan half on each cooky. Bake 10 to 15 minutes. Makes 16 to 20.

RUM SQUARES

This is a prize recipe for your holiday cooking.

1 pound light brown sugar, less
  ¾ cup
1 cup butter
4 eggs
2 heaping cups unsifted flour
2 tablespoons vanilla
½ pound English walnuts,
  chopped

8 slices candied pineapple, cut
  in small pieces
½ pound candied cherries
¼ pound citron, cut in small
  pieces
1 pound chopped pecans

Preheat oven to 200 degrees F. Use 16½×11½-inch deep pan for baking. (The old-fashioned biscuit pan is excellent.) Grease pan and flour. Cream sugar and butter, add 1 egg at a time, flour, and vanilla. Place walnuts in bottom of pan. Put stiff batter in spoonfuls in pan, spread lightly in order not to lift nuts from pan. Place all fruit and pecans on top of batter, press into batter with teaspoon. Bake 3 hours. When cake is cool, cut in squares as fudge, place in metal cake box. Give each square a good drink of rum and store to mellow. Makes about 50.

SCOTCH SHORTBREAD

This Scotch Shortbread is delightful as it is not "too sweet."

2½ cups sifted flour   ½ cup confectioners' sugar
¼ teaspoon salt   1 cup butter, do not substitute

Sift dry ingredients into bowl. Break butter into small pieces and work in with hands until dough is smooth and well blended. Roll about ½ inch thick, cut with small cutter about the size of center of doughnut cutter. Place on ungreased cooky sheet, chill for about 45 minutes. Preheat oven to 275 degrees F. Bake 40 to 45 minutes. Makes 50 to 60, using small canapé cutter.

TOASTED COCONUT BARS

A favorite cooky recipe from a favorite friend.

½ cup butter
½ cup firmly packed brown sugar
1 cup sifted flour

Preheat oven to 350 degrees F. Combine ingredients. Mix thoroughly. Spread evenly in 13½×9½-inch pan. Bake 15 to 18 minutes. Watch carefully. Remove from oven and cover with Coconut Topping, as below. Return at once to oven and continue baking in 325-degree F. oven for 20 minutes longer. Remove from oven and place on rack to cool. Cool 5 minutes. Cut in 2-inch bars. Makes 24.

COCONUT TOPPING

1 cup firmly packed brown sugar   ½ teaspoon baking powder
2 eggs, well beaten   ¼ teaspoon salt
½ teaspoon vanilla   1½ cups shredded coconut
2 tablespoons flour   1 cup chopped nuts

Combine sugar, eggs, and vanilla. Beat until light and fluffy. Sift together dry ingredients. Add to egg mixture and beat well. Add coconut and nuts. Blend thoroughly. Use as directed.

Cakes

Down South cakes are one of the popular desserts. Pound Cake, Lemon Cheese Cake, and moist and tempting Coconut Cake are but a few. Fruit Cake and Lane Cake (get out your bottle of best bourbon for this one) are for your holiday tables. Picnics and cakes are synonymous. I can remember my aunt Kate, a plump little woman, who baked the best cakes I have ever tasted. There were always several kinds on her table, which was laden with so much food it almost groaned. I know that many of you had Aunt Kates too, and will reminisce through these pages with me.

APPLE CAKE

3 eggs
2 cups sugar
1¼ cups salad oil
1 teaspoon vanilla
3 cups chopped peeled apples

1 teaspoon salt
1 teaspoon soda
3 cups flour
1 cup chopped nuts

Beat eggs well, add sugar, oil, and vanilla. Mix well. Add apples. Sift salt and soda with flour. Add apple batter to flour, add nuts blending well. Bake in 2 greased 9-inch layer pans, starting in a cold oven set at 325 degrees F. Bake for 45 minutes. Spread with following filling between layers and on top and sides of cake.

FILLING

1 cup butter or margarine
2 cups light brown sugar
½ cup evaporated milk

Combine ingredients and bring to a boil. Cool and spread. Serves 18 to 20.

BEST GINGERBREAD CAKE

½ cup butter and shortening
  mixed
½ cup sugar
1 egg, beaten
1 cup dark molasses
2½ cups flour

1½ teaspoons soda
1 teaspoon cinnamon
1 teaspoon ginger
½ teaspoon cloves
½ teaspoon salt
1 cup hot water

Preheat oven to 325 to 350 degrees F. Cream butter and shortening, and sugar. Add egg and molasses. Sift together flour, soda, cinnamon, ginger, cloves, and salt. Add to first mixture. Add hot water and beat until smooth. The batter is soft but it makes a fine cake. Bake in greased shallow pan, 13×9½ inches, 30 to 35 minutes. Makes approximately 20 squares.

BEST WHITE FRUIT CAKE

This is one of my favorite fruit cakes. You will wonder at the amount of flavoring; this is right. It is part of the secret of this cake.

1 cup butter	¼ pound chopped candied citron
1 cup white sugar	1¾ cups flour
5 large eggs	½ teaspoon baking powder
4 cups coarsely chopped nuts	½ ounce pure vanilla extract
1 pound chopped candied pineapple	½ ounce pure lemon extract
½ pound chopped candied cherries	

Cream butter. Add sugar gradually, cream until fluffy. Add eggs, which have been beaten with rotary beater, and blend. Mix nuts and fruit with part of flour. Sift remaining flour and baking powder together. Fold into mixture. Add flavorings and mix well. Fold in nuts and fruit. Pour into greased paper-lined 9-inch tube pan or 2 loaf pans, 9×5 inches. Place in cold oven and bake at 250 degrees F. for 3 hours. (Small loaves will bake in 2½ hours.) Makes about a 5-pound cake.

PETITE FRUIT CAKES

These Petite Fruit Cakes are pretty to serve and bake quickly.

Use the recipe for Best White Fruit Cake*. Place batter in fluted paper cups in muffin pans. Place in cold oven and bake at 250 degrees F. for about 1 hour. Take cakes from oven and brush tops with beaten egg white and garnish with candied cherries, bits of pineapple, and pecan halves if desired. Return to oven and bake 5 or 10 minutes longer. Makes about 4 dozen.

BROWN SUGAR POUND CAKE

1 cup butter or margarine
½ cup shortening
1 box (1 pound) plus 1 cup
   light brown sugar
5 eggs

3½ cups sifted flour
1 teaspoon baking powder
1 cup milk
2 teaspoons rum or vanilla
   flavoring

Preheat oven to 325 degrees F. Cream butter, shortening, and sugar. Add eggs, one at a time, beating well after each addition. Add flour sifted with baking powder alternately with milk. Add flavoring. Bake in greased paper-lined 9-inch tube pan for 1 hour and 20 minutes. Serves 24.

BUTTERNUT CAKE

Try this Butternut Cake for a most unusual flavor. It's a deep yellow, perfect for a Halloween cake. The men like this one!

1 cup butter or margarine
2 cups sugar
4 eggs
2½ cups cake flour

½ cup self-rising flour
1 cup milk
1 tablespoon butternut flavoring

Preheat oven to 350 degrees F. Cream butter and sugar 10 minutes on high speed in your electric mixer. Add unbeaten eggs. Mix well. Add flour, milk, and flavoring. Mix well. Bake in greased paper-lined 9-inch tube pan for 1 hour. Cool. Spread with following icing.

ICING

2 cups confectioners' sugar
½ cup shortening
4 tablespoons evaporated milk,
   let come to boil

1 tablespoon butternut flavoring
1 cup chopped very fine toasted
   pecans

Mix ingredients well. Spread on cake. Serves 24.

CANDIED FRUIT CAKE

This Candied Fruit Cake is a recipe from a friend and is so delicious I want to pass it on to those of you who may not have it. It's rich, almost a confection. It is nice to cut in finger-size pieces for a tea or pickup supper.

2 cups sifted flour
2 teaspoons baking powder
½ teaspoon salt
4 eggs
1 cup sugar
3 packages (7½ ounces each) chopped dates

1 pound candied pineapple, cut in coarse pieces
1 pound candied cherries
7 cups pecan halves

Preheat oven to 275 degrees F. Sift together 1¾ cups flour, baking powder, and salt. Beat eggs and gradually add sugar and dry ingredients. Mix fruits and nuts with remaining flour and add to mixture. Pack into 9-inch tube pan that has been greased and lined with greased paper. Bake for 1 hour and 30 minutes. Makes 5 pounds.

CARROT CAKE

Here is the recipe for a cake made with carrots. Dubious? Try it and you'll be a Carrot Cake fan too.

2 cups sugar
1½ cups salad oil
4 eggs
3 cups grated carrots

2 cups plain flour, sifted
2 teaspoons soda
2 teaspoons cinnamon
1 teaspoon salt

Preheat oven to 350 degrees F. Mix sugar, oil, and eggs. Add carrots, mix well. Add flour, soda, cinnamon, and salt, sifted together. Mix and bake in 2 greased 9-inch round layer pans. Cool and spread with following icing between layers and over cake.

ICING

1 package (8 ounce) cream cheese	2 teaspoons vanilla
	1 cup chopped toasted nuts
¼ cup margarine	
1 box (1 pound) confectioners' sugar	

Work cheese until soft. Add softened margarine. Beat in sugar gradually. Add flavoring and nuts. Mix and spread. Serves 24.

CHOCOLATE POUND CAKE

1 cup butter	¼ teaspoon salt
½ cup shortening	½ teaspoon baking powder
3 cups sugar	½ cup cocoa
6 eggs	1¼ cups sweet milk
3 cups flour	1 teaspoon vanilla

Preheat oven to 300 degrees F. Cream butter, shortening, and sugar together. Add eggs, one at a time. Sift dry ingredients together and add alternately with milk. Add flavoring. Bake in greased paper-lined 9-inch tube pan 1 hour and 25 minutes. If you wish you may ice cake with your favorite chocolate icing. Serves 24.

COCONUT CAKE

⅔ cup butter	2 teaspoons baking powder
1 cup sugar	⅔ cup milk
3 eggs	1 teaspoon vanilla
2¼ cups sifted flour	1 tablespoon light corn syrup

Preheat oven to 375 degrees F. Cream butter and sugar. Add eggs one at a time. Sift together flour and baking powder and alternately add milk. Add vanilla and syrup. Bake in two greased 9-inch round layer pans 35 minutes. When cool, spread with following icing. Serves 24.

ICING

2 cups sugar	2 egg whites
3 tablespoons white corn syrup	⅛ teaspoon salt
½ cup water	1 cup grated coconut

Mix sugar, syrup, and water. Cook to soft-ball stage (238 degrees F. on candy thermometer). Beat egg whites stiff, add salt. Beat slowly while pouring half of syrup over egg whites. Cook other part of syrup to hard-ball stage and finish pouring over whites, beating as you pour. Spread on cake. Sprinkle grated coconut over icing. Makes enough to fill and frost an 8-inch or 9-inch 2 layer cake.

DARK FRUIT CAKE

5 cups flour sifted	1½ pounds candied pineapple
3 tablespoons cinnamon	3 pounds pecans
3 tablespoons allspice	1 pound blanched almonds
1 tablespoon mace	1 pound brazil nuts
1 tablespoon nutmeg	1 pound butter
1 teaspoon cloves	2½ cups sugar
1 teaspoon salt	14 eggs, slightly beaten
3 teaspoons soda	¾ cup molasses
4 pounds raisins	1 cup grape juice or sherry
1½ pounds candied cherries	1 tablespoon vanilla

Preheat oven to 275 degrees F. Sift flour, measure and sift 4½ cups with spices, salt, and soda. Reserve ½ cup flour. Place raisins in sieve and set sieve over boiling water to plump up the raisins. Cut cherries in half, chop pineapple in small pieces, chop pecans, almonds, and brazil nuts coarsely. Mix all fruits and nuts with reserved flour. Cream butter until soft, add sugar gradually. Cream until light, beat in eggs. Add flour mixture to butter mixture alternately with molasses and grape juice. Add vanilla. Fold in floured fruits and nuts. Batter will be thick; mix thoroughly with hands. Lift batter into two 9-inch tube pans, plus two 9×5-inch loaf pans, which have been greased and lined on bottom and sides with brown or waxed paper and greased again. Bake, allowing 3 to 4 hours for smaller cakes and at least 5 hours for larger cakes. Place a shallow pan of water in oven. Remove it the last hour of baking. Cool cakes and store. Makes about 15 pounds.

FIG PRESERVE CAKE

2½ cups sugar	1 teaspoon nutmeg
¾ cup butter	1 teaspoon cinnamon
4 eggs	1 teaspoon cloves
1 teaspoon soda	2 cups fig preserves
1 cup buttermilk	1 teaspoon vanilla
3 cups flour	1 cup chopped nuts

Preheat oven to 300 degrees F. Cream sugar and butter, add well-beaten eggs. Mix soda with buttermilk and add to first mixture. Gradually add flour and spices. Add preserves, vanilla, and nuts. Bake in greased pan, 13×9½ inches, 1 hour. Spread with following icing if desired. Serves 20.

ICING

1 cup brown sugar	1 tablespoon butter
1 can (5⅓ ounce) evaporated milk	1 tablespoon vanilla

Boil sugar and milk to soft-ball stage (238 degrees F. on candy thermometer), or until a little in cold water forms a soft ball. Add butter and vanilla. Beat well and spread. Makes about 2 cups.

GERMAN CHOCOLATE CAKE

1 cup butter	1 package (4 ounce) German
2 cups sugar	chocolate, dissolved in ½ cup
4 eggs, separated	hot water
1 teaspoon soda	¼ teaspoon salt
1 cup buttermilk	1 teaspoon vanilla
2½ cups cake flour	

Preheat oven to 350 degrees F. Cream butter, sugar, and add 1 egg yolk at a time and beat well. Add soda dissolved in ½ cup buttermilk. Add flour, chocolate, salt, vanilla, and remaining buttermilk. Fold in stiffly beaten egg whites. Bake in 2 greased, 9-inch layer pans about 40 minutes.

NOTE: Do not try to handle layers until cool as they are soft and break easily. Cool and spread with following filling.

GERMAN CHOCOLATE FILLING

1 cup sugar	1 teaspoon vanilla
½ cup butter	1 cup grated coconut
1 cup evaporated milk	1 cup chopped pecans
3 egg yolks	

Mix sugar, butter, milk, and well-beaten egg yolks. Cook, stirring well until thick. Add vanilla, coconut, and pecans. This will "ice" between layers and on top. If you wish to ice entire cake, double this recipe for filling.

HERSHEY CAKE

This cake is a nice one to cover with foil after baking and tuck in refrigerator. Cut as desired.

1 cup margarine	1 cup flour
1 cup sugar	1 teaspoon salt
4 eggs	½ teaspoon vanilla
1 can (5½ ounce) chocolate syrup	1 cup chopped nuts

Preheat oven to 350 degrees F. Cream margarine and sugar. Mix and add eggs, one at a time. Add chocolate syrup and flour, which has been sifted with salt. Add vanilla and chopped nuts. (Batter will be thin.) Grease and flour 2 square pans, 9×9 inches; bake for 30 minutes. Do not remove from pans. Cool. Spread with following icing. Serves 16.

3 squares (1 ounce each)	2 tablespoons water
unsweetened chocolate	1 egg, beaten
1½ cups confectioners' sugar	4 tablespoons softened butter

Melt chocolate in double boiler. Remove from stove. Add sugar and water. Blend. Add egg and butter. Beat well, pour over cakes and spread. If the icing does not harden, slip in refrigerator for a little while. Cut in squares to serve. Makes about 2 cups.

HOT MILK SPONGE CAKE

This Hot Milk Sponge Cake is grand for peach or strawberry short cake.

3 eggs	1 teaspoon baking powder
1 cup sugar	6 tablespoons hot milk
2 teaspoons lemon juice	
1 cup cake flour, do not	
substitute, sift, then measure	

Preheat oven to 350 degrees F. Beat eggs well. Add sugar slowly and beat. Add lemon juice, flour, and baking powder. Add milk and mix with spoon. Grease 9×9-inch pan lightly; bake for 35 minutes. Serves 16.

JAPANESE FRUIT CAKE

This cake has always been served at our house for the Christmas holidays.

1 cup butter	⅛ teaspoon salt
2 cups sugar	5 eggs
3 cups plain flour	1 cup milk
1 teaspoon baking powder	

Preheat oven to 350 degrees F. Cream butter and sugar. Sift flour, measure and sift again, this time with baking powder and salt. Add eggs to sugar mixture alternately with dry ingredients and milk, beating after each addition. Fill 1 greased 9-inch layer pan with batter and to the rest of the batter add the following:

1 cup chopped or seeded raisins	1 teaspoon allspice
1 cup chopped pecans	1 teaspoon cloves
1 teaspoon cinnamon	

Pour the spicy dark mix into 2 greased 9-inch layer pans. You now have one light and two dark spicy layers. Bake plain layer about 20 minutes and dark layers about 25 minutes. Cool and spread with following filling between layers and over cake. Serves 24.

FILLING

Juice 2 lemons	1 cup boiling water
Grated rind 1 lemon	1 cup drained canned crushed
1½ cups grated fresh or frozen	pineapple
coconut	2 tablespoons cornstarch
2 cups sugar	¼ cup cold water

Put all together except cornstarch and cold water and bring to boil. Dissolve cornstarch in water and add to mixture. Cook until it drops from spoon in thick lumps. Cool and spread. Makes about 2½ cups.

LANE CAKE

Christmas down South means Lane Cake to many of us.

4 cups flour	2 cups sugar
2 teaspoons baking powder	1 cup milk
¼ teaspoon salt	2 teaspoons vanilla
1 cup butter	6 egg whites

Preheat oven to 350 degrees F. Sift flour, baking powder, and salt together 2 or 3 times. Cream butter, add sugar and cream until very light. Add to this sifted dry ingredients and milk alternately until they are all in, starting with and ending with dry ingredients. Beat well after each addition. Add vanilla. Fold in well-beaten egg whites. Bake in 3 greased 9-inch layer pans about 25 minutes or until brown. Cool and spread with following filling between layers and over cake. Serves 24.

FILLING

2 cups sugar	1 cup seeded raisins
8 egg yolks	1 cup chopped nuts
½ cup butter	½ cup bourbon

Mix sugar, beaten egg yolks, and butter and cook in double boiler until very thick. Add raisins, nuts, and bourbon. Spread. Makes 3 to 3½ cups.

LAYER FRUIT CAKE

4 cups self-rising flour	2 cups freshly grated or frozen
½ teaspoon salt	coconut
2 teaspoons cinnamon	2 quarts pecans, do not chop
2 teaspoons nutmeg	2 cups butter
2 teaspoons allspice	4 cups sugar
2 teaspoons cloves	6 eggs
1 pound seedless raisins	1 pint fig preserves
2 pounds candied cherries	1 pint watermelon rind preserves

Preheat oven to 300 degrees F. Sift flour with salt, cinnamon, nutmeg, allspice, and cloves. Place raisins in sieve and set the sieve over boiling water to plump up the raisins. Cut cherries in half. Mix fruit, coconut, and nuts with several tablespoons of flour mixture. (Save a few pecans and cherries for decorating top layer.) Cream butter until soft, add sugar gradually, mixing until smooth. Add eggs one at a time, beating well after each addition. Add flour fruit-nut mixture and preserves. Place batter in 4 greased paper-lined 8-inch layer pans and press down gently. Place reserved pecans and cherries on top of one layer. Bake for about 1 hour and 40 minutes.

Cool in pans about 10 to 15 minutes. Remove from pans and spread following filling between layers. Serves 28 to 30.

NOTE: This cake cuts easier if wrapped in foil and placed in refrigerator.

FILLING

3 cups sugar	2½ cups canned crushed
½ cup butter	pineapple
1 cup freshly grated coconut or	2 oranges, peeled and ground
1 cup frozen	

Cream sugar and butter well, add other ingredients. Mix and boil until very thick. Spread filling between cake layers. Makes 3 to 4 cups.

LEMON CHEESE CAKE

This cake almost melts in your mouth.

1 cup butter	2 teaspoons baking powder
2 cups sugar	¼ teaspoon salt
4 eggs	1 teaspoon vanilla
3 cups cake flour	1 cup milk

Preheat oven to 350 degrees F. Cream butter and sugar well. Add eggs one at a time and beat after each addition. Sift flour, measure, and mix flour, baking powder, and salt; sift again. Add vanilla to milk. Turn electric mixer to blend and add dry ingredients and liquid alternately to sugar and egg mixture; begin with dry and end with dry. Pour into 3 greased paper-lined, 9-inch layer pans. Bake for 35 minutes or until done. Spread with following icing between layers and on cake, or ice top and sides with a white icing.

LEMON CHEESE ICING

1½ cups sugar	Juice 3 lemons
½ cup flour	¾ stick butter or margarine
3 egg yolks	Grated rind of 1 lemon
¾ cup water	

Place sugar, flour, egg yolks, water, lemon juice and rind in top of double boiler. Mix well. Turn unit on high and as mix begins to heat, drop in butter. Cook until very thick, so it falls in lumps from spoon. Stir constantly. Cool and spread between layers and on top and sides of cake.

LEMON POUND CAKE

1 package (3 ounce) lemon-flavored gelatin
1 cup hot water
1 box (18½ ounce) yellow cake mix

¾ cup salad oil
1 teaspoon lemon flavoring
4 eggs

Preheat oven to 325 degree F. Dissolve gelatin in water. Set aside. Empty contents of cake mix into large mixing bowl. Add oil and flavoring. Add eggs, one at a time, beating well after each addition. Add gelatin mixture and continue beating until batter is well mixed. Use 9-inch tube pan. Put two layers of waxed paper in bottom. Grease the tube and sides of pan and dust lightly with flour. Bake for 1 hour and 10 minutes. Remove from pan immediately with spatula and glaze with the following, which you have mixed while cake is baking. This is a very moist cake and freezes well. Serves 24.

GLAZE FOR CAKE

Mix juice of 2 lemons with 2 cups of confectioners' sugar. Pour slowly or spoon over cake. Makes about ¾ cup.

LINDA'S POUND CAKE

I think that the cream may be the secret of this cake.

1 cup butter
3 cups sugar
6 eggs

3 cups sifted flour
½ pint cream
1 teaspoon vanilla

Cream butter and sugar. Add eggs one at a time, beating well after each egg. Add flour and cream alternately. Add flavoring. Place in cold oven and bake in greased paper-lined 9-inch tube pan at 300 degrees F. for 1 hour and 25 minutes. Let cool on rack a few minutes. Turn out to finish cooling. Serves 24.

OATMEAL CAKE

1 cup oatmeal	1⅓ cups flour
1¼ cups boiling water	1 teaspoon cinnamon
½ cup shortening	1 teaspoon nutmeg
1 cup white sugar	1 teaspoon salt
1 cup brown sugar	1 teaspoon soda
2 eggs	1 teaspoon vanilla

Preheat oven to 350 degrees F. Add oatmeal to water and set aside to cool. Cream shortening, sugar, and eggs; add oatmeal and beat until fluffy. Add dry ingredients sifted together. Add flavoring. Bake in greased shallow pan, 13×8 inches, 45 minutes to 1 hour. Add the following topping to cake and brown for about 10 minutes. This is a moist cake and keeps well. Serves 20.

TOPPING

½ cup melted butter	1 cup grated coconut
1 cup brown sugar	2 egg yolks, beaten
1 cup chopped pecans	Evaporated milk

Combine above and add just enough milk to spread well. Do not cook this before putting on cake. Spread on cake and return to oven to brown. Makes about 1 cup.

PHYLLIS'S PRUNE CAKE

This Prune Cake came to my attention at a bake sale. It was so good, I begged the recipe.

2 cups plain flour
1½ cups sugar
1 teaspoon soda
1 teaspoon salt
1 teaspoon cinnamon
1 teaspoon allspice
1 teaspoon cloves
1 teaspoon nutmeg

3 eggs
1 cup salad oil
1 cup buttermilk
1 teaspoon vanilla
1 cup chopped pecans
1 cup finely chopped cooked
  prunes

Preheat oven to 300 degrees F. Sift dry ingredients together. Sift in spices. Add eggs, oil, and milk. Beat well, add flavoring, pecans, and prunes. Bake in greased shallow glass baking dish, 13×9½-inches, for 45 minutes to 1 hour. About 5 minutes before cake is done make the topping below. Pour this topping over cake, slowly, after removing from oven, while cake is still in pan. Slip back in oven for 5 minutes, remove, and cut in squares to serve. Serves 15 to 20.

TOPPING

½ teaspoon soda
½ cup buttermilk
1 cup sugar

1 teaspoon white corn syrup
½ cup margarine
½ teaspoon vanilla

Mix soda in buttermilk, place all ingredients in saucepan, and boil 3 minutes. Pour over cake as directed above. Makes ¾ cup.

PINEAPPLE CAKE

1 cup butter
2 cups sugar
4 eggs
3 cups cake flour
2 teaspoons baking powder

¼ teaspoon salt
1 cup milk
1 teaspoon vanilla
2 tablespoons bourbon

Preheat oven to 350 degrees F. Cream butter and sugar. Add eggs one at a time and beat after each addition. Sift flour, baking powder, and salt together. Now add dry ingredients and milk alternately to sugar and egg mixture. Add flavoring and bourbon. Pour in 3 greased paper-lined 9-inch layer pans. Bake for 35 minutes or until done. (The whisky makes this cake mellow.) Cool. Spread between layers with Pineapple Filling. Let cake stand for several hours. Spread with Pineapple Cake Icing. Serves 24.

PINEAPPLE FILLING

2½ cups canned crushed
   pineapple
½ cup water

⅔ cup sugar
3 teaspoons cornstarch mixed
   with a little water

Put pineapple, water, and sugar in saucepan, let come to a boil. Add cornstarch mixed with water until smooth. Cook until smooth and thick, stirring constantly. Cool and spread on cake between layers. Makes about 2 cups.

PINEAPPLE CAKE ICING

2 egg whites, unbeaten
1½ cups sugar
1 tablespoon white corn syrup

5 tablespoons water
1 teaspoon vanilla

Put all ingredients in top of double boiler. Beat with rotary egg beater until thoroughly mixed. Place over boiling water and beat constantly for 7 minutes or until frosting stands in peaks. Cool and spread on cake. Makes about 2½ cups.

PINEAPPLE UPSIDE DOWN CAKE

⅓ cup butter
1 cup granulated sugar
1 egg
1 teaspoon orange or vanilla
   extract
1¾ cups flour
3 teaspoons baking powder

¼ teaspoon salt
½ cup milk
3 tablespoons butter
¾ cup brown sugar
5 to 6 slices drained canned
   pineapple

Preheat oven to 350 to 375 degrees F. Cream ⅓ cup butter and sugar together, add egg, well beaten, and flavoring. Sift together the dry ingredients and add to first mixture alternately with the milk. Cream together butter and brown sugar. Rub the bottom and sides of a heavy frying pan with the butter-sugar mixture and place the slices of pineapple on bottom and sides of pan. Pour the cake mixture in and bake in oven for about 40 minutes. Turn onto a round dish. This is delicious served hot or cold.

The butter and sugar mixture makes sufficient sauce, or if you wish serve with whipped cream. Serves 8 to 10.

NOTE: I make my cake in an iron skillet.

POUND CAKE

This is my mother's Pound Cake recipe.

1 cup butter, or more	¼ teaspoon baking powder
1¾ cups sugar	⅛ teaspoon mace
5 eggs	1 tablespoon brandy or
2 cups flour, measured after	1 teaspoon vanilla
two siftings	⅛ teaspoon salt

Preheat oven to 300 degrees F. Cream butter until fluffy. Add sugar to butter and cream until fluffy and light. Drop in 1 whole egg at a time, beating until you have used the 5. Fold in flour and baking powder sifted together. Add mace, brandy or vanilla, and salt. Mix gently. Bake in greased, paper-lined 9-inch tube pan for 1 hour. Serves 24.

PRALINE CAKE

1 cup buttermilk	2 cups flour
½ cup butter	2 heaping tablespoons cocoa
2 cups light brown sugar	1 teaspoon soda
2 eggs	1 tablespoon vanilla

Preheat oven to 350 degrees F. Warm buttermilk and butter. Put in bowl, add brown sugar and eggs, beat well. Add dry ingredients sifted together. Beat well. Add vanilla. Bake in greased, floured rectangular pan, 13×9½ inches, for 20 to 25 minutes. Spread top of cake with following icing as soon as cake is done. Turn oven to broil. Place cake on bottom rack in oven and cook until icing bubbles and is a light brown. This takes only a few minutes. Cut in squares to serve. Makes approximately 20 to 24 squares

ICING FOR PRALINE CAKE

½ cup butter	6 tablespoons light cream
1 cup brown sugar	1 cup chopped pecans

Mix all ingredients. Spread mixture on top of cake. Makes about 1½ cups.

RED VELVET CAKE

This is a beautiful red cake, nice for Christmas time. The bit of cocoa gives it an unusual flavor.

1½ cups sugar	2 tablespoons cocoa
1 cup butter	1 teaspoon salt
2 eggs	1 teaspoon soda
2 bottles (1 ounce each) red food coloring	1 cup buttermilk
	1 teaspoon vinegar
2¼ cups sifted cake flour	1 teaspoon vanilla

Preheat oven to 350 degrees F. Cream sugar and butter until fluffy. Add eggs one at a time. Beat 1 minute after each egg. Carefully mix in food coloring. Sift together flour, cocoa, salt, and soda; mix buttermilk with vinegar and vanilla; add to the creamed ingredients alternately with the dry ingredients. Beat on medium speed until well mixed. Turn into 2 greased, waxed-paper lined 9-inch layer pans. Bake for 35 to 40 minutes. Cool. Spread with following icing. Serves 24.

SPONGY WHITE ICING

1½ cups sugar   Whites 2 large eggs
1 tablespoon white corn syrup   ⅛ teaspoon salt
¾ cup cold water   1 teaspoon vanilla

Reserve 2 tablespoons sugar. Put rest of sugar, syrup, and water to boil until a long thread forms when tested, 230 degrees F. on candy thermometer. Beat stiff the whites, to which the salt has been added. Add reserved sugar. (Beat eggs while sugar mixture is boiling.) When syrup is ready pour slowly over egg whites, beating constantly. Continue beating until thick. Add the flavoring, spread on cake. Makes about 2 cups.

RUM CAKE

1 cup butter or margarine   1 teaspoon vanilla
1¾ cups sugar   2 cups flour
5 eggs

Preheat oven to 325 degrees F. Cream butter well. Add sugar, then eggs, one at a time, beating well after each addition. Add vanilla and flour, mix well. Bake 1 hour in greased 9-inch tube or Bundt pan. Glaze with following icing while cake is still hot. Serves 24.

RUM CAKE ICING

1 cup sugar
½ cup water
½ to ¾ ounce rum extract

Bring sugar and water to a boil, cool. Add rum extract. Cool icing and apply to hot cake, using pastry brush. This is more of a glaze than an icing. Makes about 1 cup.

STRAWBERRY CAKE

This cake is "easy to do," and good. It may be made ahead as it is a moist cake.

1 box (18½ ounce) white cake
   mix
½ cup salad oil
1 package (3 ounce)
   strawberry-flavored gelatin

¼ cup hot water
4 eggs
1 package (10 ounce) thawed
   frozen strawberries, drain and
   reserve juice

Preheat oven to 350 degrees F. Combine cake mix and salad oil. Add gelatin dissolved in water and cooled. Mix well. Add eggs, one at a time, beating continuously. Stir in strawberries, which have been thawed and drained. Pour into 2 greased 9-inch round cake pans and bake for approximately 35 minutes. Cool and spread with following filling. Serves 24.

FILLING

½ cup butter
1 box (1 pound) confectioners' sugar
Juice from strawberries

Have butter at room temperature. Cream butter and sugar well. Add enough strawberry juice to make of spreading consistency. Makes about 2½ cups.

WHITE CHRISTMAS FRUIT CAKE

For Christmas nothing can equal Fruit Cake. My mother used to make this one. She made "oodles" of these, to eat and give away. I remember she used to wrap them in cheese cloth dampened with wine and store in large cans in which she dropped an apple or two.

2 pounds white seedless raisins	½ teaspoon soda
½ pound finely chopped candied citron	⅓ cup milk
	1½ cups butter
½ pound candied cherries	2 cups sugar
½ pound finely chopped candied pineapple	4 cups flour
	2 teaspoons salt
2½ cups chopped nuts	1 teaspoon cream of tartar
1 cup grated fresh coconut (optional)	12 egg whites, stiffly beaten

Preheat oven to 275 degrees F. Soak raisins in water until plump, dry thoroughly. Mix with other fruit, nuts, coconut; add soda dissolved in milk. Cream butter and sugar until light and soft. Sift flour, salt, and cream of tartar together 3 times. Add to butter mixture alternately with egg whites. When thoroughly mixed, combine with fruit mixture. Mix well. Bake in 4 loaf pans, 9×5 inches, or 2 tube pans, 9½ inches each, which have been greased and lined with brown or wax paper coated with oil. Bake about 2 hours for loaf pans; for tube pans it takes about 2½ to 3 hours. Makes 10 to 12 pounds.

An orange ground in food chopper and added to this batter makes a delicious addition to cake.

WHITE FRUIT CAKE

One of the best White Fruit Cakes.

½ pound butter
2¼ cups sugar
5 eggs
3 cups flour
½ pound chopped candied
   pineapple

½ pound mixed candied fruit
½ pound candied cherries
2½ cups chopped nuts
1 cup freshly grated coconut
   (optional)
3 teaspoons vanilla

Cream butter and sugar. Add eggs one at a time, beating after each addition. Add 1 cup sifted flour and mix. Add fruit and nuts, which have been dredged in other 2 cups flour. Add coconut and flavoring, blend. Pour batter into greased paper-lined 9-inch tube pan and bake 2 hours. Bake 30 minutes in oven preheated to 250 degrees F. and increase heat to 300 degrees F. to finish baking. Makes about 5 to 7 pounds.

CAKE COOKING HINT

To make a cake-mix cake taste homemade, add ¼ cup of cooking oil (any type) to the batter.

BOILED WHITE ICING

2½ cups sugar
¾ cup water
3 large cooking spoons white
   corn syrup

3 teaspoons sugar
2 egg whites

Mix sugar, water, and syrup. Boil to soft-ball stage (238 degrees F. on your candy thermometer). Remove from stove. Add sugar to egg whites and beat stiff. Pour syrup slowly over egg whites and beat until mixture begins to get stiff. When stiff enough, frost cake.

NOTE: If icing does not seem to harden as it should, place over boiling water a minute. Makes about 2 cups.

CARAMEL ICING

1 cup buttermilk, use real buttermilk
2½ cups sugar
¼ teaspoon salt

1 teaspoon vanilla
1 teaspoon soda
¾ cup butter

Put all together except butter and let boil. Stir constantly; it browns by degrees. Cook until it creams, 238 degrees F. on your thermometer. Add butter, cool a minute, and beat as other icings. Double this for a big cake. Makes about 1½ cups.

CONFECTIONERS' ICING

1 cup confectioners' sugar
2 tablespoons white corn syrup

1 tablespoon milk
⅛ teaspoon vanilla

Combine and mix ingredients until well blended. Mix smooth. This icing is a good one to spread over the top of your fruit cakes. Makes about 1 cup.

CONFECTIONERS' CARAMEL ICING

⅓ cup melted butter
1 cup firmly packed light brown sugar
2½ cups confectioners' sugar, sifted

¼ cup milk
Dash salt

Mix butter with brown sugar. Add confectioners' sugar alternately with milk. Add salt. Beat until smooth. If icing is too thick to spread easily, beat in ½ teaspoon of milk at a time until spreading consistency. Makes about 2½ cups.

FOUR-MINUTE CHOCOLATE ICING

2 cups sugar   ½ cup butter
½ cup cocoa   1 teaspoon vanilla
⅔ cup milk

Cook sugar, cocoa, and milk 4 minutes after it begins to boil or bubble. Remove from heat and add butter and vanilla. Let stand about 15 minutes and beat until cool and thick enough to spread on cake. Makes about 2 cups.

SEVEN-MINUTE FROSTING

This Seven-minute Frosting is a white icing for you to use on many cakes. Easy and quick.

2 egg whites, unbeaten   5 tablespoons water
1½ cups sugar   1 teaspoon vanilla
1 tablespoon white corn syrup

Put all ingredients in top of double boiler. Beat with rotary egg beater until thoroughly mixed. Place over boiling water and beat constantly for 7 minutes or until frosting stands in peaks. Cool and spread on cake. Makes about 2 cups.

Pies

Somewhere I remember reading that the Romans made the first pie we know of, a meat pie. Since that time pies have come a long way, and our pies in America are for the most part dessert pies. Our Southern versions are made from fruits, vegetables, nuts, and other delectable ingredients. Pie is one of America's favorite desserts. It is served in roadside stands and in the best gourmet restaurants. Antique lovers seek the old pie cupboards of Grandmother's day. You will find these cupboards in today's homes. Do you suppose there is a piece of pie therein?

Lemon, Chess, Raisin, Pecan, Coconut, and the old-time choice Sweet Potato Pie are favorites from which to choose.

BEST EVER PIE

This Best Ever Pie was given to me by a friend a long time ago when I lived in Baltimore. I think you will find it different and delicious.

2 eggs	½ cup seedless raisins
1 cup sugar	1 tablespoon melted butter
1 teaspoon cinnamon	1 tablespoon vinegar
1 teaspoon cloves	Pastry for 8-inch pie
½ cup chopped pecans	

Preheat oven to 400 degrees F. Beat the egg yolks well, until thick and light. Gradually add sugar, which has been sifted with cinnamon and cloves. Add pecans, raisins, and butter. Beat egg whites until stiff but not dry and fold gently into sugar mixture. Do not beat in. As you fold them in, add the vinegar. Pour into pastry shell. Bake in preheated oven for 10 minutes. Now reduce heat to 350 degrees F. and bake 25 minutes more. The crust and top should be crisp and nicely browned. Cool and serve with whipped cream if desired. Serves 6.

BLACKBERRY ROLL

3 cups sifted all-purpose flour	3 to 3½ cups blackberries
1 tablespoon baking powder	1¼ cups sugar
5 to 6 teaspoons sugar	1 tablespoon flour
Dash salt	3 tablespoons melted butter or
½ cup shortening	more
1 to 1¼ cups milk	

Have oven set at 450 degrees F. Grease a long shallow baking pan. Sift flour, baking powder, 5 to 6 teaspoons sugar, and salt together in mixing bowl. Cut in shortening until mixture is mealy looking. Stir in enough milk to make a soft dough. (Use fork.)

Roll out dough on floured board into a 12×16-inch rectangle about ¼ to ½ inch thick. Wash and drain berries and mix with 1¼ cups sugar and 1 tablespoon flour. Spread berries over rectangle of dough and roll up as compactly as possible.

Seal ends of roll, press together with tines of fork. Now place in greased baking pan, brush top with melted butter. Bake for 10 minutes at 450 degrees F. and then reduce to 350 degrees F. and continue baking about 45 minutes or longer, until crust is brown.

To serve, cut roll in thick slices, serve warm with cream or hard sauce. Serves 8.

BONNIE'S COCONUT PIE

This Coconut Pie is one of the best, and one of the easiest to make.

2 eggs	⅓ cup milk
1 cup sugar	1 teaspoon vanilla
1 cup grated or flaked coconut	Pastry for 8-inch pie
½ cup melted butter or margarine	

Preheat oven to 325 degrees F. Beat eggs lightly. Add sugar, coconut, butter, milk, and vanilla. Pour into pie shell and bake for 45 to 50 minutes or until set. Serves 6.

BUTTERSCOTCH PIE

4 tablespoons butter	4 tablespoons water
1 cup brown sugar	2 egg yolks
2 cups scalded milk	1 baked 9-inch pie shell
5 tablespoons cornstarch	

MERINGUE:

2 egg whites
4 tablespoons sugar

Cook butter and sugar in skillet until thick and brown, stirring constantly. Stir in milk. Mix the cornstarch and water smooth, add slightly beaten egg yolks. Add to first mixture and cook in double boiler until thick and creamy; stir constantly. Cool and pour into baked pie shell. Cover with meringue: beat egg whites until foamy; Add 4 tablespoons sugar gradually, beating until mixture stands in peaks. Pile lightly on pie filling. Bake in preheated 350-degree F. oven 15 minutes or until meringue is delicately browned. Serves 6 to 8.

NOTE: When cutting meringue pie, dip knife in cold water to prevent sticking.

CANADIAN BUTTER TARTS

These Canadian Butter Tarts are the best ever; try these for your next buffet when the men will be present.

Pastry for 2-crust pie	¼ cup melted butter
2 eggs	1 teaspoon vanilla
1 cup seedless raisins	1 cup chopped nuts
1 cup brown sugar	3 teaspoons cream

Preheat oven to 300 degrees F. Divide pastry in half, cut each half in 5 or 6 parts. Roll in 5-inch circles. Place in ungreased muffin pans.

Beat eggs. Add remaining ingredients and mix well. Put 1 tablespoon in each unbaked pastry shell and bake. (Don't worry about the small amount placed in shell, the mixture "swells" upon cooking.) Makes approximately 16 tarts. If desired, serve with a dash of whipped cream on top.

CARROT PIE

¾ cup sugar	2 cups mashed cooked carrots
1 teaspoon ginger	3 large eggs, lightly beaten
1 teaspoon cinnamon	1 cup milk
1 teaspoon nutmeg	1 teaspoon vanilla
½ teaspoon salt	Pastry for 9-inch pie

Preheat oven to 400 degrees F. Combine sugar, spices, and salt in mixing bowl. Add carrots and eggs, mix well. Stir in milk and vanilla. Pour mixture in pie shell and bake for 40 to 50 minutes or until firm. Cool before serving. Serves 6 to 8.

CASHAW PIE

This Cashaw Pie is most delicious! The cashaw is a member of the pumpkin family and if you are not familiar with it you will be most surprised. This is Deep South cooking.

2 cups cooked and mashed
   cashaw
½ cup butter or margarine
1½ cups sugar
2 eggs

1 teaspoon lemon extract
   (be sure to use the extract,
   not flavoring)
Pastry for 9-inch pie

Preheat oven to 400 degrees F. Mix hot cashaw, butter, and sugar well. Add beaten eggs and extract. Pour into pie shell. Bake for 15 minutes. Now reduce heat to 350 degrees F. and cook about an hour or until filling sets. Serves 6 to 8.

NOTE: To cook your cashaw, cut in chunks and peel. Drop in water as you peel. Take from water and drop in a heavy pot or skillet and cook covered on medium heat until tender, about 20 minutes. It needs no water, other than the little left on from paring, as cashaw seems to have much water in it. When it becomes transparent it is done.

CHESS PIE

1 cup sugar
1 cup butter
3 egg yolks
1 egg white

3 tablespoons water
1 teaspoon vanilla
Pastry for 9-inch pie

Preheat oven to 350 degrees F. Cream sugar and butter as for making cake. Add egg yolks and white, beat well. Add water and vanilla and beat again. Pour into a pie pan lined with pastry and bake until filling sets, about 35 minutes. Serves 6 to 8.

NOTE: When done, if desired, the top may be spread with jelly and covered with a meringue.

CHOCOLATE ANGEL PIE

This is a delicious and rich pie.

MERINGUE SHELL:

2 egg whites	½ cup sugar
⅛ teaspoon salt	½ cup chopped nut meats
⅛ teaspoon cream of tartar	½ teaspoon vanilla

Preheat oven to 300 degrees F. Beat egg whites until foamy. Add salt and cream of tartar. Beat until mixture stands in soft peaks. Add sugar gradually. Beat until very stiff. Fold in nut meats and vanilla. Turn into lightly greased 8-inch pie pan. Make nest-like shell, building sides up above edge of pan. Bake for 55 minutes. Cool. Fill with following filling.

FILLING:

1 package (4 ounce) German chocolate	1 tablespoon vanilla
3 tablespoons hot water	1 cup heavy cream, whipped

Melt cake of chocolate in double boiler. Add hot water; blend and cool. Add vanilla. Fold in cream. Turn this mixture into meringue shell. Chill. Serves 6 to 8.

CHOCOLATE CREAM PIE

3 squares (1 ounce each) unsweetened chocolate	½ teaspoon salt
2½ cups milk	2 egg yolks
1 cup sugar	2 tablespoons butter
6 tablespoons flour	½ to 1 teaspoon vanilla
	1 baked 9-inch pie shell

MERINGUE:

2 egg whites
4 tablespoons sugar

Preheat oven to 350 degrees F. Add chocolate to milk and heat in double boiler. When chocolate is melted, beat with rotary beater until blended. Mix sugar, flour, and salt. Add this gradually to chocolate mixture and cook until thickened, stirring occasionally. Pour small amount of mixture over slightly beaten egg yolks, stir vigorously, return to double boiler, and cook about 2 to 3 minutes longer. Remove from double boiler, add butter and vanilla. Cool. Pour into pie shell and cover with meringue: Beat egg whites until foamy; add 4 tablespoons sugar gradually, beating until mixture stands in peaks. Pile lightly on pie filling. Bake 15 minutes or until meringue is lightly browned. Serves 6 to 8.

COCONUT CREAM PIE

⅓ cup sugar	1 tablespoon butter
2 tablespoons cornstarch	¾ cup grated or flaked coconut
¼ teaspoon salt	coconut
3 egg yolks, slightly beaten	½ teaspoon vanilla
1½ cups scalded milk	1 baked 9-inch pie shell

MERINGUE:

2 egg whites
4 tablespoons sugar

Preheat oven to 300 degrees F. Add ⅓ cup sugar, cornstarch, and salt to egg yolks. Pour milk into this, place in double boiler, stir and cook until thickened. Add butter, coconut, and vanilla. Pour into pie shell and cover with meringue: Beat egg whites until foamy; add 4 tablespoons sugar gradually. Beat until mixture stands in peaks. Pile lightly on pie filling. Place in oven to brown. Serves 6 to 8.

COOKY PEACH PIE

6 to 8 peeled peaches	Butter
¾ cup sugar	1 package (8 ounce) sugar
1½ tablespoons flour	cookies
⅛ teaspoon salt	

Preheat oven to to 350 degrees F. Slice fresh peaches in a shallow pie pan. Mix sugar, flour, and salt. Pour over peaches, dot with bits of butter. Top with package of cookies sliced approximately ¼ inch thick. Bake about 45 minutes. Serves 6 to 8.

CUSTARD PIE

Custard Pie is one to "woo" friend husband with; the secret of cooking one is to start in hot oven and then reduce temperature to finish cooking.

3 eggs, slightly beaten	2 tablespoons melted butter
2½ cups sweet milk	¼ teaspoon nutmeg, or more
¾ cup sugar	Pastry for 9-inch pie
Pinch salt	

Preheat oven to 400 degrees F. Mix ingredients (except nutmeg), put into uncooked pie shell. (Note: Do not beat eggs too much, just enough to hold whites and yolks together.) A sprinkle of nutmeg over top of pie and it is ready to slip in the 400-degree F. oven for 12 to 15 minutes. Now reduce oven heat to 300 degrees F. and cook until custard is set in the center of pie, about 30 minutes. Serves 6 to 8.

DEEP-DISH APPLE PIE

This Deep-dish Apple Pie is from Virginia.

Pare and slice 5 to 6 cups apples	¼ teaspoon cinnamon
¾ cup light brown sugar	1 tablespoon lemon juice
2 tablespoons flour	1 tablespoon butter, or more
	Pastry for 9-inch pie

Preheat oven to 400 to 425 degrees F. Place apples in 1½-quart deep pie plate or casserole. Combine sugar, flour, cinnamon, and lemon juice. Add to apples and mix together. Dot with butter. Roll pastry about ½ inch larger than dish, cut several gashes near center. Lay pastry over apples and fold under all around to fit edge. Press pastry down against dish with tines of fork. Bake about 40 minutes. Serve warm with cream or hard sauce. Serves 8 to 10.

DEEP DISH MUSCADINE PIE

1ST STEP:

2 cups muscadines
2½ cups water
1 cup sugar

Wash and separate the insides from the muscadine hulls. Put ½ cup water with the pulp and boil 5 minutes. Strain to remove seeds. Mix hulls, remaining 2 cups water, and sugar. Simmer, covered, about 25 minutes.

2ND STEP:

¼ cup margarine   ¾ cup flour
½ cup sugar   ½ cup milk

Preheat oven to 350 degrees F. Melt margarine in deep 2-quart baking dish in which pie will be baked. Make batter by mixing together sugar, flour, and milk. Pour this over melted margarine. Pour fruit mixtures over batter and bake 35 to 40 minutes or until done. The crust will rise to top. Serves 8 to 10.

ENVELOPE TARTS

Here is a quickie for that Coke or morning party.

Preheat oven to 400 degrees F. Roll out pie pastry to ⅛ inch thick. Cut in pieces 2 to 3 inches square or in rounds. Put a teaspoon of jam or marmalade on each piece. Moisten edges and fold diagonally, pressing edges together with fork. Bake 15 to 20 minutes. Make these smaller for a tea tray.

FRENCH COCONUT PIE

3 eggs
1 cup sugar
1 teaspoon vanilla
¼ cup buttermilk

¼ cup margarine
1 cup finely grated coconut
Pastry for 9-inch pie

Preheat oven to 325 degrees F. Whip eggs until fluffy; add sugar, vanilla, milk, margarine, and coconut. Pour in pie shell and bake until golden brown, for about 45 minutes. Serves 6 to 8.

GRASSHOPPER PIE

2 tablespoons melted margarine
14 chocolate cookies with
   cream filling, crushed, reserve
   a few for pie topping
24 large marshmallows

½ cup milk
4 tablespoons crème de menthe
2 tablespoons crème de cacao
1½ cups heavy cream

Mix margarine and cookies. Press into 9-inch pie pan. Melt marshmallows in milk. Let cool a few minutes. Stir in crème de menthe and crème de cacao. Fold in 1 cup cream, whipped. Pour mixture into pie shell and freeze. When ready to serve top with remaining ½ cup cream, whipped, and sprinkle reserved crumbs over top. Serve frozen. Serves 6 to 8.

JO'S APPLE PIE

I recommend this pie recipe—it's easy and so good.

4 apples
2 tablespoons flour
¾ to 1 cup sugar, reserve 1
   tablespoon for pie top

½ cup margarine
Pastry for 9-inch pie
2 tablespoons butter

Preheat oven to 350 degrees F. Peel apples, cut in wedges. Place in a 9-inch buttered pie dish. Mix flour and sugar. Crumble in margarine, sprinkle on top of apples. Bake 20 minutes. After baking this apple mixture, this is next step. Have piecrust cold, roll and cut in strips. Strip top of pie, sprinkle with reserved sugar. Dot with butter. Place in oven to brown.

VARIATIONS: Use 2 cups peaches or 2 cups red pie cherries, drained. Serves 6.

KEY LIME PIE

1 tablespoon unflavored gelatin	2 or 3 teaspoons grated lime
¼ cup cold water	peel
4 eggs, separated	Green food coloring
1 cup sugar, divide	1 baked, 9-inch pie shell
⅓ cup lime juice	½ cup heavy cream, whipped
⅛ teaspoon salt	

Soften gelatin in cold water. Beat egg yolks, add ½ cup sugar, lime juice, and salt. Cook over hot water stirring constantly until thickened. Add lime peel and gelatin. Stir until gelatin is dissolved and add food coloring to tint a soft pale green. Cool. Beat egg whites stiff, add remaining sugar slowly after each addition. Fold into lime mixture. Pour into pie shell, chill until firm. Garnish with whipped cream. Serves 6 to 8.

NOTE: If you prefer, use a meringue on this pie.

LEMON ANGEL PIE

MERINGUE CRUST:

4 egg whites
¼ teaspoon cream of tartar
1 cup sugar

Preheat oven to 275 degrees F. Beat egg whites until foamy, add cream of tartar. Continue beating until stiff and add sugar very, very gradually. Pour into buttered pie plate shaping to form crust and bake 1 hour.

FILLING:

4 egg yolks	3 tablespoons lemon juice
½ cup sugar	1 cup heavy cream
1 tablespoon grated lemon rind	

Mix eggs, sugar, rind, and lemon juice. Cook in double boiler until thick. When crust and filling are cold, add cream, whipped, and mix with filling. Pour into crust and refrigerate 12 hours. This freezes well. Serves 6 to 8.

LEMON CHESS PIE

1 tablespoon flour	⅓ cup milk
2 cups sugar	¼ cup melted butter
2 teaspoons grated lemon rind	¼ cup lemon juice
1 tablespoon corn meal	Pastry for 9-inch pie
4 eggs	

Preheat oven to 300 degrees F. Combine flour, sugar, lemon rind, and meal. Add eggs, milk, butter, and lemon juice. Pour in unbaked pie shell and bake 30 minutes. Serves 6 to 8.

LEMON CHIFFON PIE

This is a luscious pie.

1 cup sugar, divided	1 tablespoon unflavored gelatin
½ cup lemon juice	1 teaspoon grated lemon rind
½ teaspoon salt	1 baked 9-inch pie shell or
4 eggs	graham cracker crust
¼ cup cold water	½ cup heavy cream, whipped

Add ½ cup sugar, lemon juice, and salt to beaten egg yolks. Cook over boiling water until of custard consistency. Pour water in cup and sprinkle gelatin on top of water. Add to hot custard and stir until dissolved. Add lemon rind. Cool. When mixture begins to thicken fold in stiffly beaten egg whites to which the other ½ cup sugar has been added. Fill baked pie shell or graham cracker crust and chill. Just before serving spread a thin layer of whipped cream over pie. Serves 6 to 8.

LEMON PIE

⅓ cup cornstarch or ½ cup flour   3 egg yolks
½ cup sugar   ⅓ cup lemon juice
⅛ teaspoon salt   Grated rind 1 lemon
½ cup cold water   1 baked 9-inch pie shell
1 cup hot water

MERINGUE:

3 egg whites
4 tablespoons sugar

Preheat oven to 350 degrees F. Mix cornstarch, sugar, and salt. Mix with cold water until smooth. Add hot water and cook on low heat about 5 minutes. Add egg yolks and cook 3 to 4 minutes longer. Add lemon juice and rind; if too thin cook a minute longer. Pour into pie shell and cover with meringue: beat egg whites until foamy, gradually add 4 tablespoons sugar. Beat until mixture stands in peaks. Pile lightly on pie and bake 10 to 12 minutes or until meringue is lightly browned. Serves 6 to 8.

MACAROON PIE

3 egg whites   14 double crisp salt crackers,
1 cup sugar   broken
½ teaspoon baking powder   14 chopped dates
1 teaspoon almond flavoring   ½ cup chopped pecans

Preheat oven to 350 degrees F. Beat egg whites fairly stiff. Add sugar, baking powder, and flavoring. Mix crackers, dates, and nuts, fold in egg whites. Bake for 20 minutes in a greased 8- or 9-inch pie pan. Serves 6 to 8.

MALISSA'S PEACH PIE

This is a copy of a Peach Pie that our cook Malissa used to make.

3 cups peeled and sliced peaches
1 cup sugar
2 tablespoons flour
½ cup water

Dash cinnamon
Dash nutmeg
¼ cup butter
Pastry for 2-crust pie

Preheat oven to 450 degrees F. Cover the bottom of 2-quart deep pie dish or casserole with piecrust. Cover sides also if you wish more crust. Place peaches in mixing bowl. Mix sugar and flour, add water, and mix well. Pour over peaches. Mix lightly and pour into pie dish. Sprinkle a bit of cinnamon and nutmeg over top of peaches and dot with butter. Make a lattice of piecrust across the top of pan and bake 10 minutes. Now cool oven to 350 degrees F. and bake about 40 minutes longer. (This is a hint for you: After placing sliced peaches in mixing bowl, slip dish with bottom crust in oven to dry out a bit so it won't be sticky.)

This is good hot or cold, with or without cream, plain or whipped. Serves 6 to 8.

NESSELRODE PIE

4 eggs
2 cups scalded milk
1½ tablespoons cornstarch
1 cup sugar, divided
1½ tablespoons unflavored
    gelatin

4 tablespoons cold water
2 tablespoons brandy or rum
⅛ teaspoon salt
½ cup brandied fruit
1 baked 9-inch pie shell
½ cup cream, whipped

Separate eggs. Add milk slowly to beaten egg yolks. Mix cornstarch and ½ cup sugar and stir into milk and egg mixture. Cook over simmering water for 20 minutes or until custard generously coats spoon. Remove from heat. Sprinkle gelatin in water. Add to custard mixture while it is still hot. Let cool. Add brandy or rum. Next step: Beat egg whites very stiff, gradually beat in remaining ½ cup sugar and salt, add to custard while it is still soft and smooth. Carefully fold in brandied fruit and fill pie shell. Set in refrigerator to chill. Serve with a topping of whipped cream. If brandied fruit is not available, I suggest that you use candied fruit soaked in a simple syrup flavored with brandy or bourbon. Serves 6 to 8.

OATMEAL PIE

This Oatmeal Pie has the flavor of a pecan pie.

2 eggs, beaten
⅔ cup melted margarine
⅔ cup sugar
⅔ cup white corn syrup
⅔ cup uncooked oatmeal,
   regular or quick

⅛ teaspoon salt
1 teaspoon vanilla
Pastry for 8-inch pie

Preheat oven to 350 degrees F. Mix all ingredients together and pour into pie shell. Bake about 1 hour. Serves 6 to 8.

PEACH CRUNCH

8 to 10 fresh peeled peaches
1 scant cup brown sugar
1 teaspoon cinnamon

3 tablespoons flour
½ cup margarine

Preheat oven to 350 degrees F. Place sliced peaches in 9-inch pie pan or other shallow pan. Blend sugar, cinnamon, flour, and margarine together until you have small lumps, as pie dough. Crumble (do not roll) over sliced peaches. Bake about 40 minutes until brown and bubbly. Serves 6.

PECAN MINIATURE PIES

CREAM CHEESE PASTRY SHELLS:

1 package (3 ounce) cream cheese
½ cup butter
1 cup sifted flour

Have cream cheese at room temperature. Mix with softened butter and flour. Blend thoroughly. Chill dough. Pinch off 24 balls of dough and press into tiny ungreased muffin cups to form shells. (This is an approximate number, maybe a few less.)

FILLING:

¾ cup brown sugar
1 tablespoon melted butter
1 egg

¼ teaspoon salt
1 cup chopped pecans
½ teaspoon vanilla

Preheat oven to 350 degrees F. Blend all filling ingredients except pecans and beat. Spoon filling into shells, fill each not quite three-quarters full. Sprinkle chopped pecans generously on top, or you may use coconut. Bake 25 minutes. Cool on rack. Makes 2 dozen.

PECAN PIE

1¼ cups sugar
½ cup light corn syrup
¼ cup butter or margarine
3 eggs, slightly beaten

1 cup coarsely chopped
pecans, or halves
1 teaspoon vanilla
Pastry for 9-inch pie

Preheat oven to 350 degrees F. Combine sugar, syrup, and butter in 2-quart saucepan. Bring to boil on high, stirring constantly until butter is melted. Remove from stove and gradually add hot syrup to eggs; stir all the while. Add pecans to mixture and cool to luke-warm. Add vanilla. Pour into pie shell and bake for 40 to 45 minutes. Serves 6 to 8.

PINEAPPLE PIE

4 tablespoons cornstarch
¾ cup sugar
1 cup milk

3 egg yolks
1 cup canned crushed pineapple
1 baked 9-inch pie shell

MERINGUE:

3 egg whites
4 tablespoons sugar

Preheat oven to 350 degrees F. Mix cornstarch, ¾ cup sugar, and milk together. Add beaten egg yolks and put in double boiler. Cook until mixture begins to thicken. Add pineapple. Stir constantly and cook until thick enough for pie. Pour into pie shell. Cover with meringue: Beat egg whites until foamy; add 4 tablespoons sugar gradually, beating until mixture will stand in peaks. Pile lightly on pie. Bake 15 minutes or until lightly browned. Serves 6 to 8.

PUMPKIN CUSTARD PIE

1½ cups milk
¾ cup sugar
1 teaspoon cinnamon
1 teaspoon ginger
¾ teaspoon salt

1½ cups mashed canned or
   cooked fresh, pumpkin
2 eggs, slightly beaten
Pastry for 9-inch pie

Preheat oven to 425 degrees F. Heat milk to boiling point. (This is the secret of this pie.) Mix sugar, spices, and salt. Add to pumpkin and eggs. Pour into unbaked pie shell, place in oven, and bake for 15 minutes. Set oven back now to 350 degrees F. and cook 25 to 30 minutes or until set. Serves 6 to 8.

RAISIN PIE

This is the Raisin Pie my family likes best; I think you will like it too.

2 cups seedless raisins
2½ cups water
½ cup brown sugar
2 tablespoons cornstarch
1 teaspoon cinnamon

⅛ teaspoon salt
1 tablespoon butter
1 tablespoon vinegar
Pastry for 2-crust pie

Preheat oven to 425 degrees F. Boil raisins in 2 cups water for 5 minutes. Combine sugar, cornstarch, cinnamon, and salt. Moisten with remaining ½ cup cold water and add to raisins. Stir until mixture boils. Remove from fire. Add butter and vinegar. Pour into pastry-lined 9-inch pie pan; cover top with lattice pastry. Bake 25 minutes. Serves 6 to 8.

RUM PIE

1 tablespoon unflavored gelatin
4 tablespoons cold water
3 eggs
½ cup sugar

⅛ teaspoon salt
¾ cup milk
3 tablespoons rum
1 Vanilla Wafer Crust* (9 inch)

TOPPING:

½ cup heavy cream
3 tablespoons sugar
3 tablespoons rum

1 tablespoon grated sweet
chocolate

Soften gelatin in water 5 minutes. Beat egg yolks, add sugar, salt, and milk. Cook over low heat in double boiler, stirring constantly. When mixture coats spoon pour in gelatin. Cool. Beat egg whites and fold in custard with 3 tablespoons rum. Pour in crumb crust. Chill. Whip cream, add 3 tablespoons sugar gradually, flavor with 3 tablespoons rum. Cover pie with whipped cream. Sprinkle with chocolate. Serves 6 to 8.

SCUPPERNONG PIE

Another Deep South recipe. The party who gave this one to me says those who have eaten this pie admit they have been missing something.

3 or 4 cups scuppernongs	2 tablespoons cornstarch
Water	3 tablespoons butter
1 cup sugar, or more if needed	Cinnamon or apple pie spice
	Pastry for 2-crust pie

Preheat oven to 300 degrees F. Wash scuppernongs. Use 2 medium-sized enamel saucepans; squeeze pulp into one and use other for hulls. Cover hulls with water and cook until tender, drain. Cook pulp until soft enough to run through sieve to remove seeds. Add to hulls. Mix sugar and cornstarch. Add scuppernong mixture and dot with butter. Sprinkle with spice as desired. Pour into pastry-lined pie pan, cover with strips of pastry. Bake until brown. Serves 6 to 8.

STRAWBERRY PIE

This was my father's favorite pie.

Pastry for 2-crust pie	1 cup sugar
1 tablespoon melted butter or margarine	⅛ teaspoon salt
1 tablespoon flour	1 quart strawberries
3 tablespoons pastry flour	1 teaspoon lemon juice
	1 to 2 tablespoons butter

Preheat oven to 400 degrees F. Place pastry in 9-inch pie pan. Brush bottom of crust with melted butter or margarine and dust lightly with 1 tablespoon flour to prevent juices from soaking in. Mix 3 tablespoons pastry flour, sugar, and salt. Mix with berries. Add lemon juice. Fill pie shell you have prepared with berry mix and dot bits of butter over top. Cover with top crust or lattice crust. Bake 10 minutes; now reduce heat to 350 degrees F. and cook about half hour longer, until pie is browned and done. Serves 6 to 8.

SWEET POTATO PIE

There is something about Sweet Potato Pie that seems to linger in one's memory.

2 medium sweet potatoes (1½ to 2 cups)	⅛ teaspoon salt
	1 teaspoon vanilla
2 tablespoons softened butter	⅛ teaspoon soda
1 large egg	½ cup buttermilk
½ cup sugar	Pastry for 9-inch pie
1 tablespoon flour	

Preheat oven to 350 degrees F. Boil potatoes, mash. Combine potatoes, butter, and egg. Mix sugar with flour and salt, add to mixture along with vanilla. Dissolve soda in milk and add to potato mixture. Pour into pie shell. Bake for 20 minutes or until set. Serves 6 to 8.

WHITE GRAPE PIE

This Grape Pie is extra special.

½ cup sugar	1 tablespoon lemon juice
1½ tablespoons cornstarch	1 pound white seedless grapes, washed and stemmed
¾ cup boiling water	
⅛ teaspoon salt	1 baked 9-inch pie shell
1 tablespoon butter or margarine	

MERINGUE:

3 egg whites
4 tablespoons sugar

Preheat oven to 350 degrees F. Sift sugar and cornstarch together into saucepan or top of double boiler. Slowly add boiling water, stirring all the while. Bring to boiling, add salt, butter, lemon juice, and grapes. Cook over low heat or hot water in double boiler stirring for 8 minutes. Pour into pie shell. Cover with meringue as follows:

Beat egg whites until foamy, gradually add 4 tablespoons sugar. Beat until mixture stands in peaks. Pile lightly on pie. Brown meringue in oven.

GRAHAM CRACKER OR VANILLA WAFER CRUST

1¼ cups finely crushed graham crackers or vanilla wafers, plus ¼
    cup for topping if needed
½ cup sugar
½ cup melted butter

Combine all ingredients in medium bowl, blend well. Line pie plate with mixture and pat firmly into place. Chill before filling. This makes a 9-inch piecrust.

IRENE'S PIECRUST

1½ cups sifted flour   ½ cup shortening
¾ teaspoon salt   4 or 5 tablespoons ice water

Sift flour and salt together. Cut in shortening until crumbly. Add ice water to hold ingredients together, mixing to form ball. Roll approximately ⅛ inch thick on floured board. Fits into 8- to 9-inch pie pan. Fill.

Desserts

Our desserts will delight many tastes; some linger happily in our memories. Ambrosia, fresh Peach Ice Cream, a frozen lemon dessert, old-fashioned Rice Pudding, and Grated Raw Sweet Potato Pudding are all here, to name a few. I remember when Ambrosia and fruit cake were traditional desserts at our house for Thanksgiving and Christmas. Charlotte, truly a delectable end to a meal, is a congealed dessert with a bit of sherry or bourbon for flavor. In a hurry? Try Cherries Jubilee for a glamorous dessert, or if time permits and you plan ahead, serve Congealed Egg Nog. Whatever it may be, let your dessert be the "crowning glory" of your meal. As you linger with friends over dessert and coffee the talk will be of "cabbages and kings," and a lot of other things. Who could ask for anything more?

AMBROSIA

Ambrosia is one of the South's favorite desserts.

15 to 18 medium-size oranges
¾ cup sugar or to taste
1½ cups fresh or frozen grated
   coconut

1 can (13½ ounce) pineapple
   chunks, drained (optional)

Peel oranges, being careful to remove all white membrane. Cut into small slices or pieces. Mix oranges and juice with sugar. Add coconut and pineapple chunks. Place in refrigerator to chill. Note: Add more or less sugar to taste, depending on sweetness of fruit. This may also be served in orange cups. Serves 10 to 12.

APPLES AND BITTERS

6 large tart apples
1 tablespoon angostura bitters
¼ to ½ cup butter

¾ to 1 cup flour
1 cup light brown sugar
⅛ teaspoon salt

Preheat oven to 350 degrees F. Peel, slice, and core apples. Place in a buttered baking dish, 11½×7½ inches, and sprinkle bitters over. Mix the butter into flour, sugar, and salt mixture. Spread this mix over the apples and bake about 45 minutes. It is good served warm with a dab of whipped cream. Serves 6.

APPLE-CORN FLAKE DESSERT

6 cups peeled, sliced apples	½ cup corn flakes
2 tablespoons brown sugar	½ cup sifted flour
⅓ cup orange juice	½ teaspoon cinnamon
⅓ cup brown sugar	1 tablespoon grated orange or
2 tablespoons butter or	lemon rind
margarine	1 tablespoon butter or margarine

Preheat oven to 375 degrees F. Arrange apples in greased shallow baking dish, 11½×7½ inches. Sprinkle the 2 tablespoons sugar on top, now pour about half the orange juice over this. Next work the ⅓ cup sugar and 2 tablespoons butter together with spoon until creamy. Add corn flakes, flour, cinnamon, and orange rind, mix until crumbly. Spread on top of apples. Sprinkle rest of orange juice over top and dot with butter. Bake for 30 to 40 minutes. Serve warm or cold. Good with cream. Serves 6.

APPLE TORTE

1 can (1 pound 2 ounce) apples	½ cup butter
1 package (6½ ounce) jiffy	¾ cup chopped pecans
cake mix	

Preheat oven to 325 degrees F. Pour apples in buttered 9×9-inch cake pan. Sprinkle cake mix over apples. Melt butter and pour over cake mix, now spread pecans over all. Bake for 45 minutes. Serves 6.

BAKED PEARS IN LEMON SYRUP

This is another way to serve Baked Pears. If you have a pear tree this will be welcome.

Peel small but not overly ripe pears. Split in half and remove core. While doing this place your syrup on stove and it can be cooking.

Make syrup as follows: 1 cup of sugar (to 6 or 8 pears), ¾ cup of water, and the juice of half a lemon. Drop the lemon peel in syrup for "extra lemony" flavor and remove when you pour over pears. Cook for about 5 minutes. Preheat oven to 350 degrees F. Place pears in shallow baking dish, 11½×7½ inches, and pour syrup over them. Bake for about 1 to 1½ hours or until pears are tender. The syrup will cook down and thicken. Turn pears over when half done, this saves basting. Serve hot or cold. Try putting 2 or 3 halves in deep compote and placing a spoon of vanilla ice cream over . . . delicious! Serves 6 to 8.

BANANA PUDDING

¾ cup sugar	2 eggs, separated
⅓ cup flour	1 teaspoon vanilla
⅛ teaspoon salt	36 vanilla wafers, or less
2 cups milk	4 medium-size bananas, sliced

Blend ½ cup sugar, the flour, and salt together thoroughly in top of double boiler. Add ½ cup milk, stirring to make smooth. Add remaining milk. Cook over boiling water, stirring frequently until thickened. Cover and cook about 15 minutes. Beat egg yolks slightly; add hot custard slowly to yolks. Return to double boiler, cook 2 minutes. Remove from heat and add vanilla. Preheat oven to 325 degrees F. Line the bottom and sides of a 2-quart casserole with vanilla wafers. Arrange sliced bananas in layers on wafers in bottom. Pour custard over bananas and make another layer, repeating according to size of baking dish. Beat egg whites stiff but not dry, add remaining sugar 1 tablespoon at a time, beating constantly. Spread meringue over custard. Bake for 10 to 15 minutes. Serves 6 to 8.

BECK'S ICE CREAM

2 cans (15 ounces each)   Juice 1 whole lemon
  condensed milk
2 quarts milk
Large bowl peeled crushed
  peaches, sweetened to taste
  (about 3 to 4 cups)

Mix condensed milk with milk. Add peaches before last of milk
and finish with milk. Add lemon juice. Freeze. Pineapple and bananas
are good to substitute in this recipe. This makes about a gallon.

BOILED CUSTARD ICE CREAM

Old-fashioned Boiled Custard Ice Cream is hard to beat!

4 eggs   1 quart milk
1 cup sugar   2 teaspoons vanilla or lemon
⅛ teaspoon salt   flavoring

Beat eggs together, add sugar and salt, mix well. Thin with a little
of the milk. Pour this mixture into remainder of milk, which has
been heated; cook in double boiler until thick enough to coat a
spoon. (Be sure to cook this in double boiler, too much heat will
cause the milk to curdle.) The water under the inset should boil
moderately to cook mixture. When done, add the flavoring. Cool
before freezing. Freeze as any ice cream. Makes ½ gallon.

CHARLOTTE

This is another favorite dessert in the South.

3 eggs
¾ cup sugar
½ cup sherry or ¼ cup
  bourbon
1 pint heavy cream

1½ tablespoons unflavored
  gelatin
½ cup cold water
¼ cup hot water

Beat egg yolks with sugar. Add sherry. Beat egg whites stiff. Whip cream. Soak gelatin in cold water for 5 minutes. Dissolve in hot water. Add to yolk mixture. Combine whipped cream and stiffly beaten egg whites. Fold both mixes together. Chill. Serves 6.

CHERRIES JUBILEE

This recipe for Cherries Jubilee is one of my favorites. It's easy, and a conversation piece.

¾ cup currant or guava jelly
¼ cup cherry juice (from
  canned cherries)
1½ to 2 cups Bing or Dark
  Sweet pitted cherries

½ cup brandy or bourbon,
  warmed
1 quart vanilla ice cream

Melt jelly mixed with juice in a skillet or chafing dish. Heat the cherries in jelly mixture. Pour brandy in center of skillet, don't stir. Light. Spoon flaming over ice cream in serving dishes. Serves 6.

CONGEALED EGG NOG

This Congealed Egg Nog makes a grand holiday dessert.

2 tablespoons unflavored gelatin
½ cup cold water
1 cup hot milk
1 cup sugar
4 eggs

1 cup bourbon or sherry
flavoring
1 quart heavy cream
Maraschino cherries

Soften gelatin in water and dissolve in hot milk. Cool. Add sugar to beaten egg yolks and beat well. Add bourbon slowly. Whip cream and add to gelatin mixture. Add egg yolk mixture. Fold in stiffly beaten egg whites. Chill to congeal and serve with cherries for decoration. Serves 8.

CRANBERRY SHERBET

This Cranberry Sherbet is a pretty dish.

1 tablespoon unflavored gelatin
½ cup cold water
3 cups cranberry juice cocktail

1 cup sugar
3 tablespoons fresh lemon juice

Sprinkle gelatin over water to soften. Heat 1 cup cranberry juice cocktail to boiling point, now stir in softened gelatin and sugar until both are dissolved. Add remaining cranberry liquid and lemon juice. Pour into ice cube tray, set freezer control to cold point, and freeze to mushy stage. Transfer to mixing bowl and beat well. Return to tray and freeze firm. Serves 6.

CURRIED FRUIT

⅓ cup butter or margarine
¾ cup brown sugar
2 teaspoons curry powder
1 can (1 pound) pineapple
  chunks, with ¼ cup syrup

1 can (1 pound, 1 ounce)
  peach halves, drained
1 can (1 pound) pear
  halves, drained
10 maraschino cherries

Preheat oven to 325 degrees F. Melt butter in skillet. Add sugar and curry powder. Add pineapple and syrup to skillet. Mix, simmer until sugar is melted. Put fruits in buttered shallow 1½-quart baking dish. Pour sauce over. Bake 1 hour. Serve in sauce dishes. Makes 8 servings.

FERNALD'S FAVORITE DESSERT

This recipe will be a favorite with the men. It is a variation of old-fashioned bread pudding. This is about the easiest thing you can mix and bake along with any oven dinner.

3 tablespoons butter or
  margarine
2 eggs, beaten
2 cups milk
1 teaspoon vanilla

¼ cup sugar
⅛ teaspoon salt
1 generous cup bread crumbs
A few raisins (optional)
1 tablespoon brown sugar

Set oven to 375 degrees F. While mixing pudding set 1½-quart baking dish in oven to warm with butter. Mix the eggs, milk, vanilla, sugar, salt, bread crumbs, and raisins. Remove warm baking dish and over the melted butter sprinkle the brown sugar. Pour in the pudding mix and bake uncovered for about an hour or until knife comes out clean after test. A slightly warmer or cooler oven makes no difference in flavor . . . just vary the time a bit and cook along with whatever is baking for dinner. Serves 6 to 8.

FROZEN APPLESAUCE

½ cup whipping cream   2 tablespoons sugar
¼ teaspoon cinnamon   1 can (16½ ounce) applesauce

Whip cream until custardlike, now stir in cinnamon and sugar well. Add applesauce and mix only until mixture looks marblelized. Spoon into ice cube tray and freeze with control at normal setting. Serve when mixture holds its shape but is not too solid. Serves 6.

GRATED RAW SWEET POTATO PUDDING

A Grated Raw Sweet Potato Pudding has lingered in many memories.

2 eggs   ⅛ teaspoon salt
1 cup sugar   3 cups grated raw sweet potato
1½ cups milk   (reserve 1 cup potato for a
½ cup melted butter   brown crust)
2 teaspoons vanilla

Preheat oven to 350 degrees F. Beat eggs, add sugar and milk, butter, vanilla, and salt. Add 2 cups potatoes. Place in 2-quart baking dish. Sprinkle reserved cup potato over top. Bake for 25 minutes. Serves 6.

LEMON CHEESE DESSERT

FIRST STEP:

   1½ packages (3 ounces each) lemon-flavored gelatin
   1¼ cups boiling water
   Mix and chill slightly

SECOND STEP:

   2½ cups vanilla wafer crumbs
   ¼ cup butter, softened

Mix. Put about two-thirds of this crumb mixture on bottom of pan approximately 12×9 inches or a bit larger. Reserve remaining crumbs for topping.

THIRD STEP:

2 packages (8 ounces each) cream cheese	1 pint heavy cream, whipped
1 cup sugar	1 teaspoon vanilla

Cream cheese, add sugar, whipped cream, vanilla, and chilled gelatin mixture. Pour over crumb filling in pan and top with remaining crumbs. Chill. Cut in squares to serve. If desired top with additional whipped cream or thin half slice of lemon. Serves 12 to 16.

LEMON CREAM SHERBET

1 cup sugar	2 egg whites
2 cups milk	2 tablespoons sugar
Grated rind 1 lemon	1 cup heavy cream
Juice 2 lemons	Lemon for garnish

Add sugar to milk and dissolve. When dissolved, add lemon rind and juice. Stir while adding lemon juice. Turn into tray and freeze for 1 hour. Beat egg whites, adding sugar. Whip cream and combine with the beaten egg whites. Add frozen mixture and mix lightly. Return to freezing unit and freeze. Requires no stirring. Serve garnished with half slice of lemon. Serves 8 to 10.

LEMON SURPRISE

A good make-ahead dessert.

1 can (13 ounce) evaporated milk, chilled	Grated rind 1 lemon
1 cup sugar	1 cup graham cracker crumbs, or more
Juice 3 large or 4 small lemons	

Whip milk, add sugar. Now add lemon juice and rind. This is fluffy. Freeze in 2 small trays or 1 large tray lined with graham cracker crumbs in bottom of tray. Cut in squares to serve. Garnish as desired. This makes a pretty parfait if you pile it in glasses after mixing instead of freezing and eliminate the cracker crumbs. Serves 8.

LUCILE'S PEACH ICE CREAM

Peach Ice Cream is a popular dessert in our peach country. This recipe is "extra special." It is good to pack in containers after freezing to store in freezing unit for later use.

1½ quarts milk
½ pint heavy cream
1 can (13 ounce) evaporated milk
Juice of 2 lemons

2½ cups sugar
⅛ teaspoon salt
1 quart peaches, peeled and put through sieve or mashed finely
Sugar

Mix milk, cream, evaporated milk, lemon juice, 2½ cups sugar, and salt. Sweeten peaches to taste; even with sugar called for they need a bit of sugar as they are tart. Add peaches to mixture and freeze in freezer rather than refrigerator. Makes about 1 gallon.

MINCEMEAT-ICE CREAM DESSERT

Try this for a holiday dessert.

1½ cups canned mincemeat
6 tablespoons thawed frozen pineapple-grapefruit concentrate
¼ cup water

3 tablespoons brown sugar
½ cup chopped pecans
1 quart vanilla ice cream

Mix mincemeat, fruit concentrate, water, and sugar. Bring to boil and add pecans. Serve hot over ice cream. Makes about 2½ cups of sauce. Serves 8 to 10.

MINTED PEARS

These Minted Pears are nice to garnish with, cool and refreshing.

1 cup water
½ cup sugar

½ cup crème de menthe
6 to 8 canned pear halves

Boil water and sugar together for 5 to 10 minutes. Stir in crème de menthe. Place pear halves in syrup, being careful not to break. Simmer about 5 minutes, remove from heat and place in bowl. Cover and let them stand in refrigerator for 4 or 5 hours, turning occasionally in syrup. Serves 6 to 8.

MRS. BAIRD'S BAKED PEARS

Preheat oven to 300 degrees F. Take 6 to 8 pears or as many as you need, wash and dry. Do not peel; this is part of the secret, being baked whole with the peel on. Rub each pear with salad oil. Place in oblong ungreased baking dish, 11½×7½ inches, and bake for approximately 1½ to 2 hours or until tender, depending on ripeness of pears. To serve, split open and remove core. Place a dab of butter on each pear half, some may like a sprinkling of sugar. These may be served hot or cold but are especially good hot with butter. To serve cold, a bit of whipped cream might be added. Serves 6 to 8.

MY FAVORITE BAKED CUSTARD

This is the best Baked Custard I have ever tried. It is so smooth and its only flavoring is the nutmeg on top. Do not spoil it by adding any other.

4 eggs
½ cup sugar
4 cups milk or 3 cups milk and
1 cup cream

⅛ teaspoon salt
Nutmeg

Preheat oven to 300 degrees F. Beat eggs just enough to mix yolks and whites. Now stir in sugar and dissolve well. Next add milk and salt. Run this mixture through a strainer so it will be free from any stringy parts of egg protoplasm. Pour mixture into 12 individual Pyrex custard cups and place in pan of water. Sprinkle tops of custards with generous covering of nutmeg and your custards will be ready for oven. The oven temperature should be about 300 degrees F., never over 350. You must avoid a hot temperature so the water around the custards will not boil as this might curdle the custard. Cooking on low baking temperature is the secret; your custards will be smooth. Cooking time is from 30 to 40 minutes; you can tell when it is done by testing center with knife blade; if it comes out clean it is done. Serve plain or with whipped cream. Serves 12.

ORANGE SHERBET

1 package (3 ounce)   ¾ cup sugar
   orange-flavored gelatin   2 tablespoons lemon juice
1 cup hot water   1 tablespoon grated lemon rind
1 cup orange juice   2 cups milk

Dissolve gelatin in water. Add orange juice, sugar, lemon juice, and rind. Chill until syrupy and fold in milk. Freeze 1 hour, beat until smooth. Refreeze and serve. (Use fresh or canned orange juice.) Lime sherbet may be made in this manner. Serves 6.

PEACH CREAM SURPRISE

This Peach Cream Surprise is made with peach purée. It is a delightful dessert and tastes like peach ice cream. Serve it with a few slices of peaches over the top—it's a nice way to make peach ice cream in your refrigerator.

1¼ cups sweet milk   ⅛ teaspoon salt
⅔ cup sugar   2 teaspoons lemon juice
1 cup peach purée   1 egg white, stiffly beaten
1 cup heavy cream

Mix milk and sugar in saucepan. Heat, stirring constantly until sugar dissolves, and remove from stove. Now stir in purée, cream, salt, and lemon juice. Mixture may look a bit curdled, but this look will disappear when it freezes. Pour into shallow pan, 8×8 inches, or ice cube tray; freeze until firm about an inch from edge. Pour into large cold bowl and beat until fluffy smooth, now fold in egg white. Return to pan, freeze about 2 hours or until firm. Serve in dessert dishes or cut in squares. Serves 6 to 8.

PEPPERMINT ICE CREAM

1 tablespoon unflavored gelatin
¼ cup cold water
2 cups milk

½ pound peppermint stick candy
1 cup heavy cream

Soften gelatin in water. Scald the milk and dissolve broken peppermint sticks in it. Add gelatin and stir until it is dissolved. Cool until mixture is beginning to set. Now whip until it is foaming. Add cream and freeze. Makes ½ gallon.

QUICK FRIED APPLE PIES

Here is a quickie using canned biscuits for the pastry.

1 can (8 ounce) biscuits
1½ cups drained applesauce
Fat for frying

½ cup sugar
1 teaspoon cinnamon

Take each biscuit and roll out (as piecrust); roll to size of a saucer. Place on one half of this a tablespoon or two of applesauce. Fold in half, moisten and seal edges with tines of fork. Fry in 1½ inches hot fat in heavy bottomed frying pan. (I use iron skillet.) When brown on one side, turn and brown on other side. Have ready a flat pan with sugar and cinnamon mixed. Lift pie from frying pan and drain on paper toweling. Now give both sides of pie a quick sugar coating. Serve hot or cold. For a delicious dessert, top with a dab of vanilla ice cream. Serves 10.

RICE PUDDING
(*Raw Rice*)

An old-fashioned favorite—Rice Pudding.

⅓ cup raw white rice, do not use Minute Rice
⅓ cup sugar
1 quart sweet milk

¼ to ½ cup seedless raisins
⅛ teaspoon salt
½ teaspoon nutmeg
½ teaspoon vanilla

Heat oven to 325 degrees F. Mix all ingredients and put into 2-quart deep baking dish. Bake uncovered for about 3 to 4 hours. Serve warm or cold. Try putting a spoon of jelly on top of each portion before serving. Serves 6 to 8.

RICE PUDDING
(*Cooked Rice*)

This Rice Pudding is quicker; it is made with cold, cooked rice.

2 eggs
2 cups milk
1½ cups cold, cooked rice
1 cup raisins

½ cup sugar
⅛ teaspoon salt
1 teaspoon vanilla
Dash nutmeg (optional)

Preheat oven to 350 degrees F. Beat eggs until light. Add to milk and rice. Add other ingredients lightly. Place in 2-quart buttered casserole or baking dish. Bake uncovered in shallow pan of water for about an hour. Serves 6.

NOTE: If you wish place a meringue on top of this pudding.

STRAWBERRY CHARLOTTE RUSSE

2 dozen ladyfingers
1½ tablespoons unflavored
   gelatin
¼ cup cold water
½ cup sugar

2 cups strawberries
½ cup strawberry juice
1 teaspoon vanilla
⅛ teaspoon salt
1 cup heavy cream, whipped

Line a glass mold with half the ladyfingers. Soak gelatin for 5 minutes in water. Mix sugar with strawberries and let stand about 5 minutes. This will make juice. If there is not enough to make ½ cup of juice add water or orange juice to make ½ cup. Dissolve gelatin in juice heated to boiling point. Fold in berries, flavoring, salt, and whipped cream. Pour on top of ladyfingers in mold and cover with the rest of the ladyfingers. Chill for 2 hours or longer. Serves 6.

Candy

This chapter is dedicated to all those "sweet tooths" who glance within.

There was a day in yesteryear when candy pulls were in fashion. I suspect that Grandmother and Grandfather were partners at a candy pull. Old-fashioned kitchens were busy places when candy making was going on.

Today we still like homemade candies, but we are fortunate to have candy thermometers to make our candy making easy. Peanut Brittle and Fudge are delicious sweets for your candy jar. I especially recommend the Mexican Caramel Candy. You'll agree that it is one of the best candies you have ever tasted. The recipe was given to me by a friend. Fortunate indeed are her friends for whom she makes it each Christmas. The Grapefruit Peel is a tempting holiday treat; its bittersweet flavor is delightful.

CHOCOLATE CREAM FUDGE

This recipe for Chocolate Cream Fudge is one of my favorite candy recipes.

½ cup cocoa or 2 squares
(1 ounce each) bitter
chocolate
2 cups sugar
⅔ cup milk

2 tablespoons light corn syrup
⅛ teaspoon salt
1 tablespoon butter
1 teaspoon vanilla
1 cup chopped pecans

Mix cocoa, sugar, milk, syrup, salt, and cook over low or medium heat. Stir no more than necessary to keep from sticking. Cook to soft-ball stage (238 degrees F. on candy thermometer). If you use the squares of chocolate, shave fine; mix with sugar and other ingredients and cook slowly, stirring, until the chocolate has dissolved. Then continue cooking as above. When candy is done set in cool place for 5 minutes and drop the butter on the surface, don't stir it in. Add flavoring. Let the fudge become quite cool, almost cold; this is important. Then beat it until creamy, add pecans, and pour into a buttered pan in layer about ¾ inch thick. When cold, mark in squares to cut. You may substitute ¼ cup finely chopped candied orange peel for nuts for a holiday candy. Makes 25 to 30 pieces.

CRYSTALLIZED GRAPEFRUIT PEEL

Peel your grapefruit and cut peel into ¼-inch strips; boil in water to cover about 15 minutes. Change the water three times, boiling a few minutes each time. Make a syrup of 2 cups of water to 2 cups of sugar. Boil until syrup spins a thread, then add peel equal to the amount of sugar used. Boil until the peel is transparent. If the syrup becomes too thick before peel is clear, add 1 or 2 tablespoons of boiling water to thin the syrup and continue cooking.

When peel is transparent, lift out and drain well, then roll in granulated sugar. Let dry slightly and it is ready to serve or pack.

A good test when cooking the peel is to bend one strip. If it stays bent the cooking is sufficient! If it opens, continue cooking.

It is a nice idea to color your peel. Add a few drops of green food coloring a little at a time until the desired shade is obtained. This is done when peel is almost done. It seems that the green coloring takes better than the red. One grapefruit will make about 1 pound of peel.

CRYSTALLIZED GRAPEFRUIT SHELLS

Crystallized Grapefruit Shells are a pretty idea for holiday time. Make these and fill with candy and salted nuts, cover with a fancy paper mat, and tie with Christmas ribbon. A pretty and edible gift, a wonderful idea for the person who has everything.

Select grapefruit of good color, thick peel, and without blemishes. Wash carefully; now break the oil cells by grating lightly on a fine grater. Cut slice from stem end of grapefruit; remove the inside, being careful to leave all of the thick part of peel and being careful not to break the shell. Cover with cold water; bring to boil, cook gently about 10 minutes. Now drain off water and repeat the process until peel is tender and as much of the bitter flavor is removed as desired. Cool shell, put in a syrup made of equal parts of sugar and water. Be sure to use sufficient syrup to float the fruit. Cook to 220 degrees F. on your candy thermometer. Let fruit stand in syrup at least 24 hours, turn several times. Now cook to 228 degrees F. (very thick syrup). Remove from syrup and cool. If the shell is large, turn it over a glass to shape. If you wish you may add a few drops of green coloring for a pretty colored shell.

DIVINITY CANDY

Divinity Candy is as divine as its name. I use pecans for my candy, also black walnuts. You may use other nuts or chopped cherries.

2 cups sugar
½ cup water
½ cup white corn syrup
2 egg whites, large eggs

⅛ teaspoon salt
1 teaspoon vanilla
1 cup chopped nuts

Put sugar, water, and syrup into a saucepan and stir until sugar dissolves. Let it boil, after sugar dissolves, without stirring, until it reaches 265 degrees F. on your candy thermometer, or it forms a firm ball when dropped in cold water. A thermometer is particularly good to cook this kind of candy. While this is cooking, beat the egg whites until they are stiff; add salt. When the syrup is ready, pour it over the egg whites while it is very hot. Beat constantly while pouring slowly. Continue beating until mixture creams and begins to harden. Add flavoring and nuts. Pour in buttered pan or drop from spoon; watch this as it may harden fast. If you wish you may tint your candy any color preferred. Makes approximately 30 to 40 pieces.

NOTE: This candy is easier to make on a dry day!

GLAZED PECANS

2 cups sugar
1 cup water
⅛ teaspoon cream of tartar

2 tablespoons lemon juice
2 cups pecan halves toasted until lightly browned

Make a syrup of sugar and water, add cream of tartar. Boil without stirring until it reaches a temperature of 300 degrees F. on your candy thermometer (the hard-crack stage). Remove from heat and set in an outer pan of boiling water to prevent syrup from hardening. Add lemon juice. Dip nuts into the syrup and place on dish to drain. If you prefer, pour the nuts into the syrup, stir well, and remove to dish. Makes 3 cups.

KENTUCKY COLONEL BOURBON BALLS

1 cup pecan halves
4 tablespoons bourbon
1 pound confectioners' sugar
½ cup butter, do not substitute
1 teaspoon vanilla

4 squares (1 ounce each) bitter
   chocolate
1 tablespoon slivered paraffin
Extra pecan halves (optional)

Soak nuts in bourbon several hours. Mix sugar, butter, and vanilla with hands until creamy. Drain nuts and add any remaining bourbon liquid to sugar mixture. Roll into small marble-size balls around pecan halves. Chill in refrigerator 40 minutes to an hour before dipping. To dip balls I suggest that you use a fork with tines bent slightly to hold ball. This keeps you from sticking a hole in the candy. To dip: Melt chocolate, adding slivered paraffin, and dip balls one at a time until thoroughly coated. Top with half nut if desired. Makes about 30 to 40.

MINTED NUTS

This Minted Nuts recipe is so good! It is nice for your tea table or for a special holiday treat.

1 cup sugar
½ cup water
1 tablespoon white corn syrup
⅛ teaspoon salt
6 marshmallows

½ teaspoon essence of
   peppermint or 3 drops oil
   of peppermint
3 cups pecan halves or large
   broken pieces

Cook sugar, water, syrup, and salt slowly. Remove from fire just before it forms a soft ball when tried in water, 230 degrees F. with candy thermometer. Add marshmallows, stir until they are dissolved. Add peppermint and nuts and stir with circular motion until every nut is coated and mixture hardens. May be kept in tightly covered jar for at least a week.

NOTE: You may have to separate nuts after you remove from vessel after stirring in fondant. If nuts become moist while stored just leave out in open for an hour or so and they will "dry out." Makes about 4 cups.

NANCY AND CHIP'S FUDGE

4½ cups sugar
1 cup butter or margarine
1 can (13 ounce) evaporated milk

Mix and cook to 240 degrees F. on your candy thermometer, a little past a soft ball; stir occasionally. Take off stove and add:

1 jar (7 ounce) marshmallow cream
1 package (12 ounce) semi-sweet chocolate drops
1 teaspoon vanilla

Beat with mixer until creamy.
Add:

1 to 2 cups chopped nuts

Pour into buttered pans or drop from spoon. Makes 5 pounds.

NOTE: This candy freezes well.

PARTY MINTS

1 pound confectioners' sugar
4 tablespoons butter
2 tablespoons light cream
¼ teaspoon oil of peppermint

Food coloring
Green candied cherries or tiny
    green leaves

Mix sugar, butter, cream, and oil of peppermint and color as desired. Roll out and cut into tiny rounds or fancy shapes for party mints. For pumpkin or apple mints, mix and roll and shape with hands to form small balls in shapes of pumpkin and apples. Use bit of cherry or leaf for stem. Makes about 75 to 100.

PEANUT BRITTLE

1½ cups sugar
½ cup light corn syrup
2 tablespoons water
1½ cups small raw peanuts

¼ teaspoon salt
1 teaspoon baking soda
1½ teaspoons butter or
margarine

Cook sugar, syrup, and water until mixture spins a thread; add the raw peanuts and cook until the syrup is light brown. Remove from heat. Add salt, soda, and butter. Stir briskly until mixed and pour on a well-buttered slab or cooky sheet at once. Spread mixture rapidly with spatula. Loosen mixture from slab, stretch and pull with hands and spatula until brittle is so thin you can almost see through it. When cool break into pieces. Makes 25 to 30 pieces, depending on size of pieces.

PECAN PRALINES

1 cup brown sugar
1 cup white sugar
½ cup water or cream

2 tablespoons butter
1 cup chopped pecans

Combine sugars and water in large saucepan and cook over medium heat to thread stage or 230 degrees F. on candy thermometer. Now remove from heat, add butter, and cool candy to lukewarm. Beat candy with spoon until somewhat thickened. Add pecans. Drop by tablespoons on waxed paper, making patties 3 to 4 inches in diameter. Makes about 12 large pralines.

PECAN ROLL

1 cup light brown sugar
2 cups granulated sugar
1 cup evaporated milk
½ cup white corn syrup

1 teaspoon vanilla
½ cup confectioners' sugar
1 cup chopped pecans

Mix sugar, milk, and syrup and cook slowly until mixture forms a soft ball when dropped in cold water. Remove from heat and let cool to lukewarm. Add vanilla and beat until mixture will hold its shape. Turn out on board which has been dusted with confectioners' sugar. Shape into a long roll about 2 inches in diameter. Roll in chopped pecans, wrap in waxed paper, and place in refrigerator to harden. Slice with sharp knife. Makes 1 pound.

POPCORN CANDY

This Popcorn Candy is a "goody" for goblin time.

5 cups popcorn
2 marshmallows, cut in small pieces
1 cup confectioners' sugar
3 tablespoons white corn syrup

1 tablespoon butter or margarine
1½ teaspoons water
⅓ cup chopped gumdrops (optional)

Place popcorn in large bowl. Combine marshmallows, sugar, syrup, butter, and water in medium saucepan. Bring to full boil over medium heat. Stir occasionally, remove from heat, and continue to stir until marshmallows are melted. Pour syrup over popcorn, toss lightly until well coated. Let mixture stand until cool enough to handle. Grease hands and shape popcorn into lemon-size balls and, if you wish, press the gumdrops into each. Wrap each in wax paper, store at room temperature. These may be made any time within a week before serving. Makes about 1 dozen balls.

TINGLE'S MEXICAN CARAMEL CANDY

The unusual thing about this candy is the fact that you cook the nuts in the candy instead of adding last as in most candy recipes. This gives a toasted flavor that is delicious! This candy stays creamy for a long time, that is, if you can keep it that long.

3 cups sugar
1 can (5⅓ ounce) evaporated milk

½ cup butter or margarine
Pinch salt
1 cup chopped pecans

In this recipe, place sugar to caramelize and cook other mixture at the same time. Take 1 cup of the sugar and melt in iron skillet (or heavy saucepan) until caramelized. Mix remaining 2 cups sugar with milk, butter, and salt and cook slowly. When it begins to boil add the caramelized sugar and stir well. Now add the pecans and cook slowly to soft-ball stage. Cool slightly, beat, and drop from spoon. Makes about 30 to 40 pieces.

Preserving & Pickling

No Southern cookbook would be complete without a chapter on preserving and pickling. Just imagine a juicy peach pickle with a piece of baked ham.

Many pickle and preserve recipes have been handed down from mother to daughter and are guarded secrets. For instance, Watermelon Rind Pickles, Corn Relish, Pear Honey, and even old-fashioned Artichoke Pickles. Plum Sauce, spicy with a tang, is a condiment to serve with your meats. Strawberry Preserves and Peach and Plum Jam are luscious spread on that hot buttered biscuit or a piece of toast.

I could not resist including a Peach Wine recipe.

ARTICHOKE PICKLES

These Artichoke Pickles will be welcome to many of you. These are the artichokes Grandmother used to pickle. I believe some call these Jerusalem artichokes.

Wash and scrub well ½ peck artichokes. Drop in a cold weak salt water for about 2 hours. Use ½ cup salt to 1 gallon of water.

Make the following mixture:

5 cups vinegar
5 cups sugar
1 cup salad oil
2 medium onions, cut in rings
2 cloves garlic (optional)
Several hot red peppers
2 tablespoons whole cloves

4 tablespoons celery seed
4 tablespoons white and black
mustard seed
4 tablespoons whole allspice
4 tablespoons broken cinnamon
sticks

Mix mixture ingredients together; stir to melt sugar. Fill jars with artichokes, selecting those of uniform size for each jar. The larger ones may be sliced. Cover with the spiced vinegar mix to the very brim. Seal until ready to use. Let pickle ripen for at least two weeks before using. Makes 5 to 6 pints.

CANNED PECANS

We grow pecans in our locality in Georgia and I cannot resist including this recipe. These keep well.

These are canned in your oven. Use screw-top jars, screw top on firmly. Pack shelled pecans in jar and crumple a piece of brown paper in top of jar. Screw tops on and place in cold oven. Set oven temperature for 225 to 250 degrees F. Count time when oven is preheated and process for 45 minutes. Cool in oven and remove.

CANTALOUPE PEACH CONSERVE

This Cantaloupe Peach Conserve was given to me by a farmer friend.

4 cups chopped peeled
   cantaloupe
5 cups chopped peeled peaches
6 cups sugar

¼ cup lemon juice
½ teaspoon nutmeg
¼ teaspoon salt
1 teaspoon grated lemon rind

Combine cantaloupe and peaches. Simmer mixture 20 minutes, stirring until there is enough liquid to prevent fruit from sticking. Add sugar and lemon juice. Boil until thick. Add nutmeg, salt, and lemon rind. Boil 3 minutes. Ladle into hot jars, seal. Makes 5 to 6 half pints.

CHOPPED CUCUMBER PICKLE

This pickle has a taste similar to India relish.

50 small or 25 large-sized
   cucumbers
¾ cup salt
3 medium-sized onions
3 large green peppers, seeded

1 tablespoon mustard seed
1 tablespoon celery seed
3 cups vinegar
4 cups sugar

Wash and grind cucumbers, using medium chopper. Now sprinkle with salt and let stand overnight. Drain and squeeze out juice; use colander. Grind onions and peppers. Add to ground cucumbers. Add mustard seed, celery seed, vinegar, and sugar. Bring to boil and boil 10 minutes. Put in jars and seal. Makes 5 to 6 pints.

CHUTNEY

18 tart apples	1 tablespoon ground ginger
3 sweet peppers	¼ teaspoon cloves
1 large onion	¼ teaspoon allspice
1½ cups seeded raisins	½ teaspoon nutmeg
1½ cups sugar	2 bay leaves
3 cups vinegar	Salt
Juice 3 to 4 lemons	Red pepper
1½ cups tart jelly	

Pare, core, and slice apples. Seed and core peppers, chop. Chop onion. Mix apples, peppers, and onion with raisins, sugar, vinegar, lemon juice, jelly and ginger. Tie spices in piece of cheese cloth, as bag. Boil all together until thick, add salt and red pepper to taste. Remove spice bag and pour into sterilized jars and seal. Makes 4 to 5 pints.

CLEAR CRANBERRY JELLY

1 pint water
1 quart cranberries
2 cups sugar

Put water and berries together. Cook rapidly until all berries pop open, about 10 or 15 minutes. Strain through cheese cloth. Add sugar, boil quickly until mixture flakes, the same as making any jelly. Pour into molds or jelly glasses to get firm. If you wish, seal with paraffin. Makes 4 to 5 jelly glasses.

CORN RELISH

18 ears corn, husked and cleaned
1 large cabbage
4 large onions
2 green peppers, seeded
¼ pound dry mustard
1 pound sugar

½ cup salt
10 to 12 stalks celery, or
 1 tablespoon celery seed
2 teaspoons turmeric
2 quarts vinegar

Cut kernels from corn; chop cabbage, onions, and peppers very fine. Mix these ingredients with remaining ingredients and cook until tender. Stir constantly, as it burns easily. Seal in sterilized jars. Makes about 8 pints.

CRANBERRY CATSUP

This is another idea for cranberries.

4 pounds cranberries
1 pound onions
2 cups water
4 cups sugar
2 cups vinegar

1 tablespoon cloves
1 tablespoon allspice
1 tablespoon cinnamon
1 tablespoon salt
1 tablespoon pepper

Cook cranberries and onions in water until tender. Put through food chopper. Add remaining ingredients and cook until tender, about 8 minutes. Stir while cooking. Pour into hot sterilized jars. Seal at once. Makes 5 pints.

CRANBERRY RELISH

1 pound cranberries
2 oranges

2 apples
2 cups sugar

Wash cranberries, oranges, and apples. Grind in chopper using medium blade. Mix with sugar and store in refrigerator in tightly closed container. Mix must stand 24 hours to be good; keeps indefinitely. (This may be congealed as a salad with nuts added.) Makes 2 cups or more.

DILL PICKLES

4 cloves garlic	½ peck cucumbers
24 peppercorns	2 quarts vinegar
4 cloves	1 quart water
4 flowers dill or 4 teaspoons dill seed	1 cup coarse salt (bag salt)

Place in each jar 1 clove garlic, 6 peppercorns, 1 clove, and 1 flower dill or 1 teaspoon dill seed. Dry off cucumbers after washing and cut in chunks or slices to suit. Pack in sterilized jars and pour over the following, which has been heated to boiling: vinegar, water, and salt. Fill jars and seal. Let pickles ripen at least a week before serving. Makes 4 quarts.

EASY PEACH PICKLES

4 cups sugar	50 to 60 small, peeled
3 cups vinegar	pickling-size peaches
1 tablespoon allspice	Whole cloves
1 teaspoon cinnamon	

Mix sugar and vinegar. Sprinkle in allspice and cinnamon. Cook syrup 15 minutes before putting in peaches. Stick 2 whole cloves in each peach, drop in a few peaches at a time. Cook until they look a bit clear and are tender, approximately 10 to 15 minutes. Take out and put in sterilized jars; add other peaches to juice. Cook all peaches, pack in jars. Now pour the hot syrup over peaches and seal. Makes 5 to 6 pints.

FIG PRESERVES

While writing my column for the paper I had many requests for a Fig Preserves recipe. This is my answer.

6 quarts figs
2 quarts sugar
3 quarts water

Rinse and drain figs, let stand in shallow pan to dry out. Make a syrup of sugar and water, boiling them together for 10 minutes. Add figs to syrup and boil rapidly for 45 minutes or until figs are clear and transparent. Remove figs and continue cooking syrup until well thickened. Pour hot syrup over figs and let stand overnight to plump. In the morning reheat figs and syrup to boiling, pack in hot jars, and seal. Makes 5 to 6 quarts.

GREEN TOMATO PICKLES

10 pounds green tomatoes
5 pounds white onions
⅔ cup salt
1 quart vinegar
1½ quarts water

1 cup sugar
2 tablespoons white mustard
seed
2 tablespoons celery seed

Wash and slice tomatoes. Peel and slice onions. Place tomatoes and onions in large crock in alternate layers. Sprinkle each layer with salt, cover with plate. Weight down. Let stand overnight, drain. Add 2 cups vinegar and 2 cups water. Heat to boiling, drain. Add remaining vinegar and water, sugar, mustard seed, and celery seed. Boil slowly, stir occasionally, for 30 minutes. Seal in jars. Makes about 8 to 10 pints.

HOT CABBAGE PICKLE

This is an old Southern recipe.

6 pounds cabbage
6 large onions
8 red peppers

8 green peppers, seeded
3 hot peppers, seeded

Grind above ingredients, place in large enamel pan, and mix in the following:

2 tablespoons salt
5 cups sugar
4 tablespoons mustard seed

2 tablespoons turmeric
Vinegar

Cover ingredients with vinegar. Cook 20 minutes.

1 cup flour
½ cup vinegar

To thicken: Mix flour with vinegar and add slowly to mixture. Cook until thick. Place pickles in sterilized jars and seal. Makes 5 to 6 quarts.

ICED GREEN TOMATO PICKLES

3 cups lime
2 gallons water
7 pounds small green tomatoes, sliced
5 pounds sugar and 2 more cups
4½ pints vinegar
1 teaspoon whole cloves

1 teaspoon allspice
1 teaspoon ginger
1 teaspoon celery seed
1 teaspoon mace
1 teaspoon cinnamon
1 bottle (½ ounce) green food coloring

Mix the lime in 2 gallons water for lime water. Soak the tomatoes in lime water for 24 hours. Drain, wash well, being careful not to break tomatoes. Let stand in clear water 4 hours, change water every hour. Mix sugar, vinegar, and spices. Bring to boil. Add green coloring. Pour this mixture over drained tomatoes and let stand overnight. Next day bring to boil and boil 1 hour. Seal quickly in pint jars. Chill before serving. Makes 5 to 6 pints.

MY SWEET CUCUMBER PICKLES

These are so easy to make, and so good.

Wipe about 5 quarts cucumbers and cut as desired. Place in stone jar. (You may use glass if other is not available.) Make following brine:

2 cups salt
4 cups boiling water

Mix and pour over cucumbers and let stand 3 days. Drain, reheat, and pour over cucumbers again for 3 more days. Take cucumbers from briny water and make following mixture:

1 gallon boiling water
1 tablespoon alum

Dissolve alum in gallon of boiling water and pour over cucumbers, let stand 6 hours. Drain, pack in jars, and cover with this mixture.

½ gallon vinegar
1 jar (2 ounce) pimentos,
   drained and chopped
3 sticks (2 inches each)
   cinnamon

2 teaspoons whole cloves
1 teaspoon allspice
7 cups sugar

Heat this mixture to boiling point and pour over cucumbers in jars. (Note: My mother used to take a silver knife and run the blade down the sides of the jars to get out "air bubbles" . . . it works.) Seal and let stand for at least a month before serving. Makes 7 to 8 pints.

ONION RELISH

2 small red peppers, seeded
2 small green peppers, seeded
2 pounds small white onions
2 cups sugar

1 pint vinegar
1½ teaspoons salt
Dash red pepper

Grind peppers or chop fine and cover with boiling water. Let stand 3 minutes. Now drain. Slice onions very thin and add to peppers. Add other ingredients and cook gently 15 minutes after it reaches boiling. Put in jars and seal. Makes 5 half pints.

ORANGE AND PEACH JAM

This combination of oranges and peaches makes a delicious jam.

12 medium-size oranges, washed,
   quartered, and seeds removed
1 lemon, seeded
16 large peaches

Sugar
1 cup drained, cut, maraschino
   cherries

Coarsely grind oranges and lemon. Peel and pit peaches, slice and slightly crush. Measure fruits, add equal amount of sugar. Divide mixture in half. Cook each portion until thick, stirring frequently. Add cherries. Seal in hot sterilized jars or seal with paraffin. Makes 6 to 8 jelly glasses.

PEACH CHUTNEY

3 cups peeled, sliced peaches
1 cup raisins
⅓ cup finely chopped onions
1 tablespoon ginger
1 teaspoon white mustard seed
1 teaspoon celery seed

⅔ teaspoon salt
½ teaspoon paprika
1 tablespoon grated lemon rind
3 cups vinegar
1½ cups sugar
2 tablespoons lemon juice

Mix the ingredients and cook slowly until thick (about 1 hour). Pour into hot sterilized jars and seal immediately. Makes 5 to 6 half pints.

PEACH AND PLUM JAM

This recipe for Peach and Plum Jam is a favorite. Each time I make it and serve with meats it gets "rave" notices. The large blue plums are the best to use.

2 pounds peaches
1½ pounds plums

This should make 5 cups of fruit when peeled and ground.

1 package (1¾ ounce) fruit pectin
6 cups sugar

Peel and pit or core fully ripe fruit. Chop fine or grind. (Add about ½ teaspoon each cloves, cinnamon, and allspice if desired.)

Method: Measure 5 cups fruit, mix with fruit pectin in pan. Place over high heat and stir until mixture comes to hard boil. At once stir in sugar. Bring to full rolling boil, then boil 1 minute hard, stir constantly. (A full rolling boil is a steaming, tumbling boil that cannot be stirred down.) Remove from heat, skim off foam with metal spoon. Then stir and skim about 5 minutes to cool slightly and prevent floating fruit. Ladle quickly into glasses, leaving ½ inch at top. Seal. Makes 5 to 6 pints.

PEACH OR BLACKBERRY WINE

3 quarts boiling water
18 to 20 peeled peaches, or
    1½ quarts blackberries
7½ to 8 cups sugar
1 lemon

1 package (¼ ounce) active dry
    yeast
¼ cup lukewarm water
1 egg white

Pour water over slightly crushed peaches or berries. Add sugar, juice of lemon and the rind, cut in half. Cool to lukewarm. Add yeast dissolved in lukewarm water. Let stand for 48 hours. Beat egg white slightly and add to mixture. Strain into container. You should wait a week or so to bottle and cork as the wine will work off; wait until this ceases. This wine keeps well and clears beautifully in about a month. Use a bit less sugar for scuppernong or grape wine, as grapes seem to have some sugar content. Use same quantity as blackberries. Makes 1 gallon.

PEAR HONEY

This Pear Honey is grand for something to spread on your breakfast toast.

6 or 7 pears (3 cups, ground)	1 orange (½ cup, ground)
2 apples (¾ cup, ground)	3½ cups sugar

Wash, peel, quarter, and core pears and apples. Wash and quarter orange and remove white center. Grind and measure fruit. Combine in large preserving kettle. Add sugar, blend thoroughly. Place on high heat. Stir frequently and cook until thick, approximately 25 minutes. Remove from heat and pour into sterilized jars. Seal immediately. Makes about 4 to 5 pints.

PEAR MINCEMEAT

This Pear Mincemeat is delicious. It's nice for pies.

7 pounds pears, peeled, cored, and ground	2 teaspoons cloves
1 pound raisins, ground	2 teaspoons allspice
3 pounds sugar	1 teaspoon nutmeg
1 cup vinegar	1 teaspoon salt
2 teaspoons cinnamon	1 or 2 tablespoons sherry

Mix ingredients and cook uncovered about 2 hours or until thick. Makes 7 to 8 pints.

NOTE: This mincemeat makes good pies or tarts. Add apples and nuts for the pies (have apples slightly cooked), a bit of butter, and for flavoring add bourbon to taste.

PEAR RELISH

1 peck pears
5 medium onions
6 green peppers, seeded
2 pounds sugar
5 cups vinegar

1 tablespoon salt
1 tablespoon mixed spices, tied
  in bag
1 tablespoon turmeric

Peel pears and core. Grind pears, onions, and peppers. Add sugar, vinegar, salt, mixed spices, and turmeric. Cook uncovered for 30 minutes (30 minutes after it comes to boil). Remove spice bag. Pour into sterilized jars and seal. Makes 8 to 10 pints.

PICKLED FIGS

Soda
5 pounds figs with stems
1 pint vinegar

7 cups sugar
5 sticks (1 inch each) cinnamon
1 clove for each fig

Put handful of soda on figs. Cover with boiling water. Let stand 10 minutes. Wash thoroughly. Combine vinegar, sugar, and spices and bring to full rolling boil for 15 minutes. Add fruit. Bring to rolling boil again for 15 minutes. Let stand 24 hours. Bring to boil again for 15 minutes. The third day bring to boil again for 15 minutes. Now place in sterilized jars and seal. Makes 5 to 6 pints.

PICKLED OKRA

This recipe came from Texas.

Wash okra which is fresh picked and tender. Pack in sterilized jars. To each pint add 1 hot pepper pod, 1 garlic clove, 1 teaspoon dill seed. Bring to boil the following:

1 quart vinegar
½ cup salt
1 quart water

Pour this on okra and seal. This will make about 10 pints.

PLUM SAUCE

This Plum Sauce is wonderful to serve with meats.

4 pounds plums	1 teaspoon salt
½ cup water	¼ tablespoon cayenne
2 tablespoons cinnamon	1 cup vinegar
1 tablespoon cloves	1½ pounds sugar
1 tablespoon allspice	

Wash plums and remove stems. Add ½ cup water and cook covered until plums are tender. If you wish to remove seeds and hulls put through colander. For a clear sauce use whole spices tied in a bag and remove after the sauce is done. The darker sauce is made by using ground spices. After putting through colander, cook plums with spices, salt, cayenne, vinegar, and sugar until it is as thick as catsup. Seal in sterilized jars while hot. Makes approximately 6 to 8 pints.

RED PEPPER JELLY

6 large hot red peppers	Vinegar
1 lemon	1½ cups sugar

Seed and put peppers through food chopper. Cover with cold water. Bring to boil and boil 5 minutes, drain thoroughly. Add lemon, quartered and seeded, and vinegar to cover. Cook 30 minutes. Mix in sugar and boil 10 minutes. Remove lemon. Pour into jelly glasses; cover with hot paraffin. Makes 3 to 4 glasses.

SALAD DRESSING PICKLES

These Salad Dressing Pickles are a "must." They are delicious with vegetables.

12 large cucumbers	1 tablespoon turmeric
Salt	½ cup flour
12 onions	1 quart vinegar
3 cups sugar	1 jar (2 ounce) pimentos,
1 tablespoon celery seed	drained and chopped
½ teaspoon cayenne	

Peel and slice cucumbers. Let stand overnight in brine made with ½ cup salt to 3 quarts water. The next day slice thin or chop fine the onions. Mix sugar and spices with flour and vinegar; add drained cucumbers, onions, and pimentos. Cook uncovered 10 minutes on low heat. Pack while hot into sterilized jars and seal. Makes 4 pints.

STRAWBERRY PRESERVES

My mother made Strawberry Preserves in this manner. They stayed "plump" and were so good.

Wash and drain firm, ripe strawberries. Remove hulls. Combine the berries with an equal amount of sugar. (Weigh berries and sugar.) Bring to boil slowly, boil 8 minutes. Remove from heat and let stand for 24 hours. Pour without heating into sterilized jars. Seal at once. The berries will stay plump and will not rise to top of jar.

NOTE: In sealing your jars place the sealers in hot water and simmer a few minutes to warm the rubber band and your jars will seal easier.

SURPRISE FIG AND STRAWBERRY JAM

This is a surprise recipe! It really tastes like strawberry jam.

6 cups white figs, these are the large figs
6 cups sugar
2 packages (6 ounces each) strawberry-flavored gelatin

Wash and peel figs, remove stems. Mash figs well, do not use blender. Place in large pot, about 6-quart size, and add sugar. Heat until figs start to cook and then simmer uncovered for 20 minutes. Add dry gelatin and simmer for about 10 minutes, stirring often. Pour into hot, sterilized jars and seal. Makes approximately 5 to 6 pints.

WATERMELON RIND PICKLES

I have eaten these Watermelon Rind Pickles and they are the best I have ever tasted!

2 quarts cold water
1 tablespoon calcium hydroxide, formerly slaked lime (this may be purchased at drugstore)
4 pounds watermelon rind, peeled and cut in 1-inch squares

2 tablespoons whole allspice
2 tablespoons whole cloves
10 sticks (2 inches each) cinnamon
1 quart vinegar
1 quart water
4 pounds sugar

Combine water and lime. Pour mixture over rind. Let stand 1 hour. Drain, cover with fresh cold water. Simmer 1½ hours, or until tender, and drain. Tie allspice, cloves, and cinnamon in cheese cloth. Combine vinegar, water, and sugar, heat until sugar dissolves. Add spice bag and rind. Simmer gently 2 hours. Pack rind in sterilized jars and fill jars with hot juice. Seal. Makes 6 pints.

Weights and Measures

¼ cup butter	½ stick
½ cup butter	¼ pound
1 cup butter	½ pound
2 cups butter or lard	1 pound
2 cups sugar	1 pound
3 cups brown sugar	1 pound
2 to 2½ cups fresh peaches	1 pound
2 tablespoons equal	1 ounce (liquid)

OVEN CHART

Slow oven	250–325 degrees F.
Moderate oven	325–375 degrees F.
Hot oven	400–450 degrees F.
Very hot oven	450–500 degrees F.

INDEX

Alma's Cooky, 148
Ambrosia, 208
Angel Biscuits, 136
Angel Pie: Chocolate, 190
  Lemon, 195–96
Apple Cake, 160
Apple-Corn Flake Dessert, 209
Apple Pies: Deep-Dish, 192–93
  Jo's, 194–95
  Quick Fried, 220
Apple: Salad, 32
  Torte, 209
Apples and Bitters, 208
Applesauce, Frozen, 215
Artichoke Pickles, 234
Asheville Salad, 32
Asparagus: Casserole, 56
  Ham and, 66
  Pimento and, 56

Fried, 63
  and Shrimp Elegant, 123
  Vinaigrette for, 53
Aspics: Cucumber, 35
  Tomato, 46
  with Shrimp, 45
Avocado: Fingers, 12
  Grapefruit Salad, 33
  Guacamole, 16
  Sandwiches, 12

Bacon: and Crab Meat Rolls, 14
  Omelet, 134
Banana: Bread, 136
  Ice Cream, Beck's, 211
  Pudding, 210
Barbecued Chicken: in Paper Bag, 94
  with Rice Pilaf, 102–3
Barbecue Sauce, 47

Herb, Turkey with, 104
Old-Fashioned, 50–51
Beans: Baked, Quick, 68
and Chestnuts, Green, 64
Chicken Casserole with Pimentos and, 197
Onion Casserole with (Substitute for Peas), 60
Southern Style, Green or Butter, 64–65
Beck's Date Cooky, 148
Beck's Ice Cream, 211
Beef: Chicken Joyce with, 98
Chili, 75–76
Cream Cheese Rolls, Nippy, 17
Cube Steaks, Lee's Rolled, 81
Gravy, 74
Hamburger Casserole, 77
Hungarian Goulash, 79
Italian Spaghetti, 79–80
Lasagne, 80–81
London Broil, 81
Meat Balls, Sweet-Sour, 90
Meat Loaf, 82
Pepper Steak, 83–84
Pot Roast, Gourmet, 76–77
Roast, 74
Short Ribs, Braised, 75
Smothered Steak, Savory, 88
Steak,
   en Casserole, 88
   Pepper, 83–84
   Rolled Cube, 81
   Smothered, 88
Stew, Quick, 85
Stroganoff, 74–75
Sweet-Sour Meat Balls, 90
Tamale Pie, 91–92
Beets, Harvard, 66
Berry Punch, Twin, 28
Best Ever Pie, 186
Best Gingerbread Cake, 160
Best White Fruit Cake, 161
Biscuit Pizza Snacks, 137
Biscuits: Angel, 136
Cheese, Little, 17
Cinnamon, 138
Edna's, 140–41
Sweet Potato, 145
Blackberry: Roll, 186–87
Wine, 243–44
Black-Eyed Peas, 57
Bonnie's Coconut Pie, 187
Bourbon Balls, Kentucky Colonel, 227
Bread Pudding, Fernald's Favorite, 214
Breads, 135–45
Angel Biscuits, 136
Banana, 136

Biscuit Pizza Snacks, 137
Biscuits,
Angel, 136
Cheese, Little, 17
Cinnamon, 138
Edna's, 140–41
Sweet Potato, 145
Buttermilk Rolls, 137
Butterscotch, 138
Cheese Biscuits, Little, 17
Cheese Supper, Onion, 143
Cinnamon Biscuits, 138
Corn, 138–39
Crackling, 139
Deluxe, 140
Hush Puppies, 141–42
Mexican, 142–43
Muffins, 139
Pone, 139
Spoon, 145
Crackling, 139
Date Nut, 140
Deluxe Corn, 140
Edna's Biscuits, 140–41
French Toast, Puffy, 144
Gingerbread, 141
Hush Puppies, 141–42
Jewel's Rolls, 142
Mexican Corn, 142–43
Muffins, Corn Meal, 139
Nut Date, 139
Onion Cheese Supper, 143
Pizza Snacks, Biscuit, 137
Pone, 139
Potato Biscuits, Sweet, 145
Puffy French Toast, 143
Rolls,
Buttermilk, 137
Jewel's, 142
Sixty-Minute, 144
Sesame Seed Strips, 144
Sixty-Minute Rolls, 144
Spoon, 145
Sweet Potato Biscuits, 145
Broccoli Casserole, 57
Brownies with Glaze, 149
Brown Rice Casserole, 58
Brown Sugar,
Icing, 166
Pound Cake, 162
Weights and Measures, 249
Brunswick Stew, Chloe's, 100
Buena's Roast Turkey, 94–96
Butter (Weights and Measures), 249
Buttermilk Rolls, 137
Topping, 174
Butternut: Cake, 162

Icing, 162
Butterscotch: Bread, 138
Pie, 187–88
Butter Tarts, Canadian, 188

Cabbage: Casserole, 58
Coleslaw, 34
Pickle, Hot, 240
Sauerkraut Slaw, 44
Cakes, 159–81
Apple, 160
Best Gingerbread, 160
Best White Fruit, 161
Brown Sugar Pound, 162
Butternut, 162
Candied Fruit, 163
Carrot, 163–64
Chocolate,
German, 166–67
Hershey, 167–68
Pound, 164
Coconut, 164–65
Cooking Hint for Cake-Mix, 181
Dark Fruit, 165–66
Fig Preserve, 166
Fruit,
Best White, 161
Candied, 163
Dark, 165–66
Japanese, 168–69
Layer, 170–71
Petite, 161
White, 181
White, Best, 161
White Christmas, 180
German Chocolate, 166–67
Gingerbread, 141
Best, 160
Hershey, 167–68
Japanese Fruit, 168–69
Lane, 169–70
Lemon,
Cheese, 171–72
Pound, 171
Linda's Pound, 172–73
Oatmeal, 173
Petite Fruit, 161
Phyllis's Prune, 174
Pineapple, 174–75
Upside Down, 175–76
Pound, 176
Brown Sugar, 162
Chocolate, 164
Lemon, 172
Linda's, 172–73
Praline, 176–77

Prune, 174
Red Velvet, 177–78
Rum, 178
Sponge, Hot Milk, 168
Strawberry, 179
White Christmas Fruit, 180
White Fruit, 181
Best, 161
Calico Salad, 33
Canadian Butter Tarts, 188
Canapés,
Cheese Puffs, 13
Sausage Pinwheels, 18–19
Shrimp, 19
Candied Fruit Cake, 163
Candied Sweet Potatoes, 59
Candy, 223–31
Bourbon Balls, 227
Caramel, Mexican, 230–31
Chocolate,
Bourbon Balls, 227
Fudge, Cream, 224
Fudge, Nancy and Chip's, 228
Crystallized Grapefruit Peel, 224–25
Crystallized Grapefruit Shells, 225
Divinity, 226
Fudge,
Chocolate Cream, 224
Nancy and Chip's, 228
Glazed Pecans, 226
Grapefruit Peel, Crystallized, 224–25
Grapefruit Shells, Crystallized, 225
Kentucky Colonel Bourbon Balls, 227
Mexican Caramel, 230–31
Minted Nuts, 227–28
Mints, Party, 228
Nancy and Chip's Fudge, 228
Nuts. See also specific nuts
Minted, 227–28
Party Mints, 228
Peanut Brittle, 229
Pecan Pralines, 229
Pecan Roll, 229–30
Pecans,
Glazed, 226
Minted, 227–28
Popcorn, 230
Pralines, Pecan, 229
Tingle's Mexican Caramel, 230–31
Cantaloupe Peach Conserve, 235
Caramel: Candy, Mexican, 230–31
Icing, 182
Confectioners', 182–83
Carrot: Cake, 163–64
Pie, 188
Cashaw Pie, 189
Catsup, Cranberry, 237

Cauliflower Casserole, 60–61
Celery Casserole, 61
  and Mushroom, 61–62
Cereal. *See also* Corn Flake . . .
  Toasted Delight, with, 20–21
Champagne: Cup, 21
  Punch, 21
Charlotte, 212
  Russe, Strawberry, 222
Cheese, 127–29
  Biscuit, Little, 17
  Bread, Onion Supper, 143
  Cooky, Corn Flake, 12–13
  Croquettes, Rice and, 129
  Dessert, Lemon, 215–16
  Dip, 13
    Daffodil, 15
  Grits, 128
  Ham Casserole, 77
  Icing, Cream, 164
  and Macaroni, 133
    Quickie, 133
  Omelet, 134
  Pastry, Cream, 200
  Pizza Snacks, Biscuit, 137
  Pudding, 128
  Puffs, 13
  Rolls, Nippy, 17
  Salads,
    Asheville, 32
    Cucumber, Cottage, 35
    Moon, 41
    Pineapple, Frozen, 38
    Yellow, 47
  and Shrimp Casserole, 115
  Soufflé, 129
  Spread, 13
    Ginger Cream, 14–15
  Straws, 13
Cherries Jubilee, 212
Cherry Salad, Jellied Bing, 39
  Eleanor's, 36
Chess Pie, 189
  Lemon, 196
Chestnut Dressing, 96
Chestnuts and Green Beans, 64
Chicken: Barbecued, in Paper Bag, 34
  with Rice Pilaf, 102–3
  with Beans and Pimentos, 97
  Breasts Supreme, 36
  Brunswick Stew, Chloe's, 100
  Burgundy, 97
  Creamed, 89
  Curried, 100
  Fried, 101
  Gravy, 101

Ham Cones with, Hawaiian, 78
Joyce, 98
Julie, 98
Parmesan, 99
Pie, Georgia, 101–2
Salad, 34
  Pressed, 43
Soy Sauce, 103
Tetrazzini, 99
Verna's (Substitute for Pheasant or
  Quail), 109
Chiffon Pie, Lemon, 196–97
Chili, 75–76
Chloe's Brunswick Stew, 100
Chocolate: Bourbon Balls, 227
  Brownies with Glaze, 149
  Cakes,
    German, 166–67
    Hershey, 167–68
    Pound, 164
  Cookies,
    Brownies with Glaze, 149
    Drop, 149–50
  Fudge,
    Cream, 224
    Nancy and Chip's, 228
  Icing,
    Four-Minute, 183
    Special Occasion, 168
  Pie,
    Angel, 190
    Cream, 190–91
Chowder, Florida Fish, 118
Chutney, 236
  Peach, 242–43
Cinnamon Biscuits, 138
Citric Acid Punch, 22
Cocktail Sauce, 115
Coconut: Bars, Toasted, 156
  Cake, 164–65
  Frostings and Fillings,
    Pecan, 167
    Pineapple, 169
  Icing, 165
  Pie,
    Bonnie's, 187
    Cream, 191
    French, 194
  Topping, 157
    Pecan, 173
Coffee Punch, 22
  Irish, 25
  Royal, 23
Coleslaw, 34
Confectioners' Glaze, 149
Confectioners' Icing, 182

Caramel, 182–83
for Chocolate-Drop Cooky, 150
Congealed Egg Nog, 213
Conserve, Cantaloupe Peach, 235
Cookies, 147–57
  Alma's, 148
  Beck's Date, 148
  Brownies with Glaze, 149
  Cheese Corn Flake, 12–13
  Chocolate,
    Brownies with Glaze, 149
    Drop, 149–50
  Coconut Bars, Toasted, 156
  Corn Flake Cheese, 12–13
  Corn Flake Macaroons, 150
  Crescents, 151
  Date, 151
    Beck's, 148
  English Toffee, 152
  Fruit, 152–53
  Jelly-Filled Swedish, 153
  Lemon Sours, 153–54
  Macaroons, Corn Flake, 150
  Mary's Tea Cakes, 154–55
  Pecan,
    Drop, 151–52
    Wafer, 155
  Rum Squares, 155–56
  Shortbread, Scotch, 156
  Swedish Jelly-Filled, 153
  Tea Cakes, Mary's, 154–55
  Toffee, English, 152
Cooky Crust, Graham Cracker or Vanilla
  Wafer, 205
Cooky Peach Pie, 191–92
Corn. See also Corn Bread
  Custard, Deviled, 62
  Fried, 63
  Relish, 237
  and Smoked Oyster Casserole, 125
  and Tomato Pie, 62
Corn Bread, 138–39
  Crackling, 139
  Deluxe, 140
  Dressing, 95–96
  Hush Puppies, 141–42
    Eloise, 142
  Mexican, 142–43
  Muffins, 139
  Pone, 139
  Spoon, 145
Corn Flake Cookies: Cheese, 12–13
  Macaroon, 150
Corn Flake Dessert, Apple, 209
Corn Meal Muffins, 139
Cornucopias, Party, 17–18

Crab: Casserole, 116
  Seafood, 120
  Deviled, 117
  Dip, 14
  au Gratin, 112
  Rolls, Bacon and, 14
  Seafood Casserole with, 120
  Shrimp Stuffed with, 114
  Spanish, 125–26
Crackling Bread, 139
Cranberry: Catsup, 237
  Jelly, Clear, 236
  Punch, 23
  Relish, 237–38
  Salad, Jellied, 40
    Creamy, 34
  Sherbet, 213
Cream Pie: Chocolate, 190–91
  Coconut, 191
Cream Sauce, Medium, 61
Creamy Cranberry Salad, 34
Creole: Eggs, 130
  Shrimp, 116
  Spaghetti, 76
Crescents, 151
Croquettes: Cheese and Rice, 129
  Salmon, 121–22
Croutons, Garlic, 15–16
Crystallized Grapefruit Peels, 224–25
Crystallized Grapefruit Shells, 225
Cucumber Pickles: Chopped, 235
  Dill, 238
  My Sweet, 241
  Salad Dressing, 247
Cucumber Salads: Aspic, 35
  Cottage Cheese, 35
  Pineapple, 43
Curried Chicken, 100
Curried Fruit, 214
Curried Shrimp, 117
Custard: Baked, My Favorite, 218–19
  Corn, Deviled, 62
  Ice Cream, Boiled, 211
  Pie, 192
    Pumpkin, 201

Daffodil Dip, 15
Dark Fruit Cake, 165–66
Date Bread, Nut, 140
Date Cookies, 151
  Beck's, 148
Delight Punch, 24
Deluxe Corn Bread, 140
Desserts, 207–22. See also Cakes; Cookies;
  Pies
  Ambrosia, 208

Apple,
    with Bitters, 208
    Corn Flake, 209
    Quick-Fried Pies, 220
    Torte, 209
Applesauce, Frozen, 215
Banana,
    Ice Cream, Beck's, 211
    Pudding, 210
Beck's Ice Cream, 211
Blackberry Roll, 186–87
Bread Pudding, Fernald's Favorite, 214
Charlotte, 212
    Russe, Strawberry, 222
Cheese Lemon, 215–16
Cherries Jubilee, 212
Congealed Egg Nog, 213
Corn Flake Apple, 209
Cranberry Sherbet, 213
Curried Fruit, 214
Custard
    Baked, My Favorite, 218–19
    Ice Cream, Boiled, 211
Egg Nog, Congealed, 213
Fernald's Favorite, 214
Fruit. See also Apples
    Curried, 214
Ice Cream,
    Banana, Beck's, 211
    Custard, Boiled, 211
    Cherries Jubilee, 212
    Mincemeat Sauce with, 217
    Peach, Beck's, 211
    Peach, Lucile's, 217
    Peach Surprise, 219–20
    Peppermint, 220
    Pineapple, Beck's, 211
Lemon,
    Cheese, 215–16
    Cream Sherbet, 216
    Surprise, 216–17
Lucile's Peach Ice Cream, 217
Mincemeat Ice Cream, 217
Minted Pears, 218
Mrs. Baird's Baked Pears, 218
My Favorite Baked Custard, 218–19
Orange Sherbet, 219
Peach Crunch, 199
Peach Ice Cream,
Beck's, 211
    Lucile's, 217
    Surprise, 219–20
Pears,
    in Lemon Syrup, Baked, 209–10
    Minted, 218
    Mrs. Baird's Baked, 218
Peppermint Ice Cream, 220

Pineapple Ice Cream, Beck's, 211
Puddings,
    Fernald's Favorite Bread, 214
    Rice, 221
    Sweet Potato, Grated Raw, 215
Rice Pudding, 221
Salad, 36
Sherbet,
    Cranberry, 213
    Lemon Cream, 216
Strawberry Charlotte Russe, 222
Sweet Potato Pudding, Grated Raw,
    215
Dill Pickles, 238
Dips: Cheese, 13
    Daffodil, 15
    Crab, 14
Divinity Candy, 226
Doves: Jo's Fried, 105–6
    "a la Totsie," 105
Drinks. See Punches
Duck, Roast, with Stuffing, 108

Easy Fruit Punch, 24
Easy Peach Pickles, 238
Edna's Biscuits, 140–41
Egg Nog: Congealed, 213
    Southern, 27
Eggplant, Italian, 67
Eggs, 130–32. See also Egg Salad
    Creole, 130
    Deviled, 131
        Shrimp Casserole with, 118
    Hard-Cooked, 131
    Mushroom, and Potato Baskets, 132
    Omelets, 134
        Bacon, 134
        Cheese, 134
        Fruit, 134
        Ham, 134
        Spanish, 134
Egg Salad, Molded, 40
Egg and Shrimp Casserole, Deviled, 118
Eleanor's Bing Cherry Salad, 36
English Pea Salad, 37
English Toffee Cooky, 152
Envelope Tarts, 193

Fernald's Favorite Dessert, 214
Fig(s): Jam, Surprise Strawberry and, 248
    Pickled, 245
    Preserves, 239
    Cake with, 166
Fish. See also specific kinds
    Baked, 112–13
    Chowder, Florida, 118
Florida Fish Chowder, 118

Flounder: and Shrimp, Baked, 113
Sour Cream Baked, 119
Four-Minute Chocolate Icing, 183
Frankfurters, Hawaiian "Hot Dogs," 78
French Coconut Pie, 194
French Dressing, 48–49
Moss Oaks, 50
Pineapple-Lime, 51
French Toast, Puffy, 144
Frosted Fruit Shrub, 24
Frostings and Fillings. *See also* Icings;
specific cakes
Coconut Pecan, 167
Coconut Pineapple, 169
Raisin Nut, 170
Seven-Minute, 183
Fruit. *See also* Apples
Ambrosia, 208
Cake,
Best White, 161
Candied, 163
Dark, 165–66
Japanese, 168–69
Layer, 170–71
Petite, 161
White, 181
White, Best, 161
White Christmas, 180
Cookies, 152–53
Curried, 214
Drinks. *See* Punches
Omelet, 134
Preserved. *See* Preserves and Pickles
Salads. *See also* specific fruits
Dessert, 36
Frozen, 37
Ginger Ale, 38
Tropical, 46
Fudge, Chocolate: Cream, 224
Nancy and Chip's, 228

Game, 105–9
Doves,
Jo's Fried, 105–6
"à la Totsie," 105
Duck with Stuffed, Roast Wild, 108
Pheasant,
with Rice in Foil, 106
Verna's, 109
Quail,
Braised, 107
Broiled, 107
Verna's, 109
Garlic Croutons, 15–16
Georgia Chicken Pie, 101–2
German Chocolate Cake, 166–67
Ginger Ale Salad, 38

Gingerbread, 141
Cake, Best, 160
Ginger and Cream Cheese Spread, 14–15
Glaze: Confectioners', 149
Lemon, 172
Glazed Pecans, 226
Gourmet Pot Roast, 76
Graham Cracker Crust, 205
Grapefruit: Avocado Salad, 33
Peel, Crystallized, 224–25
Shells, Crystallized, 225
Grape Pie: Deep-Dish Muscadine, 193
Scuppernong, 203
White, 204–5
Grape Punch, Lemon, 25
Grasshopper Pie, 194
Gravies: Beef, 74
Chicken, 101
Pheasant, 106
Pork, 85
Salt, 86
Turkey Giblet, 95
Green Beans. *See* Beans
Greengage Plum Salad, 38–39
Green Goddess Dressing, 49
Greens, Turnip, Southern Style (Substitute for Beans), 64–65
Grits: Casserole, 131
Cheese, 128
Guacamole, 16
Gumbo Georgia Style, 65

Ham: Asparagus Casserole, 66
Baked, My, 83
Cheese Casserole, 77
Cones, Hawaiian, 78
and Corn Custard, Deviled, 62
Cornucopias Filled with, 17–18
Delights, 16
Omelet, 134
Rolls, Stuffed, 89
Shrimp Jambalaya with, 123
Spread, 16–17
Hard Sauce, 49
Harriet's Barbecue Chicken with Rice
Pilaf, 102–3
Harriet's Salad, 39
Harvard Beets, 66
Hawaiian Ham Cones, 78
Hawaiian "Hot Dogs," 78
Herb Barbecue Sauce, Turkey with, 104
Hershey Cake, 167–68
Hollandaise Sauce, 49
Hominy. *See* Grits
Hopping John, 57
Hors d'Oeuvres, 11–21

Avocado, 12
  Fingers, 12
  Guacamole, 16
  Sandwiches, 12
Bacon and Crab Meat Rolls, 14
Beef-Cream Cheese Rolls, Nippy, 17
Canapés,
  Cheese Puffs, 13
  Sausage Pinwheels, 18–19
  Shrimp, 19
Cereal,
  Corn Flake Cheese Cooky, 12–13
  Toasted Delight, 20–21
Cheese,
  Biscuit, Little, 17
  Cooky, Corn, 12–13
  Dip, 13
  Dip, Daffodil, 15
  Puffs, 13
  Rolls, Nippy, 17
  Spread, 13
  Spread, Ginger Cream, 14–15
  Straws, 13
Corn Flake Cheese Cooky, 12–13
Cornucopias, Party, 17–18
Crab and Bacon Rolls, 14
  Dip, 14
Daffodil Dip, 15
Dips,
  Cheese, 13
  Cheese, Daffodil, 15
  Crab, 14
Garlic Croutons, 15–16
Ginger and Cream Cheese Spread, 14–15
Guacamole, 16
Ham,
  Delights, 16
  Party Cornucopias, 17–18
  Spread, 16–17
Little Cheese Biscuits, 17
Nippy Rolls, 17
Nuts,
  Salted, 18
  Toasted Delight, 20–21
Olives, French-Fried, 15
Party Cornucopias, 17–18
Pecans, Salted, 18
Pretzels, Toasted Delight, 20–21
Sausage,
  Balls, Sweet-Sour, 20
  Pinwheels, 18–19
Shrimp,
  Canapés, 19
  Spread, 19
Spreads,

Cheese, 13
Cheese and Ginger, 14–15
Ham, 16–17
Shrimp, 19
Sweet-Sour Sausage Balls, 20
Toasted Delight, 20–21
Hungarian Goulash, 79
Hush Puppies, 141–42
  Eloise, 142

Ice Cream: Banana, Beck's, 211
  Custard, Boiled, 211
  Cherries Jubilee, 212
  Drinks. See Punches
  Mincemeat Dessert, 217
  Peach,
    Beck's, 211
    Lucile's, 217
    Surprise, 219–20
  Peppermint, 220
  Pineapple, Beck's, 211
Icings, 181–83. See also Frostings and Fillings; Glaze, Confectioners'
  Boiled White, 181–82
  Brown Sugar, for Fig Preserve Cake, 166
  Butternut, 162
  Caramel, 182
    Confectioners', 182–83
  Chocolate,
    Four-Minute, 183
    Special Occasion, 168
  Coconut, 165
  Confectioners', 182
    Caramel, 182–83
    for Chocolate-Drop Cooky, 150
  Cream Cheese, for Carrot Cake, 164
  Lemon, 154
    Cheese, 172
  Pecan Praline, 177
  Pineapple, 175
  Rum, 178
  Spongy White, 178
Irene's Piecrust, 205
Irish Coffee, 25
Italian Eggplant, 67
Italian Spaghetti, 79–80

Jam: Fig and Strawberry, Surprise, 248
  Peach and Orange, 242
  Peach and Plum, 243
Japanese Fruit Cake, 168–69
Jellied Salads. See Aspics; Salads
Jellies: Cranberry, Clear, 236
  Red Pepper, 246–47

Jelly-Filled Swedish Cookies, 153
Jewel's Rolls, 142
Jimpy's Salad Dressing, 50
Jo's Apple Pie, 194–95
Jo's Fried Doves, 105–6
Joye's Mushroom Eggs and Potato Baskets, 132
Judy's Guacamole, 16

Kentucky Colonel Bourbon Balls, 227
Key Lime Pie, 195

Lamb: Chops Oriental, 180
   Quick Stew, 85
Lane Cake, 169–70
Lard, Weights and Measures, 249
Lasagne, 80–81
Laurie's Seafood Casserole, 120
Lee's Rolled Cube Steaks, 81
Lemon Cake: Cheese, 171–72
   Pound, 172
Lemon: Cookies, Sours, 153–54
   Dessert, Cheese, 215–16
   Glaze, 172
   Icing, 154
      Cheese, 171–72
   Pie, 197
      Angel, 195–96
      Chess, 196
      Chiffon, 196–97
   Punch, Grape, 25
   Sauce, 141
   Sherbet, Cream, 216
   Surprise, 216–17
   Syrup, 210
Lettuce Salad, Old-Fashioned, 42
Lime Pie, Key, 195
Lime-Pineapple French Dressing, 51
Linda's Pound Cake, 172–73
Little Cheese Biscuit, 17
Lobster Thermidor, 120–21
London Broil, 81
Louie's Spareribs, 82
Lucile's Peach Ice Cream, 217

Macaroni and Cheese, 133
   Quickie, 133
Macaroon Pie, 197–98
Macaroons, Corn Flake, 150
Malissa's Peach Pie, 198
Mary's Tea Cakes, 154–55
Measures, Weights and, 249
Meat, 73–92. See also Beef; Pork
   Balls, Sweet-Sour, 90
   Loaf, 82
   Quick Stew, 85
Medium Cream Sauce, 61

Meringue: Pies. See Pies
Pie Shells, 195–96
Mexican: Caramel Candy, 230–31
   Corn Bread, 142–43
Milk Punch, 26
Mincemeat: Ice Cream Dessert, 217
   Pear, 244–45
   Salad, Ruth's, 44
Minted Nuts, 227–28
Minted Pears, 218
Mint Julep, Southern, 27–28
Mints, Party, 228
Minty Punch, 26
Mrs. Baird's Baked Pears, 218
Molded Salads. See Salads
Moon Salad, 41
Moss Oaks French Dressing, 50
Muffins, Corn Meal, 139
Muscadine Pie: Deep-Dish, 193
Mushroom: and Celery Casserole, 61–62
   Eggs and Potato Baskets, 132
Mustard Sauce, Sour Cream, 122
My Baked Ham, 83
My Favorite Baked Custard, 218–19
My Sweet Cucumber Pickles, 241

Nancy and Chip's Fudge, 228
Nectar Punch, Hot, 25
Nesselrode Pie, 198–99
Nina's Punch, 26–27
Nippy Rolls, 17
Nut: Bread, Date, 139
   Raisin Frosting and Filling, 170
Nuts. See also specific nuts
   Minted, 227–28
   Salted, 18
   Toasted Delight with, 20–21

Oatmeal: Cake, 173
   Pie, 199
Okra: Pickled, 246
   and Tomato Gumbo, 65
Old-Fashioned: Barbecue Sauce, 50–51
   Lettuce Salad, 42
Olives, French-Fried, 15
Omelets, 134
   Bacon, 134
   Cheese, 134
   Fruit, 134
   Ham, 134
   Spanish, 134
Onions: Bread, Cheese Supper, 143
   and Pea Casserole, 60
   Relish, 242
   and Potatoes au Gratin, 67–68
Orange: and Peach Jam, 242
   Sherbet, 219

Oven Chart, 249
Oyster(s): and Corn Casserole, Smoked,
    125
  Dressing, 96
  Fried, 119
  Scalloped, 122

Party Cornucopias, 17–18
Party Mints, 228
Pastry. See also Hors d'Oeuvres; Pies
  for Blackberry Roll, 186–87
  Cream Cheese, 200
  Graham Cracker or Vanilla Wafer
    Crust, 205
  Irene's Piecrust, 205
Peach(es): Chutney, 242–43
  Conserve, Cantaloupe, 235
  Crunch, 199
  Ice Cream,
    Beck's, 211
    Lucile's, 217
    Surprise, 219–20
  Jam,
    Orange and, 242
    Plum and, 243
  Pickles, Easy, 238
  Pie,
    Cooky, 191–92
    Malissa's, 198
  Salad, Pickled, 42–43
  Weights and Measures, 249
  Wine, 243–44
Peanut Brittle, 229
Pear(s): Honey, 244
  in Lemon Syrup, Baked, 209–10
  Mincemeat, 244–45
  Minted, 218
  Mrs. Baird's Baked, 218
  Relish, 245
Pea(s): Black-Eyed, 57
  Onion Casserole with, 160
  Salad, English, 37
Pecan(s): Bread, Date, 140
  Canned, 234
  Cookies,
    Drop, 151–52
    Wafers, 155
  Frosting, Coconut, 167
  Glazed, 226
  Icing, Praline, 177
  Minted, 227–28
  Pie, 200
    Miniature, 200
  Pralines, 229
  Roll, 229–30
  Salted, 18
  Topping, Coconut, 173

Wafers, 155
Pepper Jelly, Red, 246–47
Pepper Steak, 83–84
Peppermint Ice Cream, 220
Perfection Salad, 42
Petite Fruit Cakes, 161
Pheasant: Gravy, 106
  with Rice in Foil, 106
  Verna's, 109
Phyllis's Prune Cake, 174
Pickled Peach Salad, 42–43
Pickles. See Preserves and Pickles
Pies, 185–205
  Angel,
    Chocolate, 190
    Lemon, 195–96
  Apple,
    Deep-Dish, 192–93
    Jo's, 194–95
    Quick-Fried, 220
  Best-Ever, 186
  Bonnie's Coconut, 187
  Butterscotch, 187–88
  Butter Tarts, Canadian, 188
  Canadian Butter Tarts, 188
  Carrot, 188
  Cashaw, 189
  Chess, 189
    Lemon, 196
  Chicken, 101–2
  Chiffon, Lemon, 196–97
  Chocolate,
    Angel, 190
    Cream, 190–91
  Coconut,
    Bonnie's, 187
    Cream, 191
    French, 194
  Cooky Peach, 191–92
  Corn and Tomato, 62
  Cream,
    Chocolate, 190–91
    Coconut, 191
  Crusts. See also Meringue Pie Shells
    Graham Cracker or Vanilla Wafer,
      205
    Irene's, 205
  Custard, 192
    Pumpkin, 201
  Envelope Tarts, 193
  French Coconut, 194
  Graham Cracker Crust, 205
  Grape,
    Muscadine, 193
    Scuppernong, 203
    White, 204–5
  Grasshopper, 194

Irene's Piecrust, 205
Jo's Apple, 194–95
Key Lime, 195
Lemon, 197
    Angel, 195–96
    Chess, 196
    Chiffon, 196–97
Lime, Key, 195
Macaroon, 197–98
Malissa's Peach, 198
Muscadine, Deep-Dish, 193
Nesselrode, 198–99
Oatmeal, 199
Peach,
    Cooky, 191–92
    Crunch, 199
    Malissa's, 198
Pecan, 200
    Miniature, 200
Pineapple, 201
Pumpkin Custard, 201
Raisin, 202
Rum, 202
Scuppernong, 203
Strawberry, 203
Sweet Potato, 204
Tamale, 91–92
Tomato and Corn, 62
Vanilla Wafer Crust, 205
White Grape, 204–5
Pilaf, Barbecue Chicken with Rice, 102–3
Pimentos: Asparagus Casserole with, 56
    Chicken Casserole with Beans and, 97
    Squash Casserole with, 70
Pineapple: Cake, 174–75
    Upside Down, 175–76
    French Dressing, Lime, 51
    Frosting and Filling, Coconut, 169
    Ice Cream, Beck's, 211
    Icing, 175
    Pie, 201
    Salad,
        Cucumber and, 43
        Frozen, 38
        Yellow Cheese, 47
Pizza Snacks, Biscuit, 137
Plum: Jam, Peach and, 243
    Salad, Greengage, 38–39
    Sauce, 246
Pone Bread, 139
Popcorn Candy, 230
Poppy-Seed Dressing, 51
Pork. See also Bacon; Ham; Sausage
    Chops, Stuffed, 90
        and Wine, 84
    Gravy, 85
    Roast, 85

Salt, and Gravy, 86
    Battered, 86
Spareribs, Louie's, 82
Sweet-Sour, 91
Potato(es): Baskets, 132
    Biscuits, Sweet, 145
    Candied Sweet, 59
    and Onions au Gratin, 67–68
    Pie, Sweet, 204
    Pudding, Grated Raw Sweet, 215
    Salad, Molded, 41
    Shredded Yams, 68
    Soufflé, Sweet, 70–71
    Sour Cream Scalloped, 69
Poultry, 93–104. See also Chicken; Turkey
Pound Cake, 176
    Brown Sugar, 162
    Chocolate, 164
    Lemon, 172
    Linda's, 172–73
Praline(s): Cake, 176–77
    Pecan, 229
Preserves and Pickles, 233–48
    Artichoke Pickles, 234
    Blackberry Wine, 243–44
    Cabbage Pickles, Hot, 240
    Cantaloupe Peach Conserve, 235
    Chutney, 236
        Peach, 242–43
    Corn Relish, 237
    Cranberry,
        Catsup, 237
        Jelly, Clear, 236
        Relish, 237–38
    Cucumber Pickles,
        Chopped, 235
        Dill, 238
        My Sweet, 241
        Salad Dressing, 247
    Dill Pickles, 238
    Easy Peach Pickles, 238
    Fig(s),
        Jam, Surprise Strawberry and, 248
        Pickled, 245
        Preserves, 239
    My Sweet Cucumber Pickles, 241
    Okra, Pickled, 246
    Onion Relish, 242
    Orange and Peach Jam, 242
    Peach,
        Chutney, 242–43
        Conserve, Cantaloupe and, 235
        Jam,
            Orange and, 242
            Pickles, Easy, 238
            Plum and, 243
        Wine, 243–44

Pear,
  Honey, 244
  Mincemeat, 244–45
  Relish, 245
Pecans, Canned, 234
Pepper Jelly, Red, 246–47
Plum,
  Jam, Peach and, 243
  Sauce, 246
Red Pepper Jelly, 246–47
Salad Dressing Pickles, 247
Strawberry,
  and Fig Jam, Surprise, 248
  Preserves, 247
Surprise Fig and Strawberry Jam, 248
Tomato Pickles, Green, 239
  Iced, 240–41
Watermelon Rind, Pickled, 248
Pretzels, Toasted Delight with, 20–21
Prune Cake, Phyllis's, 174
Puddings: Banana, 210
  Bread, Fernald's Favorite, 214
  Cheese, 128
  Rice, 221
  Sweet Potato, Grated Raw, 215
Puffy French Toast, 143
Pumpkin Custard Pie, 201
Punches, 21–29
  Berry, Twin-, 29
  Champagne, 21
    Cup, 21
  Citric Acid, 22
  Coffee, 22
    Irish, 25
    Royal, 23
  Cranberry, 23
  Delight, 24
  Easy Fruit, 24
  Egg Nog, Southern, 27
  Frosted Fruit Shrub, 24
  Grape Lemon, 25
  Irish Coffee, 25
  Lemon Grape, 25
  Milk, 26
  Mint Julep, Southern, 27–28
  Minty, 26
  Nectar, Hot, 25
  Nina's, 26–27
  Rum, Hot Buttered, 24–25
  Sherbet, Fruit, 24
  Shower, 27
  Southern Egg Nog, 27
  Southern Mint Julep, 27–28
  Tea, Russian, 27
  Twin-Berry, 29
  Wassail Bowl, 29

Quail: Braised, 107
  Broiled, 107
  Verna's, 109

Raisin: Nut Frosting and Filling, 170
  Pie, 202
Red Pepper Jelly, 246–47
Red Velvet Cake, 177–78
Relishes: Corn, 237
  Cranberry, 237–38
  Onion, 242
  Pear, 245
Rice: Brown, Casserole, 58
  and Cheese Croquettes, 129
  Hopping John with Black-Eyed Peas, 57
  Pheasant with, 106
  Pilaf, Barbecue Chicken with, 102–3
  Pudding, 221
  Salad, 44
  and Sausage Casserole, 87
Rolls (Breads): Buttermilk, 137
  Jewel's, 142
  Sixty-Minute, 144
Rum: Cake, 178
  Hot Buttered, 24–25
  Icing, 178
  Pie, 202
  Squares, 155–56
  Topping, 202
Russian Tea, 27
Ruth's Mincemeat Salad, 44

Salad Dressing Pickles, 247
Salad Dressings, 48–53
  Cooked, 48
  French, 48–49
    Moss Oaks, 50
    Pineapple-Lime, 51
  Green Goddess, 49
  Jimpy's, 50
  Lime-Pineapple French, 51
  Moss Oaks French, 50
  Pineapple-Lime French, 51
  Poppy-Seed, 51
  Sanford House, 51–52
  Sour Cream, 52
  Thousand Island, 52
  Tomato Salad Sauce, 52
  Vinaigrette, 53
Salads, 31–47
  Apple, 32
  Asheville, 32
  Avocado-Grapefruit, 33
  Cabbage,
    Coleslaw, 34
    Sauerkraut Slaw, 44

Calico, 33
Cheese,
 Asheville, 32
 Cucumber Cottage, 35
 Moon, 41
 Pineapple, Frozen, 38
 Yellow, 47
Cherry, Jellied Bing, 39
 Eleanor's, 36
Chicken, 34
 Pressed, 43
Coleslaw, 34
Cranberry, Jellied, 40
 Creamy, 34
Creamy Cranberry, 34
Cucumber,
 Aspic, 35
 Cottage Cheese, 35
 Pineapple and, 43
Dessert, 36
Egg, Molded, 40
English Pea, 37
Frozen Fruit, 37
Frozen Pineapple, 38
Fruit. See also specific fruits
 Dessert, 36
 Frozen, 37
 Ginger Ale, 38
 Tropical, 46
Ginger Ale, 38
Grapefruit-Avocado, 33
Greengage Plum, 38–39
Harriet's, 39
Lettuce, Old-Fashioned, 42
Mincemeat, Ruth's, 44
Moon, 41
Old-Fashioned Lettuce, 42
Pea, English, 37
Peach, Pickled, 42–43
Perfection, 42
Pickled Peach, 42–43
Pineapple,
 Cucumber and, 43
 Frozen, 38
 Yellow Cheese, 47
Plum, Greengage, 38–39
Potato, Molded, 41
Rice, 44
Ruth's Mincemeat, 44
Sauerkraut Slaw, 44
Shrimp, 45
 Aspic, 45
Tomato,
 Aspic, 46
 with Shrimp, 45
 Sauce for, 52
Tropical, 46

Yellow Cheese, 47
Salmon Croquettes, 121–22
Sandwiches, Avocado, 12
Sanford House Dressing, 51–52
Sauces: Barbecue, 47
 Herb, 104
 Cocktail, 115
 Cream, Medium, 61
 Hard, 49
 Herb Barbecue, Turkey with, 104
 Hollandaise, 49
 Lemon, 141
 Mustard Sour Cream, 122
 Plum, 246
 Sour Cream Mustard, 122
 for Tomato Salad, 52
Sauerkraut Slaw, 44
Sausage: Balls, Sweet-Sour, 20
 Biscuit Pizza Snacks, 137
 Pinwheels, 18–19
 and Rice Casserole, 87
Savory Smothered Steak, 88
Scuppernong Pie, 203
Seafood, 111–26. See also specific kinds
 Casserole, Laurie's, 120
Sesame Seed Strips, 144
Seven-Minute Frosting, 183
Sherbet: Cranberry, 213
 Lemon Cream, 216
 Orange, 219
 Punches. See Punches
Shortbread, Scotch, 156
Shower Punch, 27
Shrimp: and Asparagus Elegant, 123
 Aspic, 45
 Baked Stuffed, 114
 Boiled, 114
 Canapés, 19
 and Cheese Casserole, 115
 Creole, 116
 Curried, 117
 and Deviled Egg Casserole, 118
 and Flounder, Baked, 114
 Jambalaya, 123
 Marinade, 124
 Marinated, 121
 Remoulade, 124
 Gourmet, 125
 Salad, 45
 Aspic, 45
 Seafood Casserole with, 120
 Spread, 19
 Sweet and Sour, 126
Sixty-Minute Rolls, 144
Soufflé: Cheese, 129
 Sweet Potato, 70–71

Sour Cream: Dressing, 52
  Flounder Baked in, 119
  Mustard Sauce, 122
  Scalloped Potatoes, 69
Southern Corn Bread Dressing, 95–96
Southern Egg Nog, 27
Southern Mint Julep, 27–28
Soy Sauce Chicken, 103
Spaghetti: Chicken Tetrazzini, 99
  Creole, 76
  Italian, 79–80
Spanish Crab, 125–26
Spanish Omelet, 134
Special Occasion Icing, 168
Spinach Casserole, 69
Sponge Cake, Hot Milk, 168
Spongy White Icing, 178
Spoon Bread, 145
Spreads: Cheese, 13
  and Ginger, Cream, 14–15
  Ham, 16–17
  Shrimp, 19
Squash Casserole, 69–70
  with Pimento, 70
Strawberry: Cake, 179
  Charlotte Russe, 222
  and Fig Jam, Surprise, 248
  Pie, 203
  Preserves, 247
Sugar, Weights and Measures, 249
Surprise Fig and Strawberry Jam, 248
Swedish Cookies, Jelly-Filled, 153
Sweet Potato(es): Biscuits, 145
  Candied, 59
  Pie, 204
  Pudding, Grated Raw, 215
  Shredded Yams, 68
  Soufflé, 70–71
Sweet-Sour Meat Balls, 90
Sweet-Sour Pork, 91
Sweet-Sour Sausage Balls, 20
Sweet and Sour Shrimp, 126
Syrup, Lemon, 210

Tamale Pie, 91–92
Tarts: Canadian Butter, 188
  Envelope, 193
Tea Cakes, Mary's, 154–55

Tea Punch, Russian, 27
Thousand Island Dressing, 52
Tingle's Mexican Caramel Candy, 230–31
Toasted Delight, 20–21
Toffee Cooky, English, 152
Tomato(es): Aspic, 46
  with Shrimp, 45
  Fried Green, 64
  and Okra Gumbo, 65
  Pickles, Green, 239
  Iced, 240–41
  Pie, Corn and, 62
  Salad,
    Aspic, 46
      Shrimp with, 45
  Sauce for, 52
Toppings: Buttermilk, 174
  Coconut, 157
  Pecan, 173
  Rum, 202
Torte, Apple, 209
Tropical Salad, 46
Turkey: Buena's Roast, 94–96
  Giblet Gravy, 95
  and Herb Barbecue Sauce, 104
Turnip Greens, Southern Style (Substitute for Beans), 64–65
Twin-Berry Punch, 29

Vanilla Wafer Crust, 205
Veal Cutlet, Breaded, 92
Vegetables, 55–71. See also Preserves and pickles; Salads; specific vegetables
Verna's Pheasant or Quail, 109
Vinaigrette, 53

Wassail Bowl, 29
Watermelon Rind Pickles, 248
Weights and Measures, 249
White Christmas Fruit Cake, 180
White Fruit Cake, 181
  Best, 161
White Grape Pie, 204–5
White Icing: Boiled, 181–82
  Spongy, 178
Wieners, Hawaiian "Hot Dogs," 78
Wine, Peach or Blackberry, 243–44

Yams, Shredded, 68
Yellow Cheese Salad, 47